"He Came to Teach You Your Religion"

The Hadith of the Angel Gabriel Explaining the Foundations of Islam, *Imaan* and *Ihsaan*

By

Jamaal al-Din M. Zarabozo

Al-Basheer Company for Publications and Translations

1997

"He Came to Teach You Your Religion": The Hadith of the Angel Gabriel Explaining the Foundations of Islam, *Imaan* and *Ihsaan*

By Jamaal al-Din M. Zarabozo

Published by:
Al-Basheer Company for Publications and Translations
1750 30th St. Suite #440
Boulder, CO 80301
U.S.A.

(Note: Not affiliated with Basheer Publications)

ISBN 1-891540-01-7 $11.00 Softcover

Preface

Verily, all praise is due to Allah. We praise Him, seek His help and ask for His forgiveness. We seek refuge in Allah from the evil in our own souls and from our sinful deeds. Whoever Allah guides, no one can mislead. And whoever Allah allows to go astray, no one can guide. I bear witness that there is none worthy of worship except Allah, the One, having no partner. And I bear witness that Muhammad is His servant and messenger. O believers! Have fear of Allah according to His right and die not save as Muslims. O mankind! Have fear of your Lord, the One who created you from one soul and created from it its mate and from them spread many men and women. And fear Allah from whom you demand your mutual rights and [do not cut off] ties of kinship. Surely, Allah is Ever an All-Watcher over you. O Believers! Have fear of Allah and always speak the truth. He will direct you to righteous deeds and will forgive you your sins. And whosoever obeys Allah and His Messenger has indeed achieved a great achievement.

To proceed: Verily, the truest speech is the Book of Allah. The best guidance is the guidance of Muhammad. The worst affairs are the innovated ones. Every innovated matter is a heresy. And every heresy is misguidance. And every misguidance is in the Hell-fire.

I thank Allah for the opportunity and ability to complete this work. I pray that He accepts this work from me and forgives me for any mistakes and errors that have occurred herein.

There are many people that I would like to thank for their help in this particular work. First, I must express my thanks to Dr. Mukhtar Curtis, Kamil Mufti and my wife Zainab for reviewing and commenting upon earlier versions of the manuscript. Their comments and corrections have been very helpful. I would also like to express my gratitude to those brothers and sisters of the Islamic Center of Boulder who attended the lectures based on this book. Their comments and discussions often added important insight or questions that needed to be addressed.

There are numerous others who are always deserving of mention in any of my books. Allah has blessed me by their company, encouragement, help and guidance throughout the years. I pray that Allah rewards all of them greatly. These people include but are not limited to: Nahar al-Rashid, Humaidan al-Turki, Said Lahrichi, Muhammad al-Osimi, Fahd al-Yahya, Hamad al-Shaikh, Ahmad al-Teraiqi, Muhammad Tahlawi and Jaafar Sheikh Idris. Of course, my wife deserves special mention for all of her years of encouragement, help and patience.

As mentioned in the introduction, this book is only a small portion of the larger, *Commentary on the Forty Hadith of al-Nawawi*. It was decided to publish this hadith separately, as well as in the larger work, due to its greater mass appeal. I pray that Allah makes it easy for us to complete the larger work soon.

I pray that this work is beneficial to those who read it. If anyone has any comments, corrections or suggestions for this work, they should feel free to contact me through the publisher.

Jamaal Zarabozo
Boulder, CO
U.S.A.
October 20, 1997

Chapter Index

Introduction	1
The Text of The Hadith of Angel Gabriel	3
The Pillars of Islam	13
The Concept of *Imaan*	71
The Articles of Faith	123
The Concept of *Ihsaan*	197
Signs of the Day of Judgment	211
The Angel Teaches the Religion	225
Summary of the Hadith	229
References	231
Glossary	238
Index of Figures	243
Index of Quranic Verses Cited	244
General Index	247

Introduction

The hadith known as the "hadith of Gabriel" is one of the most comprehensive hadith of the Prophet (peace be upon him). It touches upon almost every deed of Islam. Qaadhi Iyadh has pointed out that this hadith covers or points to all of the aspects of internal and outward acts of worship of Allah. It touches upon the deeds that are related to the external organs as well as that of the heart. Indeed, he stated, "[It covers the religion] to such an extent that all the religious sciences are found in it and branch out from it."[1]

As mentioned above, this hadith is known as the hadith of Gabriel; it is also called *Umm al-Sunnah* (or "the foundation of the Sunnah") in the same way that *Surah al-Faatiha* is called *Umm al-Kitaab* (or "the Foundation of the Book"). In the same way that *Surah al-Faatiha* encompasses the meaning of the Quran as a whole, this hadith encompasses the meaning of the sunnah as a whole.

According to ibn Hajr, this incident took place close to the Prophet's death. Some say that it was just before the Farewell Pilgrimage. Hence, it was as if the Prophet (peace be upon him), through the questioning of the angel Gabriel, was summarizing his mission and message. He summarized the essential concepts of *imaan*, islam and *ihsaan*. Then, at the end, he stated that the person was the Angel Gabriel who had come to teach them their religion.[2]

---

[1] Al-Qaadhi Iyaadh al-Yahsoobi, ***Kitaab al-Imaan min Ikmaal al-Muallim (sic) bi-Fawaaid Saheeh Muslim*** (Riyadh: Dar al-Watn, 1417 A.H.), vol. 1, p. 101.

[2] Cf., Ali al-Qaari, ***Mirqat al-Mafateeh Sharh Mishkat al-Masabeeh*** (Multan, Pakistan: Maktaba Haqqaaniya, n.d.), vol. 1, p. 49.

This hadith is the second hadith in al-Nawawi's famous collection of forty hadith. This author is currently finishing an extensive commentary on that work. It was felt that this particular hadith, which covers the foundation of Islam and faith, is so important that it should also be published on its own.[1]

---

[1] Some of the sections that are more appropriate for the larger, more detailed work were deleted from this work. Furthermore, this publication is actually a combination of the author's commentary to Hadith #2 and Hadith #3 from al-Nawawi's collection. The value given this hadith can be seen in the fact that this is at least the eighth book written solely on this one hadith. Al-Nafazi (d. 684 A.H.), al-Tarsoosi (c. 1120 A.H.), ibn Taahir (d. 1241), ibn al-Haaj al-Madani (d. 1378), ibn al-Uthaimin, al-Hilaali and Salaam have all written books on this hadith. For information about the first six of those books, see Yusuf al-Ateeq, *al-Tareef bima Ufrid min al-Ahadeeth bi-l-Tasneef* (Riyadh: Dar al-Sameei, 1997), pp. 58-59. Salaam's book shall be quoted later in this work.

The Text of The Hadith of Angel Jibreel

عن عُمَرَ رَضِيَ اللَّهُ عَنْهُ أيضاً قَالَ بَيْنَمَا نَحْنُ عِنْدَ رَسُولِ اللَّهِ صَلَّى اللَّهُ عَلَيْهِ وَسَلَّمَ ذَاتَ يَوْمٍ إِذْ طَلَعَ عَلَيْنَا رَجُلٌ شَدِيدُ بَيَاضِ الثِّيَابِ شَدِيدُ سَوَادِ الشَّعَرِ لا يُرَى عَلَيْهِ أَثَرُ السَّفَرِ وَلا يَعْرِفُهُ مِنَّا أَحَدٌ حَتَّى جَلَسَ إِلَى النَّبِيِّ صَلَّى اللَّهُ عَلَيْهِ وَسَلَّمَ فَأَسْنَدَ رُكْبَتَيْهِ إِلَى رُكْبَتَيْهِ وَوَضَعَ كَفَّيْهِ عَلَى فَخِذَيْهِ وَقَالَ يَا مُحَمَّدُ أَخْبِرْنِي عَنِ الإِسْلامِ فَقَالَ رَسُولُ اللَّهِ صَلَّى اللَّهُ عَلَيْهِ وَسَلَّمَ الإِسْلامُ أَنْ تَشْهَدَ أَنْ لا إِلَهَ إِلاَّ اللَّهُ وَأَنَّ مُحَمَّدًا رَسُولُ اللَّهِ صَلَّى اللَّهُ عَلَيْهِ وَسَلَّمَ وَتُقِيمَ الصَّلاةَ وَتُؤْتِيَ الزَّكَاةَ وَتَصُومَ رَمَضَانَ وَتَحُجَّ الْبَيْتَ إِنِ اسْتَطَعْتَ إِلَيْهِ سَبِيلاً قَالَ صَدَقْتَ قَالَ فَعَجِبْنَا لَهُ يَسْأَلُهُ وَيُصَدِّقُهُ قَالَ فَأَخْبِرْنِي عَنِ الإِيمَانِ قَالَ أَنْ تُؤْمِنَ بِاللَّهِ وَمَلائِكَتِهِ وَكُتُبِهِ وَرُسُلِهِ وَالْيَوْمِ الآخِرِ

وَتُؤْمِنَ بِالْقَدَرِ خَيْرِهِ وَشَرِّهِ قَالَ صَدَقْتَ قَالَ فَأَخْبِرْنِي عَنِ الإِحْسَانِ قَالَ أَنْ تَعْبُدَ اللَّهَ كَأَنَّكَ تَرَاهُ فَإِنْ لَمْ تَكُنْ تَرَاهُ فَإِنَّهُ يَرَاكَ قَالَ فَأَخْبِرْنِي عَنِ السَّاعَةِ قَالَ مَا الْمَسْئُولُ عَنْهَا بِأَعْلَمَ مِنَ السَّائِلِ قَالَ فَأَخْبِرْنِي عَنْ أَمَارَتِهَا قَالَ أَنْ تَلِدَ الأَمَةُ رَبَّتَهَا وَأَنْ تَرَى الْحُفَاةَ الْعُرَاةَ الْعَالَةَ رِعَاءَ الشَّاءِ يَتَطَاوَلُونَ فِي الْبُنْيَانِ قَالَ ثُمَّ انْطَلَقَ فَلَبِثْتُ مَلِيًّا ثُمَّ قَالَ يَا عُمَرُ أَتَدْرِي مَنِ السَّائِلُ قُلْتُ اللَّهُ وَرَسُولُهُ أَعْلَمُ قَالَ فَإِنَّهُ جِبْرِيلُ أَتَاكُمْ يُعَلِّمُكُمْ دِينَكُمْ

On the authority of Umar who said: One day while we were sitting with the Messenger of Allah (peace be upon him), there came before us a man with extremely white clothing and extremely black hair. There were no signs of travel on him and none of us knew him. He [came and] sat next to the Prophet (peace be upon him). He supported his knees up against the knees of the Prophet (peace be upon him) and put his hands on his thighs. He said, "O Muhammad, tell me about Islam." The Messenger of Allah (peace be upon him) said, "Islam is to testify that there is none worthy of worship except Allah and that Muhammad is the Messenger of Allah, to establish the prayers, to pay the zakat, to fast [the month of] Ramadhan, and

to make the pilgrimage to the House if you have the means to do so." He said, "You have spoken truthfully [or correctly]." We were amazed that he asks the question and then he says that he had spoken truthfully. He said, "Tell me about *Imaan* (faith)." He [the Messenger of Allah (peace be upon him)] responded, "It is to believe in Allah, His angels, His books, His messengers, the Last Day and to believe in the divine decree, [both] the good and the evil thereof." He said, "You have spoken truthfully." He said, "Tell me about *al-Ihsaan* (goodness)." He [the Prophet] answered, "It is that you worship Allah as if you see Him. And even though you do not see Him, [you know] He sees you." He said, "Tell me about [the time of] the Hour." He [the Prophet (peace be upon him)] answered, "The one being asked does not know more than the one asking." He said, "Tell me about its signs." He answered, "The slave-girl shall give birth to her master[1]; and you will see the barefooted, scantily-clothed, destitute shepherds competing in constructing lofty buildings." Then he went away. I stayed for a long time. Then he [the Prophet (peace be upon him)] said, "O Umar, do you know who the questioner was?" I said, "Allah and His Messenger know best." He said, "It was [the Angel] Gabriel who came to teach you your religion."

---

[1] The text may be understood as meaning "female master" but most commentators, based on other narrations of the hadith, understand it to be a generic reference to "master".

This hadith from Umar ibn al-Khattab was recorded by Muslim[1], al-Tirmidhi, al-Nasai, ibn Majah, Ahmad, Abu Dawud, al-Baihaqi, ibn Hibban, ibn Khuzaima, al-Bazaar, Abu Yala, al-Daraqutni and a number of others.[2]

The scholars of hadith differentiate hadith by their texts as well as by the Companions who narrated the hadith. This particular hadith has also been narrated through acceptable chains from the Companions Abu Huraira, ibn Umar, ibn Masud and al-Harith al-Ashari. The narration from Abu Huraira has been recorded by al-Bukhari, Muslim, ibn Majah, ibn Abu Shaiba, ibn Hibban and others.[3]

The Circumstances Behind the Hadith

In one of the narrations in *Sahih Muslim*, this hadith of Gabriel begins in the following manner:

> Abu Huraira narrated that the Messenger of Allah (peace be upon him) said, "Ask me [about matters related to the religion]." However, the people abstained from doing so because they were overawed out of profound respect for him. In the

---

[1] By studying the chains and texts of this hadith and how Imam Muslim presented them in his *Sahih*, one would appreciate the exactness and detail that Imam Muslim has demonstrated. Many such important points have been highlighted by al-Nawawi in his commentary to *Sahih Muslim*. See Yahya al-Nawawi, *Sharh Sahih Muslim* (Beirut: Dar al-Fikr, n.d.), vol. 1, pp. 151-152.

[2] Ibn Hajr points out that the reason that al-Bukhari did not record the narration from Umar ibn al-Khattab is that there was some difference of opinion concerning the acceptability of some of its narrators. [See Ahmad ibn Hajr, *Fath al-Baari bi-Sharh Sahih al-Bukhari* (Makkah: al-Maktabah al-Tijaariyah, 1993), vol. 1, p. 159.] Hence, as was his custom, al-Bukhari, even if he accepted those narrators, did not record this hadith in order to avoid any question about the hadith of his *Sahih*. However, Muslim's approach was to record such narrations in order to demonstrate that they are authentic and that the criticisms of them are not valid.

[3] Cf., Fauzi ibn Muhammad, *al-Adhwaa al-Samaawiyah fi Takhreej Ahadeeth al-Arbaeen al-Nawaiyah* (Amman, Jordan: al-Maktabah al-Islamiyah, 1413 A.H.), pp. 52-55.

> meanwhile a man came there and sat near his knees and said, "Messenger of Allah, what is Islam?"...[1]

According to al-Ubayy, the reason the Prophet (peace be upon him) said, "Ask me," is because they were asking many questions and the Prophet (peace be upon him) realized that some were asking obstinately. Therefore, he became angry and said, "Ask me, ask me, for, by Allah, you will not ask me about anything except that I shall tell you about it as long as I am standing in this place."[2] After hearing and seeing this, the people became fearful and refrained from asking any questions. When the people refrained from asking questions, Allah sent the angel Gabriel to put these important questions to the Prophet (peace be upon him).[3]

Al-Sanusi adds that such questions do not go against the prohibition of asking questions. Actually, one must ask these types of questions because the answers to them are needed. Hence, this is an application of the Quranic verse,

فَسْـَٔلُوٓاْ أَهۡلَ ٱلذِّكۡرِ إِن كُنتُمۡ

لَا تَعۡلَمُونَ

"So ask of those who know the Scripture, if you know not" (*al-Nahl* 43).[4]

In other words, there is a type of questioning that should be avoided and a type of questioning that is commanded. Questions of a useless nature or of a purely theoretical nature with no benefit to them are to be avoided. Questions for which answers are truly needed must be

---

[1] See Abdul Hameed Siddiqi, trans., *Sahih Muslim*, (Beirut: Dar al-Arabia, n.d.), vol. 1, p. 4.

[2] Actually, al-Ubayy is referring to another hadith in *Sahih Muslim*.

[3] Abu Abdullah al-Ubayy, *Sharh Sahih Muslim* (Riyadh: Maktaba Tabariyyah, n.d), vol. 1, pp. 77-78.

[4] Muhammad al-Sanusi, *Sharh al-Sanusi*, on the margin of al-Ubayy, vol. 1, p. 77.

asked. Hence, Allah sent the angel Gabriel to the Prophet (peace be upon him) to ask him these questions and to demonstrate that important questions like these are to be asked of the people of knowledge.

"One day while we were sitting with the Messenger of Allah (peace be upon him)... put his hands on his thighs. He said, 'O Muhammad...'"

The different narrations of the hadith, referred to earlier, describe the appearance of the angel Gabriel who came to the Prophet (peace be upon him) in the appearance of a bedouin Arab. Bedouins were known for their coarse and rough nature. The Angel spoke from the back of the mosque, "Peace be upon you, o Muhammad, may I come forward?" The Prophet (peace be upon him) told him to come forward and he continued asking until he came directly to the Prophet (peace be upon him), walking over the people as he came to the front of the mosque. He then sat directly in front of the Prophet (peace be upon him), putting his hands on the Prophet's thighs. Then he began to ask the Prophet (peace be upon him) his questions. His calling the Prophet (peace be upon him) by his first name only, his walking over the necks of the people and his sitting directly in front of the Prophet (peace be upon him) all added to his appearance of being an apparently ignorant or ill-mannered bedouin Arab.

At the end of the hadith, the Prophet (peace be upon him) explained that the bedouin-looking person was the Angel Gabriel who had come to teach them their religion. According to al-Haitami and others, his teaching was both in the form of his questions and also in his behavior. Hence, some conclusions can be made from his appearance and behavior.[1]

It is not clear to this author whether the commentators noticed that they seem to be making two contradictory suggestions here. First they are stating that the angel came in a very rude fashion and then they are suggesting that his example is one that can be followed. It seems that the key is to distinguish between what the angel did in order to get attention and to make sure that everyone would pay attention to him from what he did as an example for others to follow.

"extremely white clothing and extremely black hair."

In other narrations, it also states that his clothing was so clean that there were no traces of dirt upon them. Scholars understand from Gabriel's appearance that it is recommended to have a good appearance and to be clean.[2] This is especially true when one is going to the mosque and when one is attempting to attain knowledge. White clothing is a preferred clothing, especially for the people of knowledge. According to al-Haitami, Umar recommended it for the reciters of the Quran.[3] Cleanliness is also an important characteristic of the true Muslim and, like all characteristics of true Muslims, must be even more-so emphasized for the scholars and the students of knowledge. They should set the examples for others.

There may be another aspect of note here. Islam places emphasis on both the outward and inward aspects of a human being. Neither aspect is neglected. One can understand from many texts that there is a strong

---

[1] Ahmad al-Haitami, *Fath al-Mubeen li-Sharh al-Arbaeen* (Beirut: Dar al-Kutub al-Ilmiyah, 1978), p. 59.
[2] Al-Haitami, *Fath*, p. 59.
[3] Al-Haitami, *Fath*, p. 59.

relationship between the two. If one wants to attain knowledge, one must approach that knowledge in the proper manner by first having the correct intention and also by having the proper respect for the knowledge that he seeks to attain. Having proper respect for the knowledge includes being willing to sacrifice one's time and wealth for it as well as outwardly showing respect for it by sitting and appearing in a proper manner while attaining knowledge or passing on knowledge.

"There were no signs of travel on him and none of us knew him."

He was not from the people of Madina and yet there were no signs that he had come from travel. Hence, his appearance was something special and immediately attracted the people's attention to him. Perhaps, Allah knows best, this was so the people would watch and listen to what he did very carefully. In this way, they would pay close attention to him, grasp his words and the Prophet's response and then pass it on to others who came afterwards.

Umar said that none of them knew the man. This was not simply conjecture on Umar's part. In other narrations, it explicitly states that the people looked at each other and had no idea who this man was.[1]

---

[1] Ibn Hajr, *Fath*, vol. 1, p. 160.

"He [came and] sat next to the Prophet (peace be upon him). He supported his knees up against the knees of the Prophet (peace be upon him)"

This should be the attitude of those who are truly seeking knowledge. They should try to get close to the teacher so that they can understand and hear everything he says correctly. Unfortunately, one does not always find such an attitude among Muslims today. They have more of a desire to sit in a comfortable way, with their backs against a wall, for example, rather than getting close to the teacher so that they can absorb as much as possible.

"and put his hands on his thighs"

Al-Nawawi declares that the Angel Gabriel put his own hands on his own thighs. However, in the narrations from ibn Abbas and Abu Amr al-Ashari, it explicitly states that the Angel put his hands on the thighs of the Prophet (peace be upon him). This was also the conclusion of al-Baghawi, al-Taimi and al-Tibi. Al-Turabashti also argues that this is the correct interpretation as this is the way a student should sit in front of his teacher. Perhaps it was done so he could best listen to the Prophet (peace be upon him) and absorb everything the Prophet (peace be upon him) had to say in response to the important questions he was about to pose. It shows that the questioner should be humble and polite in front of the one he is questioning.[1]

On the other hand, Ibn Hajr points out that, once again, this abrupt manner of coming all the way to the Prophet (peace be upon him) and putting his hands on the Prophet's thighs may have been just another means by

---

[1] See ibn Hajr, *Fath*, vol. 1, p. 160.

which he is showing himself to be a rough, ill-mannered bedouin Arab.[1] Hence, it could have been simply another act to attract the people's complete attention.

He said, "O Muhammad..."

Allah has said in the Quran,

لَّا تَجْعَلُوا۟ دُعَآءَ ٱلرَّسُولِ بَيْنَكُمْ كَدُعَآءِ بَعْضِكُم بَعْضًا

"Make not the calling of the Messenger among you as your calling of each other" (*al-Noor* 63). In this hadith, the Angel addressed the Prophet (peace be upon him) by saying, "O Muhammad." This has caused some concern. Such a way of addressing the Prophet (peace be upon him) is not considered proper and is censored in the above verse of the Quran. How is it that the angel addressed him in that manner? Three answers have been given to this question: (1) The prohibition of such address applies to humans only and not to the angels; (2) this event occurred before the prohibition of such address (although this explanation seems unlikely since the event took place so late in the Prophet's life); and (3) this was done to further the appearance that he was a bedouin Arab.[2]

---

[1] Ibid.
[2] Al-Haitami, *Fath*, p. 61.

The Pillars of Islam

"tell me about Islam"

In his reply, the Prophet (peace be upon him) did not give the linguistic meaning of the word Islam, in the same way that he did not give the linguistic meaning of the word *Imaan* when asked about that. Perhaps, the concepts were something very clear and the Prophet (peace be upon him) realized that the person was asking about what makes up Islam and *Imaan* and not the definition of those two terms.

Lexically speaking, the word *islaam* implies submission. In its particular sense related to the religion of Islam, Nomani wrote,

> Literally, Islam denotes self-surrender or to give oneself up to someone and accept his overlordship in the fullest sense of the term. The religion sent down by God and brought into the world by His Apostles has been called Islam for the simple reason that, in it, the bondsman yields completely to the power and control of the Lord and makes the rendering of whole-hearted obedience to Him the cardinal principle of his life. This is the sum and substance of the Islamic creed...[1]

---

[1] Mohammad Manzoor Nomani, *Meaning and Message of the Traditions* (Lucknow, India: Academy of Islamic Research and Publications, 1975), vol. 1, p. 54.

"The Messenger of Allah (peace be upon him) said, 'Islam is to testify that there is none worthy of worship except Allah'"

The testimony of faith or *shahaadah* is a combination of negation and affirmation. The negation comes first followed by the exception of affirmation. This is considered the strongest form of all-inclusiveness in the Arabic language. The *shahaadah*, therefore, means: There is absolutely none worthy of worship and there is no true God except Allah and only Allah.

In essence, one is testifying to his belief in the Islamic concept of *tauheed*, as shall be discussed in detail under the heading "Belief in Allah."

The Conditions of *La ilaaha illa-llah*[1]

Muslims know that the key to Paradise is the statement, "There is none worthy of worship except Allah." Yet many Muslims simply rely upon this statement and believe that as long as they have said it, nothing will harm them. Because of this mere verbal statement of the *shahaadah*, they think they will be granted Paradise However, the mere saying of the statement is not sufficient for salvation. In fact, the hypocrites used to say, "I testify

[1] The conditions of the testimony of faith are well-known and discussed in numerous works. Most of the above information has been derived from Haafidh ibn Ahmad Hakimi, *Maarij al-Qubool bi-Sharh Sullim al-Wusool ila Ilm al-Usool fi al-Tauheed* (Beirut: Dar al-Kutub al-Ilmiyah, 1983), vol. 1, pp. 307-315; Abdullah ibn Jibreen, *al-Shahadataan* (no city or publisher given, 1990), pp. 77-86. This author also presented most of this material on the two parts of the *shahaadah* in his *The Friday Prayer: Part II: Khutbahs (I)* (Aurora, CO: IANA, 1994), pp. 4-19; *The Friday Prayer: Part III: Khutbahs (II)* (Ann Arbor, MI: IANA, 1995), pp. 35-42.

that none is worthy of worship except Allah and.. " yet Allah describes them as liars and says that they shall abide in the lowest abyss of the Hell-fire.

As many scholars have stated, this statement or testimony is the key to Paradise. However, its saying must meet certain conditions. Al-Hasan al-Basri once told a person, "What have you prepared for death?" He replied, "The testimony that there is none worthy of worship except Allah." Al-Hasan told him, "That has some conditions to it. And beware of defaming chaste women."[1] The famous Follower Wahb ibn Munabbih was once asked, "Isn't the statement of *la ilaha illa-llah* the key to Paradise?" He answered, "Yes, but every key has ridges. If you come with the key that has the right ridges, the door will open for you. Yet if you do not have the right ridges, the door will not open for you." These ridges are conditions that differentiate Muslims who will benefit from that statement from those who will not benefit from that statement, no matter how many times a day they may have made that statement.

Before discussing the conditions of the *shahaadah*, there is one more point that should be made. Some people have a tendency to take one hadith or one verse and then, based on that one text, make a general conclusion solely based on that one text. For example, one could conclude from some hadith that whoever simply says, "There is no God except Allah," will enter Paradise. But, actually, one must realize that all of the Quran and hadith complement each other and explain one another. To find the correct position on any one question, one must bring together all of the related verses and hadith and see what the true Islamic position is on that question. The same is true for the conditions of the *shahaadah*.

---

[1] The person al-Hasan was speaking to was a poet who would defame the pious women and that is why al-Hasan made that point to him. See Jamaal Baadi, *Al-Athaar al-Waarada an Aimmat al-Sunnah fi Abwaab al-Itiqaad* (Riyadh: Dar al-Watn, 1416 A.H.) vol. 1, pp. 162-164.

A study of the verses of the Quran and the hadith of the Prophet (peace be upon him) will show find that the conditions of the *shahaadah* are seven, eight or nine in number depending on how one views them. It is important that every Muslim ensures that he is meeting these conditions in his own life with respect to his own testimony of faith.

The first condition is knowledge: One must have the necessary basic understanding of what is meant by the *shahaadah*. One must understand what the *shahaadah* is affirming and what the *shahaadah* is denying. Allah says in the Quran,

فَاعْلَمْ أَنَّهُۥ لَآ إِلَٰهَ إِلَّا ٱللَّهُ وَٱسْتَغْفِرْ لِذَنۢبِكَ
وَلِلْمُؤْمِنِينَ وَٱلْمُؤْمِنَٰتِ

"So know that there is no God save Allah, and ask forgiveness for your sin and for the believing men and the believing women" (*Muhammad* 19). Similarly, the Prophet (peace be upon him) said,

مَنْ مَاتَ وَهُوَ يَعْلَمُ أَنَّهُ لا إِلَهَ إِلاَّ اللَّهُ دَخَلَ الْجَنَّةَ

"Whoever dies knowing that there is no one worthy of worship except Allah shall enter Paradise." (Recorded by Muslim.)

In fact, the *shahaadah* itself is a testimony. When one testifies to something, one must know what it is that he is testifying concerning. Obviously, a testimony about something that one does not have any knowledge of is unacceptable. Allah says in the Quran,

إِلَّا مَن شَهِدَ بِٱلْحَقِّ وَهُمْ
يَعْلَمُونَ

"Save him who bears witness unto the truth knowingly" (*al-Zukhruf* 86).

Therefore, the basics of the *shahaadah* must be understood by the person testifying to it. If he does not understand, for example, that Allah is the only one worthy of worship and that all other gods are false gods, then he does not even have the most elementary understanding of what it is he claims to be testifying to. Such a *shahaadah* cannot be considered a proper one that is acceptable to Allah.

The second condition of the *shahaadah* is certainty or *al-yaqeen*. This is the opposite of doubt and uncertainty. In Islam, in fact, any kind of doubt concerning anything confirmed in the Quran or the sunnah is equivalent to *kufr* or disbelief.[1] One must, in his heart, be absolutely certain of the truth of the *shahaadah*. One's heart must not be wavering in any way when one testifies to the truth of, "There is none worthy of worship except Allah." Allah describes the true believers as those who have belief in Allah and then their hearts waver not. Allah says,

إِنَّمَا ٱلْمُؤْمِنُونَ ٱلَّذِينَ ءَامَنُوا۟ بِٱللَّهِ وَرَسُولِهِۦ ثُمَّ لَمْ يَرْتَابُوا۟ وَجَـٰهَدُوا۟

بِأَمْوَٰلِهِمْ وَأَنفُسِهِمْ فِى سَبِيلِ ٱللَّهِ ۚ أُو۟لَـٰٓئِكَ هُمُ ٱلصَّـٰدِقُونَ

"The (true) believers are only those who believe in Allah and His messenger and afterward doubt not, but strive with their wealth and their lives for the cause of Allah. Such are the sincere" (*al-Hujuraat* 15). Similarly, the Messenger of Allah (peace be upon him) said,

[1] An exception to this is related to the case of ignorance where one is doubtful about something and is not aware that it is proven in the Quran and sunnah. But once the person knows that something is definitively confirmed in the Quran or sunnah, there is no excuse for him to have any doubt about it.

أشْهَدُ أنْ لا إلَهَ إلاَّ اللَّهُ وَأنِّي رَسُولُ اللَّهِ لا يَلْقَى اللَّهَ بِهِمَا عَبْدٌ غَيْرَ شَاكٍّ فِيهِمَا إلاَّ دَخَلَ الْجَنَّةَ

"No one meets Allah with the testimony that there is none worthy of worship but Allah and I am the Messenger of Allah, and he has no doubt about that statement, except that he will enter Paradise." (Recorded by Muslim.)

On the other hand, Allah describes the hypocrites as those people whose hearts are wavering. For example, Allah says,

إِنَّمَا يَسْتَـْٔذِنُكَ ٱلَّذِينَ لَا يُؤْمِنُونَ بِٱللَّهِ وَٱلْيَوْمِ ٱلْـَٔاخِرِ وَٱرْتَابَتْ قُلُوبُهُمْ فَهُمْ فِى رَيْبِهِمْ يَتَرَدَّدُونَ

"They alone seek leave of you [not to participate in jihad] who believe not in Allah and the Last Day and whose hearts feel doubt, so in their doubt they waver" (*al-Tauba* 45).

Many scholars have stated that the diseases of the heart, or the doubts and suspicions that one allows into one's heart, are more dangerous for a person's faith than lusts and desires. This is because lusts and desires may be satisfied at some time yet the person still knows them to be wrong. He may then eventually be able to control himself, repent and give up those evil deeds. On the other hand, doubts and suspicions may linger in the heart, with no cure, until the person finally leaves Islam entirely or continues to practice Islam while, in fact, in his heart he does not have the true faith.

One of the greatest cures for these doubts is knowledge. A sound knowledge of the Quran and sunnah removes most, or all, of these doubts. By study and understanding, one may attain certainty. And as one studies and learns more, his certainty will be made firmer and firmer.

The third condition of the *shahaadah* is acceptance or *al-qabool*. If a person has the knowledge of and certainty in the *shahaadah*, this must be followed by acceptance, with the tongue and heart, of whatever that *shahaadah* implies. Whoever refuses to accept the *shahaadah* and its implications, even if he knows that it is true and is certain about its truth, is a disbeliever. This refusal to accept is sometimes due to pride, envy or other reasons. In any case, the *shahaadah* is not a true *shahaadah* without its unconditional acceptance.

The scholars talk about this condition as a general condition in the manner just described. However, there is also a more detailed aspect that one must be aware of. This condition also means that he believes in whatever is stated in the Quran or stated by the Prophet (peace be upon him), without any right to choose what he wants to believe and what he wants to reject. Allah says in the Quran,

أَفَتُؤْمِنُونَ بِبَعْضِ ٱلْكِتَـٰبِ وَتَكْفُرُونَ
بِبَعْضٍ ۚ فَمَا جَزَآءُ مَن يَفْعَلُ ذَٰلِكَ مِنكُمْ إِلَّا خِزْىٌ فِى ٱلْحَيَوٰةِ
ٱلدُّنْيَا ۖ وَيَوْمَ ٱلْقِيَـٰمَةِ يُرَدُّونَ إِلَىٰٓ أَشَدِّ ٱلْعَذَابِ ۗ

"Do you believe in part of the Book and reject part of it? And what is the reward of those who do so save ignominy in the life of the world, and on the Day of Resurrection they will be consigned to the most grievous doom" (*al-Baqara* 85). Allah has also said,

وَمَا كَانَ لِمُؤْمِنٍ وَلَا مُؤْمِنَةٍ إِذَا قَضَى ٱللَّهُ وَرَسُولُهُۥٓ أَمْرًا أَن يَكُونَ لَهُمُ
ٱلْخِيَرَةُ مِنْ أَمْرِهِمْ ۗ وَمَن يَعْصِ ٱللَّهَ وَرَسُولَهُۥ فَقَدْ ضَلَّ ضَلَـٰلًا مُّبِينًا

"It is not for a believing man or believing woman, when Allah and His Messenger have decreed a matter, to have any option in their decision. And whoever disobeys Allah and is Messenger has indeed strayed in plain error" (*al-Ahzaab* 36).

The fourth condition of the *shahaadah* is submission and compliance or *al-inqiyaad.* This implies the actual physical enactment by deeds of one's *shahaadah.* This is one of the main meanings of the word Islam itself, "the submission to the will and commands of Allah." Allah commands this in the Quran,

وَأَنِيبُوٓاْ إِلَىٰ رَبِّكُمۡ وَأَسۡلِمُواْ لَهُۥ

"Turn unto Him repentant, and surrender unto Him" (*al-Zumar* 54). Allah has praised those who submit to His command by their actions. Allah says,

وَمَنۡ أَحۡسَنُ دِينٗا مِّمَّنۡ أَسۡلَمَ وَجۡهَهُۥ لِلَّهِ وَهُوَ مُحۡسِنٞ

"Who is better in religion than he who surrenders his purpose to Allah while doing good" (*al-Nisaa* 125).

Allah has made it a condition of faith that one submits to the command of Allah and His messenger. Allah says,

فَلَا وَرَبِّكَ لَا يُؤۡمِنُونَ حَتَّىٰ يُحَكِّمُوكَ فِيمَا شَجَرَ
بَيۡنَهُمۡ ثُمَّ لَا يَجِدُواْ فِيٓ أَنفُسِهِمۡ حَرَجٗا مِّمَّا قَضَيۡتَ
وَيُسَلِّمُواْ تَسۡلِيمٗا

"But nay, by your Lord, they will not truly believe until they make you [the Messenger of Allah] judge of what is in dispute between them and find within themselves no dislike of that which you decide, and submit with full submission" (*al-Nisa* 65).

As shall be discussed in the discussion on *imaan*, the *shahaadah* is a testimony of faith that must be implemented in one's heart, tongue and actions. In one's heart, for example, one must have love for Allah, fear of

Allah and hope in Him. With one's tongue, one must testify to the *shahaadah*. With one's actions, one is supposed to implement what the testimony of faith requires of him. Anyone who claims to be a Muslim and yet performs no corresponding acts, either does not understand Islam whatsoever or is bearing testimony against himself that his testimony of faith is not a true and correct testimony of faith.

This does not mean that the true believer never falls into sin. Indeed, true believers do commit sins. But as long as they recognize that what they did is not correct and it is inconsistent with their obligation of submitting to Allah, then they have not violated the soundness of their testimony or *shahaadah*.

The fifth condition is truthfulness as opposed to hypocrisy and dishonesty. This means that when one says the *shahaadah*, he is saying it honestly, actually meaning it. He is not lying when it comes to his testimony of faith or simply trying to deceive or fool anyone. The Prophet (peace be upon him) said,

مَا مِنْ أَحَدٍ يَشْهَدُ أَنْ لا إِلَهَ إِلاَّ اللَّهُ وَأَنَّ مُحَمَّدًا رَسُولُ اللَّهِ صِدْقًا مِنْ قَلْبِهِ إِلاَّ حَرَّمَهُ اللَّهُ عَلَى النَّارِ

"No one bears testimony to there being no one worthy of worship save Allah, sincerely from his heart, except that Allah makes the Hell-fire forbidden for him." (Recorded by al-Bukhari.)

Most people have heard of those who say the testimony of faith yet they are not saying it honestly. They do not believe in it. They are simply saying it in order to protect themselves or to get some gain from doing so. These are the hypocrites. Allah has described them in the opening of the Quran with the following words,

وَمِنَ ٱلنَّاسِ مَن يَقُولُ ءَامَنَّا بِٱللَّهِ وَبِٱلْيَوْمِ ٱلْءَاخِرِ وَمَا هُم بِمُؤْمِنِينَ ﴿٨﴾
يُخَٰدِعُونَ ٱللَّهَ وَٱلَّذِينَ ءَامَنُوا۟ وَمَا يَخْدَعُونَ إِلَّآ أَنفُسَهُمْ وَمَا يَشْعُرُونَ ﴿٩﴾
فِى قُلُوبِهِم مَّرَضٌ فَزَادَهُمُ ٱللَّهُ مَرَضًا ۖ وَلَهُمْ عَذَابٌ أَلِيمٌۢ بِمَا كَانُوا۟
يَكْذِبُونَ

"And of mankind are some who say, 'We believe in Allah and the Last Day,' when they believe not. They think to beguile Allah and those who believe, and they beguile none save themselves, but they perceive not. In their hearts is a disease, and Allah increases their disease. A painful doom is theirs because they lie" (*al-Baqara* 8-10).

The *shahaadah* of those who become Muslims only to benefit from being Muslim and not because they believe in Islam will be rejected by Allah in the Hereafter. They will face a painful punishment duc to their lying.

The sixth condition is a pure sincerity or *ikhlaas*. When one declares the *shahaadah*, one must do that solely for the sake of Allah. One must not do it for any other reason or anyone else's sake. In this manner, the meaning of purity is the opposite of *shirk* or ascribing partners with Allah. One becomes and remains Muslim solely to serve Allah, to avoid His anger and punishment and to gain His mercy and reward. Allah says in the Quran,

فَٱعْبُدِ ٱللَّهَ مُخْلِصًا لَّهُ ٱلدِّينَ

"Worship Allah, making religion pure for him" (*al-Zumar* 2). Allah also says,

وَمَآ أُمِرُوٓا۟ إِلَّا لِيَعْبُدُوا۟ ٱللَّهَ مُخْلِصِينَ لَهُ ٱلدِّينَ حُنَفَآءَ وَيُقِيمُوا۟ ٱلصَّلَوٰةَ
وَيُؤْتُوا۟ ٱلزَّكَوٰةَ ۚ وَذَٰلِكَ دِينُ ٱلْقَيِّمَةِ

"And they are ordered not else than to serve Allah, keeping religion pure for Him, as men by nature upright and to establish worship and to pay the poor-due. That is the true religion" (*al-Bayyinah* 5). The Prophet (peace be upon him) also said,

إنَّ اللّٰهَ قَدْ حَرَّمَ عَلَى النَّارِ مَنْ قَالَ لا إلَهَ إلاَّ اللّٰهُ يَبْتَغِي بِذَلِكَ وَجْهَ اللّٰه

"Allah has forbidden for the Hell-fire anyone who says, 'There is no one worthy of worship except Allah,' and says so desiring the face [and pleasure] of Allah." (Recorded by Muslim.)

This is something that all Muslims should think about, but especially those who grew up in Muslim families and were born Muslim. Everyone should be clear to himself that he is Muslim only for the sake of Allah. A Muslim cannot be a Muslim for the sake of his parents, friends, family, community or worldly goal. It must be clear in the mind that one is a Muslim for the sake of Allah first, last and only.

The seventh condition is love. That is, the believer loves this *shahaadah*, he loves in accordance with the *shahaadah*, he loves the implications and requirements of the *shahaadah* and he loves those who act and strive on the basis of this *shahaadah*. This is a necessary condition of the *shahaadah*. If a person makes the *shahaadah* but does not love the *shahaadah* and what it stands for, then, in fact, his faith is not complete. It is not the faith of a true believer. If he has no love for this *shahaadah* or if he actually feels hatred for it, he has negated his *shahaadah*.

The true believer puts no one as an equal to Allah in his love. Allah says in the Quran,

وَمِنَ ٱلنَّاسِ مَن يَتَّخِذُ مِن دُونِ ٱللَّهِ أَندَادًا يُحِبُّونَهُمْ كَحُبِّ ٱللَّهِۖ وَٱلَّذِينَ ءَامَنُوٓاْ أَشَدُّ حُبًّا لِّلَّهِۗ

"Yet of mankind are some who take unto themselves (objects of worship which they set as) rivals to Allah, loving them with a love like (that which is due to) Allah only. However, those who believe are stauncher in their love of Allah" (*al-Baqara* 165). Elsewhere Allah says,

قُلْ إِن كَانَ ءَابَآؤُكُمْ وَأَبْنَآؤُكُمْ وَإِخْوَٰنُكُمْ وَأَزْوَٰجُكُمْ وَعَشِيرَتُكُمْ وَأَمْوَٰلٌ ٱقْتَرَفْتُمُوهَا وَتِجَٰرَةٌ تَخْشَوْنَ كَسَادَهَا وَمَسَٰكِنُ تَرْضَوْنَهَآ أَحَبَّ إِلَيْكُم مِّنَ ٱللَّهِ وَرَسُولِهِۦ وَجِهَادٍ فِى سَبِيلِهِۦ فَتَرَبَّصُوا۟ حَتَّىٰ يَأْتِىَ ٱللَّهُ بِأَمْرِهِۦ ۗ وَٱللَّهُ لَا يَهْدِى ٱلْقَوْمَ ٱلْفَٰسِقِينَ

"Say: If your fathers, your sons, your brethren, your wives, your tribe, the wealth you have acquired, merchandise for which you fear that there will be no sale, or dwellings you desire are dearer to you than Allah and His messenger and striving in His way: then wait till Allah brings His command to pass. Allah guides not wrongdoing folk" (*al-Tauba* 24). The Prophet (peace be upon him) said,

ثَلاثٌ مَنْ كُنَّ فِيهِ وَجَدَ حَلاوَةَ الْإِيمَانِ أَنْ يَكُونَ اللَّهُ وَرَسُولُهُ أَحَبَّ إِلَيْهِ مِمَّا سِوَاهُمَا

"Whoever has three characteristics has tasted the sweetness of faith. [The first of these] is that he loves Allah and His Messenger more than he loves anyone else..." (Recorded by al-Bukhari and Muslim.)

An eighth condition of the *shahaadah* is that the person who makes the *shahaadah* must deny every other object of worship. Although that is clear in the words of the testimony of faith, it does not seem clear to everyone who makes that testimony. Therefore, it needs to be mentioned explicitly.

In *surah al-Baqara*, Allah reminds Muslims of this important aspect of the *shahaadah.* The *shahaadah* is not merely an affirmation but it is both an affirmation and a negation. Allah states,

فَمَن يَكْفُرْ بِٱلطَّـٰغُوتِ

وَيُؤْمِنۢ بِٱللَّهِ فَقَدِ ٱسْتَمْسَكَ بِٱلْعُرْوَةِ ٱلْوُثْقَىٰ لَا ٱنفِصَامَ لَهَا

"And he who rejects false deities and believes in Allah has grasped a firm handhold which will never break" (*al-Baqara* 256). The Prophet (peace be upon him) emphasized this point when he said,

مَنْ قَالَ لا إِلَهَ إِلاَّ اللَّهُ وَكَفَرَ بِمَا يُعْبَدُ مِنْ دُونِ اللَّهِ حَرُمَ مَالُهُ وَدَمُهُ وَحِسَابُهُ عَلَى اللَّهِ

"Whoever says there is no one worthy of worship except Allah and denies whatever is worshipped besides Allah, then his wealth and blood are protected and his accounting will be with Allah." (Recorded by Muslim.)

Although this condition should be obvious to everyone who says the words of the *shahaadah*, one can still find Muslims who say the *shahaadah* and then make acts of worship for beings or things other than Allah. One can find them going to the graveyards and worshipping those in the graves. They will perform acts of worship, not for the sake of Allah, but for the sake of the dead "saints" (*auliyaa*) in the grave.

The ninth condition of the *shahaadah* is that the Muslim adheres to the *shahaadah* until he dies. This is a must if the *shahaadah* is to mean anything in the Hereafter. One cannot rest on his laurels of what he may have done in the past. No, indeed, the *shahaadah* must be his banner until death. Allah says in the Quran,

يَـٰٓأَيُّهَا ٱلَّذِينَ ءَامَنُوا۟ ٱتَّقُوا۟ ٱللَّهَ حَقَّ تُقَاتِهِۦ وَلَا تَمُوتُنَّ إِلَّا وَأَنتُم مُّسْلِمُونَ

"O believers, observe your duty to Allah with right observance, and die not save as Muslims [surrendering yourselves to Allah]" (*ali-Imraan* 102).

"and that Muhammad is the Messenger of Allah"

Most everyone knows that to enter into Islam one must bear witness that there is none worthy of worship save Allah and that Muhammad is the Messenger of Allah (peace be upon him). Many times the first part of the *shahaadah* or testimony is discussed in detail. However, it is just as important to understand the meaning and the implications of the second part of the *shahaadah.* Indeed, sometimes one strays from the Straight Path and from Islam itself because he is not implementing the second part of the *shahaadah* properly.

When one testifies that Muhammad is the Messenger of Allah, he is stating his belief that the Prophet Muhammad (peace be upon him) was chosen by Allah to be His Messenger and to convey His Message. Allah says in the Quran,

وَرَبُّكَ يَخْلُقُ مَا يَشَآءُ وَيَخْتَارُ

"And your Lord creates whatsoever He wills and He chooses" (*al-Qasas* 68). Allah creates and has power to do all things. Allah specifically chose the Prophet Muhammad (peace be upon him) to be His Messenger. In another verse, Allah says,

ٱللَّهُ

أَعْلَمُ حَيْثُ يَجْعَلُ رِسَالَتَهُۥ

"Allah knows best with whom to place His Message" (*al-Anaam* 124).

This implies some characteristics of the Prophet Muhammad (peace be upon him) as obviously Allah, due to His justice, wisdom and mercy, would not choose one who is treacherous or lying to be His Messenger. Allah would not choose anyone for such an important mission whom He knew would not convey the message or who would use the position to his own advantage. If anyone claims that the Prophet (peace be upon him) did not actually convey the entire message or that he distorted it in any way, he is actually saying that Allah did not know who was the correct or best person to be a messenger. This is obvious disbelief.

Second, when one makes the *shahaadah*, he is also testifying that the Prophet (peace be upon him) has been sent for all of mankind until the Day of Judgment. Allah says in the Quran,

قُلْ يَـٰٓأَيُّهَا ٱلنَّاسُ إِنِّى رَسُولُ ٱللَّهِ إِلَيْكُمْ جَمِيعًا

"Say [O Muhammad]: O mankind! Verily, I am sent to you all as the Messenger of Allah" (*al-Araaf* 158). Furthermore, the Prophet (peace be upon him) said,

أُعْطِيتُ خَمْسًا لَمْ يُعْطَهُنَّ أَحَدٌ مِنَ الْأَنْبِيَاءِ قَبْلِي... وَكَانَ النَّبِيُّ يُبْعَثُ إِلَى قَوْمِهِ خَاصَّةً وَبُعِثْتُ إِلَى النَّاسِ كَافَّةً

"I have been given five aspects that were not given to any prophet before me... [One of which is] every prophet was sent only to his people while I have been sent to all of mankind." (Recorded by al-Bukhari and Muslim.)

It is obligatory upon everyone from the time of the Prophet (peace be upon him) until the Day of Judgment to believe in and follow the Prophet (peace be upon him). If the message of Islam clearly reaches a person and he still refuses to believe in and follow the Prophet (peace be upon him), he is a disbeliever and will be in the Hell-fire forever— unless he repents and embraces Islam.

However, this also implies that the Prophet's teachings and his sunnah are valid and obligatory upon all of mankind until the Day of Judgment. That is, his example and teaching was not simply for the people of Arabia at his time. Instead, it is just as valid and just as important for each and every Muslim today, whether he be in New York or Malaysia.

Some people seem to try to resist the idea that they have to follow the Prophet (peace be upon him). When they do so, they must realize that they are going against what they have testified to. They have testified that the Prophet's message, which includes both the Quran and his inspired sunnah, is for all of mankind— including each and everyone alive today.

Third, when one declares the *shahaadah*, he is testifying that he believes with certainty that the Prophet Muhammad (peace be upon him) conveyed the message— he conveyed it correctly, he conveyed all of it, and he conveyed it clearly. Allah says in the Quran,

وَمَا عَلَى ٱلرَّسُولِ إِلَّا ٱلْبَلَٰغُ ٱلْمُبِينُ

"The Messenger's duty is only to convey (the message) in a clear way" (*al-Noor* 54). The Prophet (peace be upon him) himself said,

قَدْ تَرَكْتُكُمْ عَلَى الْبَيْضَاءِ لَيْلُهَا كَنَهَارِهَا لاَ يَزِيغُ عَنْهَا بَعْدِي إِلاَّ هَالِكٌ

"I left you on a bright path whose night and day are alike. No one strays from it after me except he is destroyed."[1]

The Prophet (peace be upon him) conveyed all of the guidance and revelation that he received from Allah. He conveyed and explained it in a clear manner. Therefore, when one makes the *shahaadah*, he is also testifying that the Prophet (peace be upon him) conveyed all the aspects of the religion– its fundamental as well as its secondary aspects. There is no part of the religion that one needs for his guidance that was not conveyed to mankind or that Allah or the Prophet (peace be upon him) may have possibly forgotten.

Therefore, when this complete and clear guidance from the Prophet (peace be upon him) is present, there is no need for any Muslim to turn to other sources for guidance. There is no need for one to turn to the books of the Jews or Christians. Indeed, the Prophet (peace be upon him) told Umar, when he saw him reading the Torah, that if the Prophet Moses were alive at his time, he would also have to follow the Prophet Muhammad (peace be upon him). There is no need for any Muslim to turn to the Greek philosophers, for example, to learn about theology. In fact, there is no need for Muslims to turn the religious or spiritual teachings of any non-Muslims to get guidance. All that is needed is to be found in the Quran and sunnah. This is part of what the Muslim is testifying to. The Muslim bears witness that the Prophet (peace be upon him) conveyed the entire message. This is all part of the meaning of the *shahaadah*.

When one declares, "Muhammad is the Messenger of Allah," one is also declaring that he is the final prophet sent by Allah. Allah says in the Quran,

---

[1] Recorded by Ahmad and al-Baihaqi. According to al-Albani, it is *sahih*. See Muhammad Nasir al-Din al-Albani, *Sahih al-Jami al-Sagheer* (Beirut: al-Maktab al-Islami, 1986), vol. 2, p. 805.

مَّا كَانَ مُحَمَّدٌ أَبَآ أَحَدٍ مِّن رِّجَالِكُمْ وَلَٰكِن رَّسُولَ ٱللَّهِ وَخَاتَمَ ٱلنَّبِيِّـۧنَ

"Muhammad is not the father of any man among you, but he is the Messenger of Allah and the Last of the Prophets" (*al-Ahzaab* 40).

There is to be no prophet who is going to come after the time of the Prophet Muhammad (peace be upon him). No new prophet and no new scripture will come that will abrogate what the Prophet Muhammad (peace be upon him) brought. Furthermore, if anyone after the time of the Prophet Muhammad (peace be upon him) claims to be a prophet, it is known automatically that such a person is a liar and a deceiver.[??] He must be opposed and it should be declared to all that his claim to prophethood is false. To accept anyone as a prophet after the Prophet Muhammad (peace be upon him) is to falsify one's declaration of the *shahaadah*.

When one makes the testimony of faith or the *shahaadah*, this not only implies that he believes in certain things but it also implies that he accepts certain responsibilities that stem from that *shahaadah*. For example, when he says that there is none worthy of worship except Allah, for that *shahaadah* to be a correct form of *shahaadah*, it means that he is now taking on the responsibility of worshipping no one other than Allah. Similarly, when one says, "I testify that Muhammad is the Messenger of Allah," he is taking on certain responsibilities with respect to the Prophet Muhammad (peace be upon him). When he is lacking in any of these responsibilities, then he is lacking in his complete fulfillment of his testimony of faith. It can even get to the point that he negates his *shahaadah* completely by refusing to fulfill his

---

[1] It is true that the Prophet Jesus (peace be upon him) will return. However, when he returns, he will not do so in the role of a prophet or messenger. He will be only a follower of the Prophet Muhammad (peace be upon him) and his Shariah.

responsibility to the Prophet Muhammad (peace be upon him).

One of these obligations toward the Prophet (peace be upon him) is to love him. This does not just imply any form of love but complete *imaan* requires that one loves the Prophet (peace be upon him) more than anyone or anything else of this world. Allah says in the Quran,

قُلْ إِن كَانَ ءَابَآؤُكُمْ وَأَبْنَآؤُكُمْ وَإِخْوَٰنُكُمْ وَأَزْوَٰجُكُمْ وَعَشِيرَتُكُمْ وَأَمْوَٰلٌ ٱقْتَرَفْتُمُوهَا وَتِجَٰرَةٌ تَخْشَوْنَ كَسَادَهَا وَمَسَٰكِنُ تَرْضَوْنَهَآ أَحَبَّ إِلَيْكُم مِّنَ ٱللَّهِ وَرَسُولِهِۦ وَجِهَادٍ فِى سَبِيلِهِۦ فَتَرَبَّصُوا۟ حَتَّىٰ يَأْتِىَ ٱللَّهُ بِأَمْرِهِۦ ۗ وَٱللَّهُ لَا يَهْدِى ٱلْقَوْمَ ٱلْفَٰسِقِينَ

"Say: If your fathers, your sons, your brothers, your wives, your kindred, the wealth that you have gained, the commerce in which you fear a decline, and the dwellings in which you delight are dearer to you than Allah and His Messenger, and striving hard and fighting in His cause, then wait until Allah brings about His Decision (torment). And Allah guides not the people who are disobedient" (*al-Tauba* 24).

Second, when one makes the testimony of faith, this means that he is accepting the Prophet Muhammad (peace be upon him) as his example of how to live and behave in a way that is correct and pleasing to Allah. Allah says in the Quran,

لَّقَدْ كَانَ لَكُمْ فِى رَسُولِ ٱللَّهِ أُسْوَةٌ حَسَنَةٌ لِّمَن كَانَ يَرْجُوا۟ ٱللَّهَ وَٱلْيَوْمَ ٱلْـَٔاخِرَ وَذَكَرَ ٱللَّهَ كَثِيرًا

"Indeed in the Messenger of Allah you have an excellent example to follow for him who hopes in (a good meeting with) Allah and the Last Day and remembers Allah much" (*al-Ahzaab* 21). Allah also says,

قُلْ إِن كُنتُمْ تُحِبُّونَ ٱللَّهَ فَٱتَّبِعُونِى يُحْبِبْكُمُ ٱللَّهُ وَيَغْفِرْ لَكُمْ ذُنُوبَكُمْ

"Say (O Muhammad): If you love Allah, then follow me and Allah will love you and forgive you your sins" (*ali-Imraan* 31)

It is very strange that some people can declare the testimony of faith and declare that Muhammad is the Messenger and Prophet of Allah– yet at the same time they do not consider him an example of the way of life that a believer should follow. Not only do they not take him as an example for themselves, they actually oppose others who do take the Prophet (peace be upon him) as their example. This is nothing but a clear sign that such a person does not have a clear understanding of the meaning and implications of the testimony of faith that he made.

The Prophet (peace be upon him) has said,

أَمَا وَاللَّهِ إِنِّي لَأَخْشَاكُمْ لِلَّهِ وَأَتْقَاكُمْ لَهُ لَكِنِّي أَصُومُ وَأُفْطِرُ وَأُصَلِّي وَأَرْقُدُ وَأَتَزَوَّجُ النِّسَاءَ فَمَنْ رَغِبَ عَنْ سُنَّتِي فَلَيْسَ مِنِّي

"I swear by Allah that I am the most fearful of Allah and most conscious of Him than all of you. But I also [as part of my sunnah] fast and break my fast, pray and sleep [at night] and I marry women. Whoever turns away from my sunnah is not from me [that is, is not one of my true followers]." (Recorded by al-Bukhari.) In this hadith, the Prophet (peace be upon him) explained that he is the most fearful of Allah and God-conscious. Therefore, there is no excuse for anyone not to follow his example and guidance. But he also stated that the one who turns away from his practice and example is not from him. One cannot truthfully claim to believe in and accept the Prophet Muhammad (peace be upon him) and, at the same time, refuse to accept his life as the example that one must strive to emulate.

Ruling Concerning One who Violates the *Shahaadah*

Anyone who knowingly and willingly violates the *shahaadah* becomes a disbeliever. There is agreement of all the scholars on this point. For example, if anyone worships anything or anybody else along with his worship of Allah, such as worshipping Jesus along with worshipping Allah, then that person becomes a disbeliever. Similarly, if anyone curses the Prophet (peace be upon him) or claims that he was a liar, this person has violated the second portion of his testimony of faith and, thereby, falls outside of the fold of Islam.

"to establish the prayers"

The Meaning of *salat* ("prayer")

Salat is a word that existed in the Arabic language before the time of the Prophet Muhammad (peace be upon him). However, its meaning in Islam is something different and special. The Prophet Muhammad (peace be upon him) demonstrated the proper manner of prayer that is pleasing to Allah. Hence, he said,

صَلُّوا كَمَا رَأَيْتُمُونِي أُصَلِّي

"Pray in the manner that you have seen me praying."[1]

---

[1] This is one of the strongest evidences for the place of the sunnah in Islam. Without referring to the sunnah, no one could possibly know the correct form of prayer, although it is something essential to Islam. Those who claim to follow the Quran and yet refuse to follow the sunnah of the Prophet (peace be upon him) are

Although the *shariah* definition of the term *salat* is quite clear, many times an understanding of a word's root or derivation sheds more light on the understanding of the concept itself. The generally accepted view is that the word *salat* lexically means *dua* (supplication). The *salat* itself is composed of a number of supplications.[1]

Prayer and supplications are from the most important aspects of worship. The worshipper turns to the one he worships and invokes him. On this point, Muhammad Rasheed Ridha wrote,

> *Salat* is the showing of one's need and dependence upon the worshipped one, by speech, action or both. This is what is meant by their statement, "The meaning of *salat* is supplication," as one demonstrates his need for the Great, the Noble, even if just in action, in order to bring about some need, continuation of some bounty or repelling of some harm or punishment.[2]

Rasheed Ridah states about the form of the Islamic prayer,

---

simply displaying their ignorance because it is not possible to know how the Quran is to be applied without reference to the Prophet's explanation and implementation of the Quran itself. This is above and beyond the fact that it is the Quran that obliges Muslims to follow and obey the Prophet (peace be upon him).

[1] Although *dua* is generally considered the meaning of the word *salat*, ibn al-Jauzi mentions other possible derivations. One interpretation is that the word comes from the expression, *salait al-ood*. That is where one softens and straightens a piece of wood by burning it. The person who prays also becomes softened and humbles himself before Allah through the prayer. Al-Qurtubi adds yet some other possible derivations, including it being derived from "constancy or continuance". In other words, when one is continually burned by a fire, the expression is *saliya bi-l-naar*. In this way, the word implies, says al-Qurtubi, that one must continue to worship Allah in the manner that He has so prescribed. Cf., Abdul Rahman ibn al-Jauzi, *Zaad al-Masair fi Ilm al-Tafseer* (Beirut: Dar al-Fikr, 1987), vol. 1, p. 20; Muhammad al-Qurtubi, *al-Jaami li-Ahkaam al-Quran* (Beirut: Dar Ihya al-Turath al-Arabi, n.d.), vol. 1, p. 169.

[2] Muhammad Rasheed Ridha, *Tafseer al-Quran al-Hakeem* (Beirut: Dar al-Fikr, n.d.), vol. 1, p. 128.

Prayer, in the manner we have just mentioned [where one demonstrates his need and reliance upon his Lord] is demonstrated in Islam in the best way possible. This is the prayer that Allah has made obligatory upon the Muslims. These statements and actions, starting with the opening statement of "Allah is greatest" and ending with the salutations, in the way that the confirmed sunnah has shown, is one of the best ways to express the feeling of need for the worshipped. It also demonstrates the soul's admiration and awe [for the one who is worshipped], if the person establishes it and performs it in its proper manner.[1]

The Meaning of "Establishing the Prayers"

A very important aspect that one should note about this hadith of the Prophet (peace be upon him) is that what is commanded is not simply the "performance" of prayer. In the Quran also, Allah is not ordering or praising those who simply perform the prayer.

Al-Raaghib al-Isfahaani points out that the word for "performer of prayer" is rarely used in the Quran. In fact, one of the few verses in which Allah ever describes the "performers of prayers" is in the verse,

فَوَيْلٌ لِّلْمُصَلِّينَ ﴿٤﴾ ٱلَّذِينَ هُمْ عَن صَلَاتِهِمْ سَاهُونَ

"So woe unto those performers of prayers who delay their prayer from its stated fixed time" (*al-Ma'oon* 4-5). Allah is ordering something very different from the simple act of "performing prayers". Allah is requiring from the believers *iqaamat al-salat* ("the establishment of the prayers"). Hence, one of the pillars of Islam is not simply praying but it is something special, which Allah and His Prophet (peace

[1] Ibid., vol. 1, pp. 128-129.

be upon him) called, "establishing the prayer." Only if one performs the prayer properly and correctly is one deserving of praise. This points out that the number of people who pray are many while the number that establish the prayer are few. This is like the statement narrated from Umar about the *Hajj*, "The number who performed the Hajj are few while the riders [present at the *Hajj*] are many."[1]

Al-Dausiri also pointed out one difference between the two phrases of "establishing the prayer" and "performing the prayer." He said, "[Allah] did not say 'performers of prayer' but He said, 'those who establish the prayer.' Allah distinguished between them in order to distinguish between the true and real prayer and the prayer in form only. The true prayer is the prayer of the heart and soul, the prayer of humility, the prayer of those who stand silently and in fear in front of Allah."[2] The prayer "in form only" was never the goal of the command.

Definitely part of the establishing of the prayer is the establishment of the spiritual and inward aspects of the prayer, as al-Dausiri has alluded to. But that is certainly not the only difference between the two as can be seen in the definition or statements about "establishing the prayer" as given by many of the scholars of Islam. For example, the famous commentator on the Quran, ibn Jarir al-Tabari wrote, "Establishing it means to perform it within its proper limits, with its obligatory aspects, with what has been made obligatory concerning it by the one upon whom it has been made obligatory." Then he quoted the Companion ibn Abbas as saying, "Establishing the prayer is to perform its bowing, prostrations and reciting in a complete manner as well as having fear of Allah and complete attention to it."[3]

---

[1]Cf., Al-Raaghib al-Isfahaani, *Mu'jam Mufradaat Alfaadh al-Quran* (Beirut: Dar al-Fikr, n.d.), p. 433.

[2] Abdul Rahman al-Dausiri, *Safwat al-Athaar wa al-Mafaheem min Tafseer al-Quran al-Adheem* (Kuwait: Dar al-Arqam, 1981), vol. 2, p. 8.

[3]Muhammad ibn Jareer al-Tabari, *Jami al-Bayaan an Taweel Ayi al-Quran* (Beirut: Dar al-Fikr, 1988), vol. 1, p. 104.

The early scholar Qatada also stated, "The establishing of the prayer is to stick to and guard its timing, ablution, bowing and prostration."[1]

Al-Raazi has made the following conclusion concerning its meaning,

> [The praise that is bestowed upon those who establish the prayer] is only for those who establish it on a continual basis without any shortcoming in fulfilling its pillars and conditions. In the same way, the one who 'establishes'[2] the provision for the soldiers is described as such only when he fulfills everyone's rights without any stinginess or shortcoming.[3]

In general, one can say that the "establishing of the prayer," as mentioned in this hadith means that one performs and executes the prayer in the proper manner as prescribed in the Quran and sunnah. This includes both the outward as well as the inward aspects of the prayer. Neither of the two are sufficient in themselves to truly establish the prayer. One must be in a state of purity for the prayer. One must perform the prayer in its proper time. One should, in the case of men, perform the prayer in congregation in a mosque. One must perform the prayer according to its rules and regulations, at the same time, though, the physical acts must be accompanied with diligence, submission, humbleness, calmness and so on. One must perform all of the acts of the prayer properly and in the manner demonstrated by the Messenger of Allah (peace be upon him). These are all part of establishing the prayer. These are essential aspects of this very important foundation of the entire structure of Islam.

---

[1] Quoted in Ismail ibn Katheer, *Tafseer al-Quran al-Adheem* (Kuwait: Dar al-Arqam, 1985), vol. 1, p. 168.

[2] This expression used for the one who supplies, or "establishes", the soldiers with their food and provisions is from the same root as "the establishing" of the prayer.

[3] Al-Fakhar al-Raazi, *Al-Tafseer al-Kabeer* (Beirut: Dar Ihya al-Turath al-Arabi, n.d.), vol. 2, p. 29.

From all of the above it is clear that what Allah is referring to is not something light or something that can be taken lightly. It is to fulfill the prayers in the best way that one can do so, according to the sunnah of the Prophet (peace be upon him), with the correct intention and with the proper attention on the prayer.

It is clear, therefore, that this pillar of Islam is something specific. If a person performs it properly and correctly, then one can say that he has "prayed" and he has "established the prayer". But if one does not do so, then, as the Prophet (peace be upon him) himself alluded to, the act of prayer may itself be negated. This was the case when the Prophet (peace be upon him) told the person in the mosque three times, after he had performed the prayer in an inadequate manner,

ارجع فصل فإنك لم تصل

"Go back and pray for you have not prayed." (Recorded by al-Bukhari and Muslim.)

However, it may be that the person establishes the prayer to some extent. The person has, from a legal point of view, performed his prayer but the reward from Allah for that prayer may be lacking. As the Prophet (peace be upon him) has said,

إِنَّ الرَّجُلَ لَيَنْصَرِفُ وَمَا كُتِبَ لَهُ إِلاَّ عُشْرُ صَلاتِهِ تُسْعُهَا ثُمْنُهَا
سُبْعُهَا سُدْسُهَا خُمْسُهَا رُبْعُهَا ثُلُثُهَا نِصْفُهَا

"A person may finish from [the prayer] and all that is recorded for him of his prayer is one-tenth of it, one-ninth, one-eighth, one-seventh, one-sixth, one-fifth, one-fourth, one-third or one-half."[1]

The meaning of "establishment of the prayer" has been stressed here because that is what the pillar of Islam is. This pillar is not simply the performance of the prayer. It is not performing it in any way or with just physical motions. Nor is it simply praying in the heart without any physical parts to it whatsoever. Nor is it praying the prayer at the time one finds convenient. One must be careful to perform this pillar of Islam in the best and correct manner. On this point, Nadwi wrote,

> *Salat* [prayer] is not merely the name of certain physical movements. It is not a wooden, lifeless ritual or something of a military discipline in which one's choice or volition has no place. It is an act in which all the three aspects of human existence, physical, mental and spiritual, find their due expression. The body, the mind and the heart participate in it jointly and in an ideal manner. The acts of standing erect, kneeling and prostration appertain to the body, recitation appertains to the tongue, reflection and contemplation to the mind, and fear, repentance and lamentation to the heart...
>
> Human personality is a many-sided thing. It is made up of the body, the mind and the heart. All the fundamental aspects of human existence are represented in *Salat* which is the foremost manifestation of faith. Some religious legists, men of prayer and devoutness, and Jews of the last phase saw only physical action in it while among the Oriental mystics and intellectuals some held it merely to be a form of contemplation and meditation. Yet again, many an ignorant Christian monk and so-called Muslim ascetic thought that it was symbolic of love and devotion, grace and

---

[1] Recorded by Abu Dawud and Ahmad. According to al-Albani, it is *sahih*. Al-Albani, *Sahih al-Jami*, vol. 1, p. 335.

adoration, warmth and ardor, sorrow and broken-heartedness and awe and repentance alone. They all stopped at what they imagined, but, as a little reflection will show, these people were sadly misguided and ignorant of the marvelous comprehensiveness of the institution of *Salat*.[1]

The Importance of the Prayer

The importance of the prayer in Islam cannot be understated. It is the first pillar of Islam that the Prophet (peace be upon him) mentioned after mentioning the testimony of faith, by which one becomes a Muslim. It was made obligatory upon all the prophets and for all peoples. Allah has declared its obligatory status under majestic circumstances. For example, when Allah spoke directly to Moses, He said,

وَأَنَا ٱخْتَرْتُكَ فَٱسْتَمِعْ لِمَا يُوحَىٰٓ ﴿١٣﴾ إِنَّنِىٓ أَنَا ٱللَّهُ لَآ إِلَـٰهَ إِلَّآ أَنَا۠ فَٱعْبُدْنِى وَأَقِمِ ٱلصَّلَوٰةَ لِذِكْرِىٓ

"And I have chosen you, so listen to that which is inspired to you. Verily, I am Allah! There is none worthy of worship but I, so worship Me and offer prayer perfectly for My remembrance" (*Taha* 13-14).

Similarly, the prayers were made obligatory upon the Prophet Muhammad (peace be upon him) during his ascension to heaven. Furthermore, when Allah praises the believers, such as in the beginning of *surah al-Muminoon*, one of the first descriptions He states is their adherence to the prayers.

Once a man asked the Prophet (peace be upon him) about the most virtuous deed. The Prophet (peace be upon

---

[1] Abul Hasan Ali Nadwi, *The Four Pillars of Islam* (Lucknow, India: Academy of Islamic Research and Publications, 1976), pp. 22-23.

him) stated that the most virtuous deed is the prayer. The man asked again and again. The first three times, the Prophet (peace be upon him) again answered, "The prayer," then on the fourth occasion he stated, "Jihad in the way of Allah."[1]

The importance of the prayer is demonstrated in many of the Prophet's statements. For example, the Prophet (peace be upon him) said,

أول ما يحاسب به العبد يوم القيامة الصلاة فإن صلحت صلح سائر عمله وإن فسدت فسد سائر عمله

"The first matter that the slave will be brought to account for on the Day of Judgment is the prayer. If it is sound, then the rest of his deeds will be sound. And if it is bad, then the rest of his deeds will be bad."[2]

The importance of the prayers lies in the fact that no matter what actions one performs in his life, the most important aspect is one's relationship to Allah, that is, one's faith (*imaan*), God-consciousness (*taqwa*), sincerity (*ikhlaas*) and worship of Allah (*'ibaadah*). This relationship with Allah is both demonstrated and put into practice, as well as improved and increased, by the prayer. Therefore, if the prayers are sound and proper, the rest of the deeds will be sound and proper; and if the prayers are not sound and proper, then the rest of the deeds will not be sound and proper, as the Prophet (peace be upon him) himself stated.

In reality, if the prayer is performed properly— with true remembrance of Allah and turning to Him for

---

[1] This is from a hadith recorded by Ahmad and ibn Hibban. According to al-Albani, the hadith is *hasan*. Muhammad Nasir al-Din al-Albani, *Sahih al-Targheeb wa al-Tarheeb* (Beirut: al-Maktab al-Islami, 1982), vol. 1, p. 150.

[2] Recorded by al-Tabarani. According to al-Albani, it is *sahih*. Al-Albani, *Sahih al-Jami*, vol. 1, p. 503.

forgiveness— it will have a lasting effect on the person. After he finishes the prayer, his heart will be filled with the remembrance of Allah. He will be fearful as well as hopeful of Allah. After that experience, he will not want to move from that lofty position to one wherein he disobeys Allah. Allah has mentioned this aspect of the prayer when He has said,

إِنَّ ٱلصَّلَوٰةَ تَنْهَىٰ عَنِ

ٱلْفَحْشَآءِ وَٱلْمُنكَرِ

"Verily, the prayer keeps one from the great sins and evil deeds" (*al-Ankaboot* 45). Nadwi has described this effect in the following eloquent way,

> Its aim is to generate within the subliminal self of man such spiritual power, light of faith and awareness of God as can enable him to strive successfully against all kinds of evils and temptations and remain steadfast at times of trial and adversity and protect himself against the weaknesses of the flesh and the mischief of immoderate appetites.[1]

The overall affect that the properly performed prayers should have upon humans is described in other verses in the Quran:

إِنَّ ٱلْإِنسَٰنَ خُلِقَ هَلُوعًا ﴿١٩﴾ إِذَا مَسَّهُ ٱلشَّرُّ جَزُوعًا ﴿٢٠﴾ وَإِذَا مَسَّهُ

ٱلْخَيْرُ مَنُوعًا ﴿٢١﴾ إِلَّا ٱلْمُصَلِّينَ ﴿٢٢﴾ ٱلَّذِينَ هُمْ عَلَىٰ صَلَاتِهِمْ دَآئِمُونَ

"Verily, man was created impatient, irritable when evil touches him and niggardly when good touches him. Except for those devoted to prayer, those who remain constant in their prayers..." (*al-Maarij* 19-23).

---

[1] Nadwi, p. 24.

As for the Hereafter, Allah's forgiveness and pleasure is closely related to the prayers. The Messenger of Allah (peace be upon him) said,

خَمْسُ صَلَوَاتٍ افْتَرَضَهُنَّ اللَّهُ تَعَالَى مَنْ أَحْسَنَ وُضُوءَهُنَّ وَصَلاَّهُنَّ لِوَقْتِهِنَّ وَأَتَمَّ رُكُوعَهُنَّ وَخُشُوعَهُنَّ كَانَ لَهُ عَلَى اللَّهِ عَهْدٌ أَنْ يَغْفِرَ لَهُ وَمَنْ لَمْ يَفْعَلْ فَلَيْسَ لَهُ عَلَى اللَّهِ عَهْدٌ إِنْ شَاءَ غَفَرَ لَهُ وَإِنْ شَاءَ عَذَّبَهُ

"Allah has obligated five prayers. Whoever excellently performs their ablutions, prays them in their proper times, completes their bows, prostrations and *khushu'*[1] has a promise from Allah that He will forgive him. And whoever does not do that has no promise from Allah. He may either forgive him or He may punish him."[2]

The prayers are a type of purification for a human being. He turns and meets with his Lord five times a day. As alluded to above, this repeated standing in front of Allah should keep the person from performing sins during the day. Furthermore, it should also be a time of remorse and repentance, such that he earnestly asks Allah for forgiveness for those sins that he committed. In addition, the prayer in itself is a good deed that wipes away some of the evil deeds that he performed. These points can be noted in the following hadith of the Prophet (peace be upon him):

---

[1] *Khushu'* in the prayer is where the person's heart is attuned to the prayer. This feeling in the heart is then reflected on the body. The person remains still and calm. His gaze is also lowered. Even his voice is affected by this feeling in the heart. For more details on this concept (as well as the difference between it and *khudhu'*), see Muhammad al-Shaayi, *Al-Furooq al-Laughawiyyah wa Atharahaa fi Tafseer al-Quran al-Kareem* (Riyadh: Maktabah al-Ubaikaan, 1993), pp. 249-254.

[2] Recorded by Malik, Ahmad, Abu Dawud, al-Nasa`i and others. According to al-Albani, it is *sahih*. Al-Albani, *Sahih al-Jami*, vol. 1, p. 616.

أَرَأَيْتُمْ لَوْ أَنَّ نَهرًا بِبَابِ أَحَدِكُمْ يَغْتَسِلُ فِيهِ كُلَّ يَوْمٍ خَمْسًا مَا تَقُولُ ذَلِكَ يُبْقِي مِنْ دَرَنِهِ قَالُوا لا يُبْقِي مِنْ دَرَنِهِ شَيْئًا قَالَ فَذَلِكَ مِثْلُ الصَّلَوَاتِ الْخَمْسِ يَمْحُو اللَّهُ بِهِ الْخَطَايَا

"If a person had a stream outside his door and he bathed in it five times a day, do you think he would have any filth left on him?" The people said, "No filth would remain on him whatsoever." The Prophet (peace be upon him) then said, "That is like the five daily prayers: Allah wipes away the sins by them." (Recorded by al-Bukhari and Muslim.)

In another hadith, the Prophet (peace be upon him) said,

الصَّلَوَاتُ الْخَمْسُ وَالْجُمْعَةُ إِلَى الْجُمْعَةِ كَفَّارَاتٌ لِمَا بَيْنَهُنَّ

"The five daily prayers and the Friday Prayer until the Friday Prayer are expiation for what is between them." (Recorded by Muslim.)

The Ruling Concerning One Who Does not Pray

There is a difference of opinion among the scholars concerning the one who fails to perform this ever important pillar of Islam. The question is whether or not one who does not perform the prayer still remains in the fold of Islam. That is, does one become a disbeliever by the fact that he does not pray? In general, one may break down those who do not pray into the following categories:[1]

---

[1] Cf., Abdul Aziz al-Abdul Lateef, *Nawaaqidh al-Imaan al-Qauliyyah wa al-Amaliyyah* (Riyadh: Dar al-Watn, 1414 A.H.), pp. 452-455.

(1) Those who, by agreement, are not disbelievers. This includes those people who may have missed a prayer due to forgetfulness or sleep. Obviously, such people are not considered disbelievers.

(2) Those who, by agreement of all scholars, are disbelievers. This category includes the following groups of people:

(i) The one who does not perform the prayer and rejects the idea that it is obligatory to pray. This person is a disbeliever by consensus as he is going against numerous and definitive evidences from the Quran and sunnah.

(ii) The one who refuses to pray out of pride or envy. This is the person who recognizes the truth of Islam yet he does not want to submit to Islam or perform the prayer out of hatred for the religion, out of pride that he does not feel that he must perform such an act and so forth.

(iii) The one who does not pray out of disdain and ridicule for the prayer. This person is disdaining or ridiculing one of the foundations of Islam and, for that reason, this takes him out of the fold of Islam.

(iv) The one who refuses to pray even though he is being threatened by the proper authorities with being killed as a punishment for not praying. This person is considered a disbeliever since he refuses to submit even with a threat of death.

(v) The one who simply disregards the prayer completely, without recognizing that it is obligatory or rejecting it as an obligation.

(3) Concerning the third category, there is a difference of opinion whether or not these people fall outside of the fold of Islam. These are the people who accept the obligation of prayer and do not deny its importance. They recognize that they are committing a sin by not praying. Yet, still, out of laziness, remiss or such, they do not perform the prayer. Some scholars say that such

a person falls completely out of the fold of Islam, he shall be in the Hell-fire forever and, in fact, Muslims cannot perform the funeral prayer for him in this world. Other scholars state that such a person is truly an evildoer, he is committing a lesser form of *kufr* and is at the doorstep of falling out of the fold of Islam. However, he does stay within the overall fold of Islam and is not to be treated like or considered a disbeliever.

This is not the proper place for a detailed discussion of this very important question.[1] One of the strongest pieces of evidence for those who say that such a person does become a disbeliever is the hadith of the Prophet (peace be upon him),

إِنَّ بَيْنَ الرَّجُلِ وَبَيْنَ الشِّرْكِ وَالْكُفْرِ تَرْكَ الصَّلاةِ

"Between a man and polytheism (*al-shirk*) and disbelief (*al-kufr*) is the abandoning of the prayer." (Recorded by Muslim.) In this hadith, the Prophet (peace be upon him) used the definitive *al-shirk* and *al-kufr*, which is a reference to something known and understood. This is understood to refer to the *kufr* that takes one out of the fold of Islam. Furthermore, both the words *shirk* and *kufr* have been used, and this is another sign that the act must take one out of the fold of Islam.

---

[1] A discussion of this point may be found in al-Abdul Lateef, pp. 456-498. For numerous hadith, statements of Companions and others' statements that clearly state that abandoning the prayer is tantamount to disbelief, see Ubaidullah ibn Battah, *Al-Ibaanah an Shareeah al-Firq al-Naajiyah wa Mujaanibah al-Firq al-Madhmoomah* (Riyadh: Dar al-Raayah, 1988), vol. 2, pp. 669-684. Ibn Uthaimin is a scholar who believes that one who does not pray becomes an unbeliever. His arguments may be found in Muhammad ibn Uthaimin, *Hukm Taarik al-Salaat* (Fairfax, VA: IIASA, n.d), *passim*. Al-Albani says that such a person is not a disbeliever. His arguments may be found in a book by the same name, Muhammad Nasir al-Din al-Albani, *Hukum Taarik al-Salaat* (Riyadh: Dar al-Jalalain, 1992), *passim*. In English, a brief discussion with a partial discussion of some related evidences may be found As-Sayyid Sabiq, *Fiqh us-Sunnah* (Indianapolis: American Trust Publications, 1985), vol. 1, pp. 77-80.

One of the strongest pieces of evidence for those who say that such a person does not leave the fold of Islam is a hadith mentioned earlier:

خَمْسُ صَلَوَاتٍ افْتَرَضَهُنَّ اللَّهُ تَعَالَى مَنْ أَحْسَنَ وُضُوءَهُنَّ وَصَلاَّهُنَّ لِوَقْتِهِنَّ وَأَتَمَّ رُكُوعَهُنَّ وَخُشُوعَهُنَّ كَانَ لَهُ عَلَى اللَّهِ عَهْدٌ أَنْ يَغْفِرَ لَهُ وَمَنْ لَمْ يَفْعَلْ فَلَيْسَ لَهُ عَلَى اللَّهِ عَهْدٌ إِنْ شَاءَ غَفَرَ لَهُ وَإِنْ شَاءَ عَذَّبَهُ

"Allah has obligated five prayers. Whoever excellently performs their ablutions, prays them in their proper times, completes their bows, prostrations and *khushu'* has a promise from Allah that He will forgive him. And whoever does not do that has no promise from Allah. He may either forgive him or He may punish him."[1]

However, it is important to note the conclusion that both sets of scholars come to. Those who say that the person falls out of the fold of Islam state that the person is to be killed as an apostate, if he does not repent. Most of those scholars who say that he does not fall outside of the fold of Islam state that he must be commanded to pray and if he refuses to pray, then he should be killed as a punishment for his refusal to pray.[2] Hence, the conclusion of the majority of the scholars is the same. Abandoning the prayer, this pillar of Islam, is such a heinous act that these scholars agree that such a person is not deserving to live. So regardless of whether one follows the scholars that say that such a person is a disbeliever or not, both sides definitely agree that the importance of the prayer is extremely great

[1] Recorded by Malik, Ahmad, Abu Dawud, al-Nasa`i and others. According to al-Albani, it is *sahih*. Al-Albani, *Sahih al-Jami*, vol. 1, p. 616.

[2] Some Hanafis state that he should be imprisoned and advised to repent.

and no Muslim who is true to his claim to Islam should ever consider abandoning the prayer.

Siddiqi's words showing the importance of prayer are a good summary to this whole discussion. He wrote,

> Prayer is the soul of religion. Where there is no prayer, there can be no purification of the soul. The non-praying man is rightly considered to be a soulless man. Take prayer out of the world, and it is all over with religion because it is with prayer that man has the consciousness of God and selfless love for humanity and inner sense of piety. Prayer is, therefore, the first, the highest, and the most solemn phenomenon and manifestation of religion.[1]

The Prophet (peace be upon him) stated its place in Islam when he said,

رَأْسُ الأَمْرِ الإِسْلاَمُ وَعَمُودُهُ الصَّلاَةُ وَذِرْوَةُ سَنَامِهِ الْجِهَادُ

"The head of the matter is Islam. Its pillar is prayer. And its apex is jihad."[2]

"pay the zakat"

The Meaning of Zakat

Linguistically, the root of the word zakat implies purification, blessing and growth. Allah has stated in the Quran,

[1] Siddiqi, vol. 1, p. 206.
[2] An authentic hadith recorded by Ahmad, al-Tirmidhi and others.

قَدْ أَفْلَحَ مَن تَزَكَّىٰ

"Indeed whosoever purifies himself (*tazakkaa*) shall achieve success" (*al-Ala* 14). Another word used in the Quran and hadith for the zakat is *sadaqa*. This word is derived from *sidq* (the truth). Siddiqi explains the significance of these two terms as they are used here,

> Both these words are highly meaningful. The spending of wealth for the sake of Allah purifies the heart of man of the love of material wealth. The man who spends it offers that as a humble gift before the Lord and thus affirms the truth that nothing is dearer to him in life than the love of Allah and that he is fully prepared to sacrifice everything for His sake.[1]

In the *shariah*, its technical meaning is in reference to a specific portion of one's varied wealth that one must give yearly to a specific group of recipients.

The Importance of Zakat

There is no question that among the pillars of Islam, zakat ranks very close to that of prayer. They are often mentioned together in the Quran— in eighty two instances to be exact.

The importance of zakat can also be seen in the following verse of the Quran where Allah orders the Companions to fight the *mushrikeen* (polytheists) wherever they can:

[1] Siddiqi, vol. 2, p. 465.

فَإِذَا ٱنسَلَخَ ٱلْأَشْهُرُ ٱلْحُرُمُ فَٱقْتُلُوا۟ ٱلْمُشْرِكِينَ حَيْثُ وَجَدتُّمُوهُمْ
وَخُذُوهُمْ وَٱحْصُرُوهُمْ وَٱقْعُدُوا۟ لَهُمْ كُلَّ مَرْصَدٍ ۚ فَإِن تَابُوا۟ وَأَقَامُوا۟
ٱلصَّلَوٰةَ وَءَاتَوُا۟ ٱلزَّكَوٰةَ فَخَلُّوا۟ سَبِيلَهُمْ ۚ إِنَّ ٱللَّهَ غَفُورٌ رَّحِيمٌ

"Then when the sacred months have passed, kill the polytheists wherever you find them, and capture them and besiege them, and prepare for them each and every ambush. But if they repent and offer prayer and give zakat, then leave their way free. Verily, Allah is Oft-Forgiving, Most Merciful" (*al-Tauba* 5). In this verse, Allah orders the Companions to fight them until they repent, establish the prayer and pay the zakat.

Shortly afterwards in the same *surah*, following the same line of discussion, Allah says,

فَإِن تَابُوا۟ وَأَقَامُوا۟ ٱلصَّلَوٰةَ وَءَاتَوُا۟ ٱلزَّكَوٰةَ فَإِخْوَٰنُكُمْ فِى
ٱلدِّينِ ۗ

"But if they repent, offer prayer and give the zakat, then they are your brethren in religion" (*al-Tauba* 11).

These two verses clearly prove the importance of zakat in Allah's sight. The disbelievers will become a part of this religion when they repent, pray and give the zakat. Hence, the payment of zakat is a true sign that a person is a Muslim and submitting himself to Allah.

One can also see from the Quran, that one of the keys to receiving Allah's mercy in the Hereafter is the payment of zakat. In *surah al-Tauba*, verse 71, Allah states,

وَٱلْمُؤْمِنُونَ وَٱلْمُؤْمِنَٰتُ بَعْضُهُمْ أَوْلِيَآءُ بَعْضٍ ۚ يَأْمُرُونَ بِٱلْمَعْرُوفِ
وَيَنْهَوْنَ عَنِ ٱلْمُنكَرِ وَيُقِيمُونَ ٱلصَّلَوٰةَ وَيُؤْتُونَ ٱلزَّكَوٰةَ وَيُطِيعُونَ ٱللَّهَ
وَرَسُولَهُۥٓ ۚ أُو۟لَٰٓئِكَ سَيَرْحَمُهُمُ ٱللَّهُ ۗ إِنَّ ٱللَّهَ عَزِيزٌ حَكِيمٌ

"The believers, men and women, are helpers and supporters of one another, they enjoin what is right and forbid what is evil, they offer their prayers perfectly, they give the zakat and they obey Allah and His Messenger. Allah will bestow His mercy on them. Surely, Allah is All-Mighty, All-Wise."

The payment of zakat should purify a person. It also purifies his wealth. Allah said to the Prophet (peace be upon him),

خُذْ مِنْ أَمْوَٰلِهِمْ صَدَقَةً تُطَهِّرُهُمْ وَتُزَكِّيهِم

"Take (O Muhammad) alms from their wealth in order to purify them and sanctify them with it" (*al-Tauba* 103). Beyond that, it can purify a believer's soul by cleansing him of the diseases of stinginess and miserliness.

It also purifies the wealth of the person by removing any evil effect from it. The Prophet (peace be upon him) once said,

من أدى زكاة ماله فقد ذهب عنه شره

"Whoever pays the zakat on his wealth will have its evil removed from him."[1]

Zakat also has a very important role to play for society as a whole. There are some obvious factors that may be stated here. For example, zakat helps the poor of society as they receive wealth that they need. This should also help to strengthen the ties of brotherhood within a Muslim society, as the poor know that the rich will come to their aid through zakat and other means of charity. Even for those who are not very rich, it makes them realize that they can afford to give for the sake of Allah. They may realize that

---

[1] Recorded by ibn Khuzaima and al-Tabarani. According to al-Albani, it is *hasan*. Al-Albani, *Sahih al-Targheeb wa al-Tarheeb*, vol. 1, p. 312.

they will not starve or die if they give some of their wealth for the sake of Allah. Furthermore, it can make those who possess wealth realize that such wealth has actually come as a blessing from Allah. Hence, the person must use it in the way that is pleasing to Allah. One of the most pleasing aspects is to fulfill one's responsibility of paying zakat upon such wealth.

There are other important social aspects that can be deduced from the Quran and sunnah. For example, one of the keys to the establishment of a Muslim community and Muslim state is the giving of zakat. Allah says in the Quran,

ٱلَّذِينَ إِن مَّكَّنَّـٰهُمْ فِى ٱلْأَرْضِ أَقَامُوا۟ ٱلصَّلَوٰةَ وَءَاتَوُا۟ ٱلزَّكَوٰةَ وَأَمَرُوا۟ بِٱلْمَعْرُوفِ وَنَهَوْا۟ عَنِ ٱلْمُنكَرِ ۗ وَلِلَّهِ عَـٰقِبَةُ ٱلْأُمُورِ

"Those who, if We give them power in the land, (they) order for the establishment of the prayer, to pay the zakat, and they enjoin the good and forbid the evil. And with Allah rests the end of all matters" (*al-Hajj* 41).

Muslims who do not pay their zakat are not only harming themselves but they can actually harm the entire Muslim *ummah*. The Messenger of Allah (peace be upon him) said,

وَلَمْ يَمْنَعُوا زَكَاةَ أَمْوَالِهِمْ إِلاَّ مُنِعُوا الْقَطْرَ مِنَ السَّمَاءِ وَلَوْلا الْبَهَائِمُ لَمْ يُمْطَرُوا

"A people do not keep from giving the zakat on their wealth except that they will be kept from having rain falling from the sky. If it were not for the animals, it would not rain at all."[1]

---

[1] Recorded by ibn Majah. According to al-Albani it is authentic. See Muhammad Nasir al-Din al-Alb *Silsilaat al-Ahadeeth al-Saheeha* (Beirut: al-Maktab al-Islami, 1979), vol. 1, hadith no. 106,

Allah and His prophet have made it clear that not paying zakat is an act that is displeasing to Allah. Indeed, Allah has threatened a great punishment for such behavior. For example, the following verse of the Quran is a reference to those who do not pay the zakat on their wealth:

وَلَا يَحْسَبَنَّ ٱلَّذِينَ يَبْخَلُونَ بِمَآ ءَاتَىٰهُمُ ٱللَّهُ مِن فَضْلِهِۦ هُوَ خَيْرًا
لَّهُم ۖ بَلْ هُوَ شَرٌّ لَّهُمْ ۖ سَيُطَوَّقُونَ مَا بَخِلُوا۟ بِهِۦ يَوْمَ ٱلْقِيَـٰمَةِ ۗ
وَلِلَّهِ مِيرَٰثُ ٱلسَّمَـٰوَٰتِ وَٱلْأَرْضِ ۗ وَٱللَّهُ بِمَا تَعْمَلُونَ خَبِيرٌ

"And let not those who covetously withhold of that which Allah has bestowed on them of His Bounty (wealth) think that it is good for them. Nay, it will be worse for them. The things which they covetously withheld shall be tied to their necks like a collar on the Day of Resurrection. And to Allah belongs the heritage of the heavens and the earth, and Allah is Well-Acquainted with all that you do" (*ali-Imran* 180).

The Prophet (peace be upon him) described the punishment that will come to those who do not pay the proper zakat on their wealth. In one hadith in *Sahih al-Bukhari*, Abu Huraira narrated that the Prophet (peace be upon him) said,

تَأْتِي الْإِبِلُ عَلَى صَاحِبِهَا عَلَى خَيْرِ مَا كَانَتْ إِذَا هُوَ لَمْ يُعْطِ
فِيهَا حَقَّهَا تَطَؤُهُ بِأَخْفَافِهَا وَتَأْتِي الْغَنَمُ عَلَى صَاحِبِهَا عَلَى خَيْرِ
مَا كَانَتْ إِذَا لَمْ يُعْطِ فِيهَا حَقَّهَا تَطَؤُهُ بِأَظْلَافِهَا وَتَنْطَحُهُ
بِقُرُونِهَا... وَلا يَأْتِي أَحَدُكُمْ يَوْمَ الْقِيَامَةِ بِشَاةٍ يَحْمِلُهَا عَلَى رَقَبَتِهِ
لَهَا يُعَارٌ فَيَقُولُ يَا مُحَمَّدُ فَأَقُولُ لا أَمْلِكُ لَكَ شَيْئًا قَدْ بَلَّغْتُ وَلا

يَأْتِي بِبَعِيرٍ يَحْمِلُهُ عَلَى رَقَبَتِهِ لَهُ رُغَاءٌ فَيَقُولُ يَا مُحَمَّدُ فَأَقُولُ لا أَمْلِكُ لَكَ مِنَ اللَّهِ شَيْئًا قَدْ بَلَّغْتُ

"[On the Day of Resurrection] camels will come to their owner in the best state of health they have ever had (in the world), and if he had not paid their zakat on them, they would tread him with their feet; similarly, sheep will come to their owner in the best state of health they ever had in this world and, if he had not paid their zakat, would tread him with their hooves and would butt him with their horns... I do not want anyone of you to come to me on the Day of Resurrection carrying over his neck a sheep that will be bleating. Then he says, 'O Muhammad (please intercede for me).' I will say, 'I can't help you for I conveyed Allah's message to you.' Similarly, I do not want anyone of you to come to me carrying over his neck a camel that will be grunting. Such a person will say, 'O Muhammad (intercede for me).' I will say to him, 'I cannot help you for I conveyed Allah's Message to you.'"

The Prophet (peace be upon him) warned of the consequences of not paying such zakat. Note the following hadith from *Sahih al-Bukhari*:

مَنْ آتَاهُ اللَّهُ مَالاً فَلَمْ يُؤَدِّ زَكَاتَهُ مُثِّلَ لَهُ مَالُهُ يَوْمَ الْقِيَامَةِ شُجَاعًا أَقْرَعَ لَهُ زَبِيبَتَانِ يُطَوَّقُهُ يَوْمَ الْقِيَامَةِ ثُمَّ يَأْخُذُ بِلِهْزِمَتَيْهِ يَعْنِي بِشِدْقَيْهِ ثُمَّ يَقُولُ أَنَا مَالُكَ أَنَا كَنْزُكَ

"Whoever is made wealthy by Allah and does not pay zakat on his wealth, then on Day of Resurrection his wealth will be made like a bald-headed poisonous snake with two poisonous glands. It will encircle his neck and bite his cheeks and say, 'I am your wealth, I am your treasure.'"

After stating that, the Prophet (peace be upon him) then recited the above verse from *surah ali-Imran.*

In another verse that also includes those who do not pay zakat, Allah has said,

وَٱلَّذِينَ يَكْنِزُونَ ٱلذَّهَبَ

وَٱلْفِضَّةَ وَلَا يُنفِقُونَهَا فِى سَبِيلِ ٱللَّهِ فَبَشِّرْهُم بِعَذَابٍ أَلِيمٍ ﴿٣٤﴾ يَوْمَ

يُحْمَىٰ عَلَيْهَا فِى نَارِ جَهَنَّمَ فَتُكْوَىٰ بِهَا جِبَاهُهُمْ وَجُنُوبُهُمْ وَظُهُورُهُمْ

هَٰذَا مَا كَنَزْتُمْ لِأَنفُسِكُمْ فَذُوقُوا۟ مَا كُنتُمْ تَكْنِزُونَ

"[There are] those who hoard up gold and silver and spend it not in the way of Allah– announce unto them a painful torment. On the Day when that wealth will be heated in the fire of hell and it will brand their foreheads, flanks and backs. [It will be said to them], 'This is the treasure which you hoarded for yourselves. Now taste of what you used to hoard'" (*al-Tauba* 34-35).

Ruling Concerning One who Does not Give Zakat

Zakat is one of the pillars of Islam, as is clear from this hadith under discussion. If a person denies the obligation of zakat or says that it is not a part of Islam, then such a person is a disbeliever according to the consensus of the scholars.[1]

The question once again is: What is the status of a person who accepts zakat as an obligation but due to laziness, stinginess or remiss he does not give zakat? Does he remain a Muslim? For the majority of the scholars, the

[1] Of course, there is always the exception of a new Muslim who has not heard of the obligation of zakat.

person does remain a Muslim.[1] The zakat is to be taken from him by force by the authorities and he is also to be punished according to judicial discretion.[2]

However, there are reports from the Companion Abdullah ibn Masood that he did not consider a person who abandons the zakat to be a Muslim. He said, "The one who leaves paying the zakat is not a Muslim." He also said, "The one who establishes the prayer but does not give the zakat actually has no prayer for him."[3]

If a group of people believe in zakat yet they refuse to pay it, they can be fought. This is exactly what happened during the time of the Companions. After the death of the Prophet (peace be upon him), some of the tribes became apostates and others refused to pay the zakat. Abu Bakr, the first *khalifah*, fought them and declared, "By Allah, I will fight anyone who distinguishes between prayer and zakat. Zakat is the compulsory right to be taken from the property. By Allah! If they refuse to pay me even a she-kid which they used to pay at the time of Allah's Messenger (peace be upon him), I would fight them for withholding it." (Recorded by Muslim.)

---

[1] Ahmad, for example, stated in his creed, "Whoever leaves the prayer has committed *kufr*. And there is no deed whose abandonment is *kufr* except the prayer. Whoever leaves it becomes a disbeliever and Allah permits the taking of his life." Quoted in Hibatullah al-Laalakai, *Sharh Usool Itiqaad Ahl al-Sunnah wa al-Jamaah min al-Kitaab wa al-Sunnah wa Ijmaa al-Sahaabah wa al-Tabieen min Badihim* (Riyadh: Dar Taiba, n.d.), vol. 1, p. 159.

[2] There is a hadith in *Sunan Abu Dawud* which states, "He who pays zakat with the intention of getting rewarded will get rewarded. If anyone evades zakat, we shall take half the property from him as a due from the dues of our Lord, the Exalted." According to al-Albani, this hadith is *hasan*. [Muhammad Nasir al-Din al-Albani, *Sahih Sunan Abi Dawud* (Riyadh: Maktab al-Tarbiyah al-Arabiya li-Duwal al-Khaleej, 1991), vol. 1, p. 296.] This seems to be Ahmad ibn Hanbal's opinion. However, Ahmad Hasan wrote, "But this injunction was valid in the early days of Islam. Later on it was repealed." [Ahmad Hasan, trans., *Sunan Abu Dawud* (Lahore: Sh. Muhammad Ashraf, 1984), vol. 2, 412.] Allah knows best.

[3] These quotes may be found in ibn Battah, vol. 2, p. 681; Abdullah ibn Abu Shaiba, *al-Musannaf* (Beirut: Dar al-Fikr, 1989), vol. 3, pp. 7-9. According to al-Haitami, these narrations are authentic from ibn Masud. Cf., Ahmad ibn Hajr al-Haitami, *al-Zawaajir an Iqtiraaf al-Kaba`ir* (Beirut: Dar al-Marifah, 1987), vol. 1, p. 170.

That incident was very important for many reasons. It demonstrates the attitude of the Companions toward a group of people who refused to pay the zakat. It is not reported that the Companions asked them whether they still believed in zakat Instead, they fought them and treated them in the same manner as those who had openly apostatized. In other words, they considered them outside of the fold of Islam due to their actions.[1]

"fast [the month of] Ramadhan"

The Meaning of *Siyaam*

Linguistically, *siyaam* means to abstain from something, such as abstaining from speaking. In the *shariah*, it is a direct reference to abstaining from food, drink and sexual intercourse during the days of the month of Ramadhan. This practice is one of the pillars of Islam, as noted in this hadith.

The Importance of *Siyaam*

Fasting is a source of self-restraint, piety and God-consciousness. It was prescribed by Allah for the prophets before Prophet Muhammad (peace be upon him). In the verses obligating the fast of the month of Ramadhan, Allah has pointed out its goal or purpose:

---

[1] Cf., Safr al-Hawaali, *Dhaahirah al-Irjaa fi al-Fikr al-Islaami* (Cairo: Maktab al-Tayyib, 1417 A.H.), vol. 2, pp. 650-652.

يَـٰٓأَيُّهَا ٱلَّذِينَ ءَامَنُوا۟ كُتِبَ عَلَيْكُمُ ٱلصِّيَامُ كَمَا كُتِبَ عَلَى ٱلَّذِينَ مِن قَبْلِكُمْ لَعَلَّكُمْ تَتَّقُونَ

"O believers! Fasting is prescribed for you as it was prescribed for those before you, that you may attain *taqwa* [self-restraint, piety and God-consciousness]" (*al-Baqara* 183).

The Prophet (peace be upon him) said that fasting is a protection from the Hell-fire:

الصيام جنة من النار كجنة أحدكم من القتال

"Fasting is a shield from the Hell-fire like one of your shields used in fighting."[1] Furthermore, it will also come as an intercessor on the Day of Judgment. The Prophet (peace be upon him) has said,

الصيام والقرآن يشفعان للعبد يوم القيامة يقول الصيام أي رب منعته الطعام والشهوات بالنهار فشفعني فيه ويقول القرآن منعته النوم بالليل فشفعني فيه قال فيشفعان

"The fast and the Quran shall come as intercessors on the Day of Resurrection. The fast shall say, 'O Lord, I prevented him from his food and drink during the day, so let me intercede for him.' The Quran will say, 'I kept him from sleep during the night, so let me intercede for him.' Then they will be allowed to intercede."[2]

---

[1] Recorded by Ahmad, al-Nasai and others. According to al-Albani, it is *sahih*. Al-Albani, *Sahih al-Jami*, vol. 2, p. 720.

[2] Recorded by Ahmad. According to al-Albani, it is *sahih*. Al-Albani, *Sahih al-Jami*, vol. 2, p. 720.

It is an act that demonstrates one's sincerity to Allah. Only Allah is aware if a person truly fasted or not. No one can know if he secretly broke his fast. Therefore, Allah has a special reward for those who fast. This is stated in the following hadith *qudsi*,

يَتْرُكُ طَعَامَهُ وَشَرَابَهُ وَشَهْوَتَهُ مِنْ أَجْلِي الصِّيَامُ لِي وَأَنَا أَجْزِي بِهِ وَالْحَسَنَةُ بِعَشْرِ أَمْثَالِهَا

Allah has said, "He leaves his food, drink and desires because of Me. Fasting is for My sake and I shall reward it. And every good deed shall be rewarded ten-fold." (Recorded by al-Bukhari.)

By Allah's grace and mercy, if a person fasts the month of Ramadhan with faith in Allah and hoping for its reward, Allah will forgive all of his previous minor sins. The Prophet (peace be upon him) said,

مَنْ صَامَ رَمَضَانَ إِيمَانًا وَاحْتِسَابًا غُفِرَ لَهُ مَا تَقَدَّمَ مِنْ ذَنْبِهِ

"Whoever fasts the month of Ramadhan with faith and hoping for its reward shall have all of his previous sins forgiven for him." (Recorded by al-Bukhari and Muslim.)

Ibn al-Qayim noted some of the beneficial and important aspects of fasting when he wrote,

> The purpose of fasting is that the spirit of man was released from the clutches of desires and moderation prevailed in his carnal self, and, through it, he realized the goal of purification and everlasting felicity. It is aimed at curtailing the intensity of desire and lust by means of hunger and thirst, at inducing man to realize how many were there in the world like him who had to go even without a small quantity of food, at making it difficult for the Devil to deceive him, and at

> restraining his organs from turning towards things in which there was the loss of both worlds. Fasting, thus, is the bridle of the God-fearing, the shield of the crusaders and the discipline of the virtuous.[1]

There is also a hadith of the Prophet (peace be upon him) that warns of the punishment for one who breaks his fast improperly. In this hadith, the Prophet (peace be upon him) said,

بينما أنا نائم أتاني رجلان فأخذا بضبعي فأتيا بي جبلا وعرا فقالا اصعد فقلت إني لا أطيقه فقال أنا سنسهله لك فصعدت حتى إذا كنت في سواء الجبل إذا بأصوات شديدة قلت ما هذه الأصوات قالوا هذا عواء أهل النار ثم انطلق بي فإذا أنا بقوم معلقين بعراقيبهم مشققة أشداقهم تسيل أشداقهم دما قال قلت من هؤلاء قال الذين يفطرون قبل تحلة صومهم

"While I was sleeping, two men came to me and took hold of my arms. They brought me to a steep mountain and said, 'Climb.' I said, 'I am not able to.' They said, 'We will make it easy for you.' So I climbed until I came to the summit of the mountain where I heard terrible cries. I said, 'What are these cries?' They said, 'Those are the cries of the inhabitants of the Fire.' Then they took me further until I came to a people who were strung up by their hamstrings, and their jawbones were torn and flowing with blood. I said, 'Who are these people?' He said, 'Those are the people who break their fast before the time it was permissible to do so.'"[2]

---

[1] Quoted in Nadwi, p. 173.

[2] Recorded by ibn Hibban and ibn Khuzaima. According to al-Albani, it is *sahih*. Al-Albani, *Sahih al-Targheeb wa al-Tarheeb*, vol. 1, p. 420.

The Ruling Concerning One who Does Not Fast

If a person denies the obligation of the fast, he becomes a disbeliever. Its obligatory status is confirmed in the Quran and numerous hadith of the Prophet (peace be upon him).

As for the one who believes in the fast but does not fast, there is a hadith which states,

عرى الإسلام وقواعد الدين ثلاثة عليهن أسس الإسلام من ترك واحدة منهن فهو بها كافر حلال الدم شهادة أن لا إله إلا الله والصلاة المكتوبة وصوم رمضان

"The bare essence of Islam and the basics, upon which Islam has been established, are three. Whoever leaves one of them becomes an unbeliever and his blood may legally be spilled. [These acts are:] Testifying that there is no God except Allah, the obligatory prayers and the fast of Ramadhan." This hadith was recorded by Abu Yala and al-Dailami. Some scholars have called it *hasan*. However, the correct view seems to be that of al-Albani, that the hadith is weak. But, most likely, it seems that it is a statement of the Companion ibn Abbas and not that of the Prophet (peace be upon him).[1] Therefore, it cannot be considered an overriding proof in this matter, especially if there is no record that the other Companions agreed with him on this point.

However, a Companion coming to such a conclusion demonstrates the importance of this act of fasting. No scholar would make such a statement, not to

---

[1] See Muhammad Nasir al-Din al-Albani, *Silsilat al-Ahadith al-Dhaeefah* (Beirut: al-Maktab al-Islami, 1398 A. H.), vol. 1, pp. 131-2.

speak of a Companion, unless that act was of great importance in Islam. Although the majority and the strongest opinion is that such a person does not become a disbeliever, those Muslims who refuse to fast the month of Ramadhan should consider ibn Abbas' statement very carefully as there is a likelihood that what he said is correct.

Furthermore, al-Dhahabi once wrote,

> According to the established believers, anyone who leaves the fast of Ramadhan without being sick is worse than a fornicator or an alcoholic. In fact, they doubt his Islam and they suspect that he might be a *zandiqah* (renegade against Islam) and one of those who destroy Islam.[1]

"and make the pilgrimage to the House if you have the means to do so."

The Meaning of *Hajj*

The next pillar of Islam mentioned in this narration of this hadith is making the pilgrimage to the House of Allah, or the Kaaba. Linguistically, *hajj* means, "He repaired, or betook himself, to, or towards a person... or towards an object of reverence, veneration, respect or honour."[2] In the *shariah*, it means a particular going or traveling at a particular time to a particular place for the purpose of worshipping Allah. In other words, it is the

---

[1] Quoted in Sabiq, vol. 3, p. 111.

[2] E. W. Lane, *Arabic-English Lexicon* (Cambridge, England: The Islamic Texts Society, 1984), vol. 1, p. 513.

journeying to Makkah during the months designated for the performance of Hajj as an act of worship for the sake of Allah.

The Importance of Hajj

The performance of *Hajj* is an obligation upon every Muslim who has the means to perform it. This can be clearly proven from the Quran and sunnah. However, it is much more than an obligation. It is one of the foundations or pillars of Islam itself.

The reward for the performance of the *Hajj* is great. The Prophet (peace be upon him) said,

مَنْ حَجَّ لِلَّهِ فَلَمْ يَرْفُثْ وَلَمْ يَفْسُقْ رَجَعَ كَيَوْمِ وَلَدَتْهُ أُمُّهُ

"Whoever performs the Hajj for the sake of Allah and does not commit any lewdness or sins returns like the day in which his mother gave him birth," that is, without any sins. (Recorded by al-Bukhari and Muslim.)

The Prophet (peace be upon him) also said,

الْعُمْرَةُ إِلَى الْعُمْرَةِ كَفَّارَةٌ لِمَا بَيْنَهُمَا وَالْحَجُّ الْمَبْرُورُ لَيْسَ لَهُ جَزَاءٌ إِلاَّ الْجَنَّةُ

"One *Umrah*[1] until the next *Umrah* is an expiation for what is between them. And the Hajj that is accepted by Allah and performed properly has no reward other than Paradise." (Recorded by al-Bukhari and Muslim.)

Another hadith reads:

---

[1] *Umrah* is sometimes called the "lesser pilgrimage". It contains less rites and may be done throughout the year.

أَنَّ رَسُولَ اللَّهِ صَلَّى اللَّهُ عَلَيْهِ وَسَلَّمَ سُئِلَ أَيُّ الْعَمَلِ أَفْضَلُ فَقَالَ إِيمَانٌ بِاللَّهِ وَرَسُولِهِ قِيلَ ثُمَّ مَاذَا قَالَ الْجِهَادُ فِي سَبِيلِ اللَّهِ قِيلَ ثُمَّ مَاذَا قَالَ حَجٌّ مَبْرُورٌ

The Messenger of Allah (peace be upon him) was asked, "What is the best deed?" He stated, "Belief in Allah and His Messenger." He was then asked, "What next?" He said, "Jihad in the way of Allah." He was again asked, "What next?" He replied, "The Hajj which is performed correctly and accepted by Allah." (Recorded by al-Bukhari and Muslim.)

Furthermore, Hajj is equivalent to jihad for women and people who are not capable of jihad. In one hadith, the Prophet was asked whether or not women are required to take part in jihad. He answered,

نَعَمْ عَلَيْهِنَّ جِهَادٌ لا قِتَالَ فِيهِ الْحَجُّ وَالْعُمْرَةُ

"Yes, upon them is the jihad which does not contain fighting: Hajj and Umrah."[1]

Hajj has numerous benefits to it. Besides those mentioned in the hadith, one can note that it is a place for Muslims from all around the world to come and worship Allah together. This is an excellent opportunity for Muslims to meet each other, understand each other and get closer to each other. Furthermore, all differences between them are swept away as they all dress in a similar fashion and perform the same rituals. The poor, the rich and all others are all standing in the same manner in front of Allah.

Siddiqi describes the significance of Hajj in the following manner,

---

[1] Recorded by Ahmad and ibn Majah. According to al-Albani, it is *sahih*. Muhammad Nasir al-Din al-Albani, *Irwa al-Ghaleel fi Takhreej Ahadith Manar al-Sabeel* (Beirut: al-Maktab al-Islami, 1979), vol. 4, p. 151.

It is rightly said that it [the Hajj] is the perfection of faith since it combines in itself all the distinctive qualities of other obligatory acts. It represents the quality of *salat* [prayer] since a pilgrim offers prayers in the Kaba, the House of the Lord. It encourages spending of material wealth for the sake of the Lord, the chief characteristic of Zakat. When a pilgrim sets out for Hajj, he dissociates himself from his hearth and home, from his dear and near ones to please the Lord. He suffers privation and undertakes the hardship of journey— the lessons we learn from fasting and *itikaf.*[1] In Hajj one is trained to be completely forgetful of the material comforts and pomp and show of worldly life. One has to sleep on stony ground[2], circumambulate the Kaba, run between Safa and Marwa and spend his night and day wearing only two pieces of unsewn cloth. He is required to avoid the use of oil or scent or any other perfume. He is not even allowed to get his hair cut or trim his beard. In short, he is commanded to abandon everything for the sake of Allah and submit himself before his Lord, the ultimate aim of the life of a Muslim. In fact, physical pilgrimage is a prelude to spiritual pilgrimage to God, when man would bid goodbye to everything of the world and present himself before Him as His humble servant saying: "Here I am before Thee, my Lord, as a slave of Thine."[3]

Hajj is Obligatory on One who Has the Means

Allah says in the Quran,

---

[1] *Itikaf* is were one secludes himself in the mosque for personal worship and devotion. Most commonly, this is done at the end of the month of Ramadhan.

[2] This is not a must but it is how many pilgrims spend their nights.

[3] Siddiqi, vol. 2, p. 577. The last statement he made is very close to what the pilgrims chant during the pilgrimage.

وَلِلَّهِ عَلَى ٱلنَّاسِ

حِجُّ ٱلْبَيْتِ مَنِ ٱسْتَطَاعَ إِلَيْهِ سَبِيلًا ۚ وَمَن كَفَرَ فَإِنَّ ٱللَّهَ غَنِيٌّ عَنِ ٱلْعَـٰلَمِينَ

"And Hajj to the House is a duty that mankind owes to Allah, those who can afford the expenses. And whoever disbelieves, then Allah stands not in need of any of the worlds" (*ali-Imran* 97). Similarly, when responding to the question of Gabriel, the Prophet (peace be upon him) also specifically pointed out that Hajj is obligatory upon the one who has the means to perform it.

Scholars differ as to exactly how this condition is to be met.[1] In general, though, it shows that Hajj is not meant to be a hardship. It is a great act of worship that people should do their best to perform but only if it is feasible for them. In general, this feasibility includes having the physical health, financial well-being and the provisions needed to undertake the Hajj. Some scholars also add that the journey should not be so treacherous that the pilgrim's life is put at risk. In addition, women must have a *mahram* [male relative or husband] to travel with them as they are not allowed to travel alone, although some scholars allow them to travel in "trustworthy" groups made up of men and women.

If one does not meet these conditions, one is not obliged to perform the Hajj. He must wait until he has the ability to perform it. When he does have the ability to perform it, there is a difference of opinion over whether he must perform it immediately at that time or if he may delay it until a future year. That is the next topic of discussion.

---

[1] Further details may be found in as-Sayed Sabiq, *Fiqh*, vol. 5, pp. 7-9.

The Question of Delaying the Performance of Hajj

There is a difference of opinion over whether or not the performance of Hajj may be delayed. That is, suppose there is a person who has not fulfilled the obligation of Hajj and he has the means and ability to make Hajj this year. If he decides to delay its performance until some later year, is he considered sinful or not? Is it permissible for him to delay it or must he perform it the first time that he has the opportunity to perform it?

Malik, Abu Hanifa, Ahmad and some Shafi'is state that one must perform Hajj at its first feasible opportunity. Otherwise, one is being sinful. Evidence for this position includes:

The Prophet (peace be upon him) said,

مَنْ كُسِرَ أَوْ عَرِجَ فَقَدْ حَلَّ وَعَلَيْهِ الْحَجُّ مِنْ قَابِلٍ

"If anyone breaks [a bone] or becomes lame, he comes out of the sacred state and he must perform the Hajj the following year."[1] The deduction from this hadith is that if one can perform the Hajj whenever he wishes, the Prophet (peace be upon him) would not have explicitly mentioned that the person should perform the Hajj in the following year.

Another hadith states,

تَعَجَّلُوا إِلَى الْحَجِّ يَعْنِي الْفَرِيضَةَ فَإِنَّ أَحَدَكُمْ لا يَدْرِي مَا يَعْرِضُ لَهُ

[1] Recorded by Ahmad, Abu Dawud, al-Nasai and others. According to al-Albani, it is *sahih*. Al-Albani, *Sahih al-Jami*, vol. 2, p. 1112.

"Hurry to perform the Hajj, that is, the obligatory one, as none of you knows what may happen to him."[1]

It is also narrated that Umar ibn al-Khattab once said, "I considered sending men to those lands to see who had the means but did not perform the Hajj. They should have the *jizya*[2] applied to them as they are not Muslims, they are not Muslims."[3]

One of the strongest pieces of evidence presented for saying that one is allowed to delay his performance of Hajj, even though he has the ability to perform it, is the fact that Hajj was made obligatory in the 6th year after the Hijrah and the Messenger of Allah (peace be upon him) himself did not perform the Hajj until the tenth year. However, Al-Shaukaani has offered the following response to this argument,

> [First,] there is a difference of opinion concerning when Hajj became an obligation. One of the opinions is that it became obligatory in the 10th year. Hence, there was no delay [on the part of the Messenger of Allah (peace be upon him)]. If it is accepted that it was obligatory before the 10th year, the Messenger of Allah (peace be upon him) delayed his performance because of his dislike to perform the Hajj in the company of the polytheists, as they would perform the Hajj and circumambulate the Kaaba in the nude. When Allah purified the House of those people, the Messenger of Allah (peace be upon him) made Hajj. Hence, he delayed his Hajj due to an excuse. [That is

---

[1] Recorded by Ahmad. According to al-Albani, it is *sahih*. Al-Albani, *Sahih al-Jami*, vol. 1, p. 569.

[2] *Jizya* is a tax paid to the state by the non-Muslim citizens in lieu of military service.

[3] This narration was recorded by Saeed ibn Mansur and al-Baihaqi. According to al-Haitami, this is an authentic narration. Al-Haitami, *al-Zawajir*, vol. 1, p. 198.

acceptable,] the dispute is only concerning one who delays his Hajj without any valid excuse.[1]

The Ruling Concerning One who Does not Perform Hajj until He Dies Although He had the Means

The one who denies the obligation of the Hajj is a disbeliever. The person who intentionally delays his performance of Hajj, although he had the means, until he dies is a *faasiq* or evildoer. He has left himself open to the punishment and displeasure of Allah in the Hereafter.

"He said, 'You have spoken truthfully [or correctly].' We were amazed that he asks the question and then he says that he had spoken truthfully."

The behavior of the angel was something very strange for the people. First, he had asked the Prophet (peace be upon him) some questions. In general, when a person asks a question, it implies that he does not know the answer. Therefore, it is strange that he should comment that the answer was correct. Second, more importantly, this was information that was known only from the Prophet's

[1] Muhammad ibn Ali al-Shaukaani, *Nail al-Autaar*, (Riyadh: Dar Zamam, 1993), vol. 4, pp. 337-338. Ibn Uthaimin states that the Hajj was made obligatory in the ninth year and the number of delegations coming to meet with the Prophet (peace be upon him) in Madina is one of the reasons that the Prophet (peace be upon him) was not able to perform the Hajj. See Muhammad ibn Uthaimin, *Al-Sharh al-Mumti ala Zaad al-Mustaqni* (Riyadh: Muassassat Asaam, 1996), vol. 7, pp. 17-18.

teachings. This man who had come to ask the questions was not known to any of the people and, so, he was not known to have been someone who learned from the Prophet (peace be upon him). This made it all the more surprising that he had the boldness to state that the Prophet's replies were correct.

The Concept of *Imaan*

"He said, 'Tell me about *Imaan* (faith).'"

In this narration, after asking about Islam, the Angel asked the Prophet (peace be upon him) about *Imaan* or faith. Once again, the Prophet (peace be upon him) understood that he was not asking about the nature of faith but he was, instead, asking about what is to be believed in. However, before discussing the aspects that the Prophet (peace be upon him) mentioned, it is important that one have the correct understanding of the concept of *Imaan* derived from the Quran and sunnah. Therefore, the following pages will be a discussion of the concept of faith.

The Concept of *Imaan*

What is *Imaan* (faith)? Who is a believer? What is disbelief? Who is a disbeliever? These questions appeared very early in the history of Islam. Unfortunately, they also led to differences of opinion as well as division among the Muslims. In the first century of Islam, the Khawarij had developed their own theory of faith and began to call many of the Muslims of that time disbelievers. In response to them came groups such as the Murjia, Jahamiyah and others whose definitions of Islam embraced everyone regardless of their deeds. Another group, the Mutazila, developed their own theory which was termed the "position between the two positions". Through all of this, though, by the grace of Allah, the position of the Quran and sunnah on these questions was clear and propagated by the true followers of Islam.

In the opening pages to his work, *Haqiqat al-Imaan ind ahl al-Sunnah wa al-Jamaah*, Muhammad Abdul Hadi al-Misri makes a very important point.[1] This important point is not only valid for the question of faith and disbelief but is valid for practically all aspects of the faith. If Muslims would keep this principle in mind, many of the differences among them would be removed and they would be guided to the true teachings of the Quran and sunnah. The point he made is this: When it comes to any concept from the Quran and sunnah, historically speaking, there have been two approaches to determine its correct meaning. The first approach is to discover the meaning of that concept from the Prophet (peace be upon him) as he passed on such knowledge to his Companions and them to their followers. The second approach is to go directly to the word itself and, based on presupposed premises, discover its meaning from a linguistic and logical point of view without first studying how Allah and the Prophet (peace be upon him) explained those terms. The first approach is the approach of the *ahl al-Sunnah wa al-Jamaah* while the second approach is that of the heretical groups. In fact, these two approaches are what really distinguishes the correct way of Islam from the distorted, later-invented views of the religion.

On this point, ibn Taimiya wrote,

> One must understand that if any term is found in the Quran or hadith, and its explanation is known

---

[1] Muhammad Abdul Hadi al-Misri, *Haqiqat al-Imaan ind Ahl al-Sunnah wa al-Jamaah* (Dar al-Furqan, 1991), p. 9.

> and its purport made clear by the Prophet (peace be upon him), there is then no need to use as evidence the statements of the linguists or others.... The words *salat*, *zakat*, *siyaam* (fasting), *hajj* found in the words of Allah and His messenger have had their meanings clarified by the Messenger of Allah (peace be upon him). The same is true for the word *khamr* (intoxicant) and others. From him, one knows their meanings. If anyone wants to explain such terms in any way other than how the Prophet (peace be upon him) explained that term, such an explanation will not be accepted... The terms *Imaan*, Islam, *nifaaq* (hypocrisy) and *kufr* are more important than all of those terms [just mentioned]. The Prophet (peace be upon him) explained the meanings of those terms in such a way that it is not necessary to look for their linguistic origins or how they were used by the [pre-Islamic] Arabs and so forth. Therefore, it is a must that, while trying to determine the meanings of such terms, one looks at how Allah and His Messenger explained those terms. Their explanation is clear and sufficient... The heretics have been misled on this matter. They turn away from this method [just described]. Instead, they begin to explain the religion of Islam based on some premises that they believe to be sound, either concerning linguistic meaning or rational thought. They do not ponder or consider the explanation of Allah and His Messenger. Every premise that goes against the clarification from Allah and His Messenger is certainly misguidance.[1]

Al-Misri adds that the one who will truly follow the methodology of going to the Quran and sunnah is the one who firmly believes that the Prophet (peace be upon him) explained the entire religion in a clear manner to his Companions and that those Companions passed that clear

---

[1] Ahmad ibn Taimiya, *Kitaab al-Imaan* (Beirut: al-Maktab al-Islami, 1988), pp. 271-273.

knowledge on to their followers and so forth.[1] Everything that essentially needs to be known of the meaning of the Quran has been given by the Prophet (peace be upon him) himself. This fact should be something fundamental and obvious to all Muslims. In theory it may be so. In practice, however, many people fail to apply this point and start looking elsewhere concerning matters that have already been made clear in the Quran and sunnah. The question of *Imaan* is a very clear illustration of this point.

Turning to the Quran and sunnah, one can attempt to answer some basic questions concerning *Imaan*. These basic questions are the following:

(1) What is true *Imaan* or who is a true believer (*mu`min*)?

(2) What is the locus of *imaan* and what are the essential components of *Imaan*?

(3) What is the relationship between *Imaan* and deeds?

(4) What are the articles of *Imaan*? In other words, what is a person supposed to believe in? This is what the Prophet (peace be upon him) explained to the Angel Gabriel. These topics shall be discussed in some detail as they are mentioned in the hadith.

The Definition of *Imaan* According to the Quran and Sunnah

Opinions differ about the exact composition of *Imaan*.[2] The different views can be summarized as follows (they are also presented in Figures 1a-d):

---

[1] al-Misri, p. 10.

[2] Cf., al-Hawaali, vol. 2, pp. 405-421; Ali ibn Abu al-Izz, *Sharh al-Aqeedah al-Tahaawiyah* (Beirut: Muassasah al-Risaalah, 1988), vol. 2, pp. 459-462.

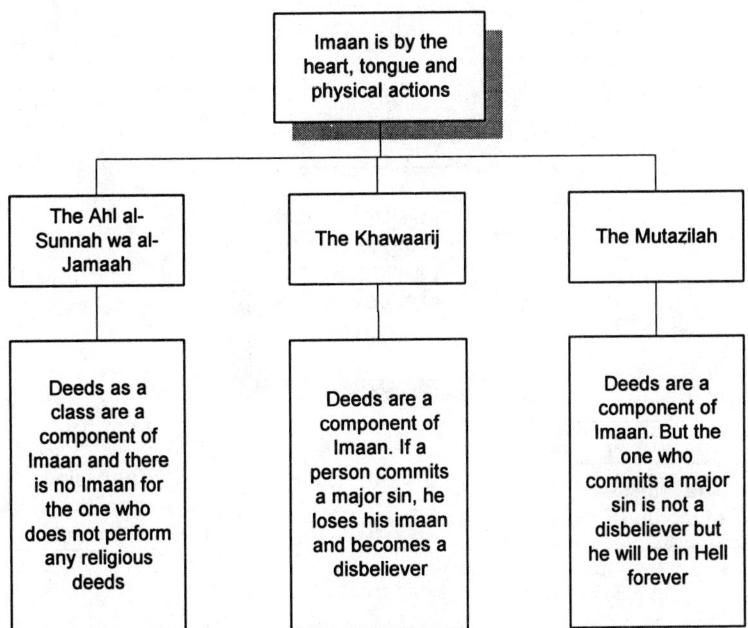

Figure 1a. The Components of *Imaan* as Viewed by Different Sects

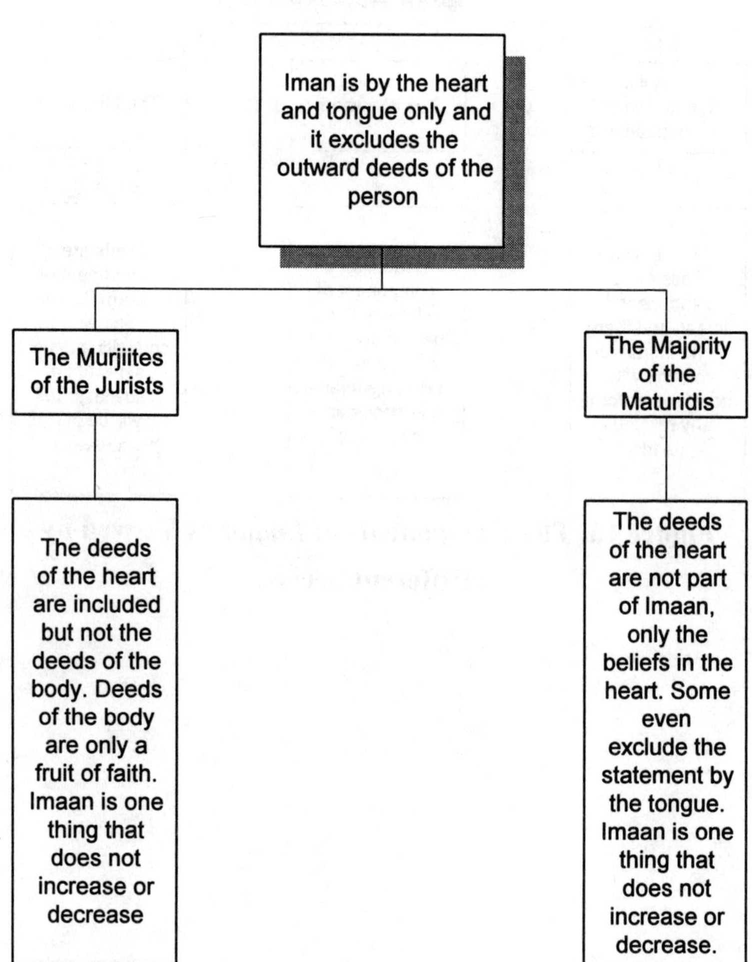

Figure 1b. The Components of *Imaan* as Viewed by Different Sects

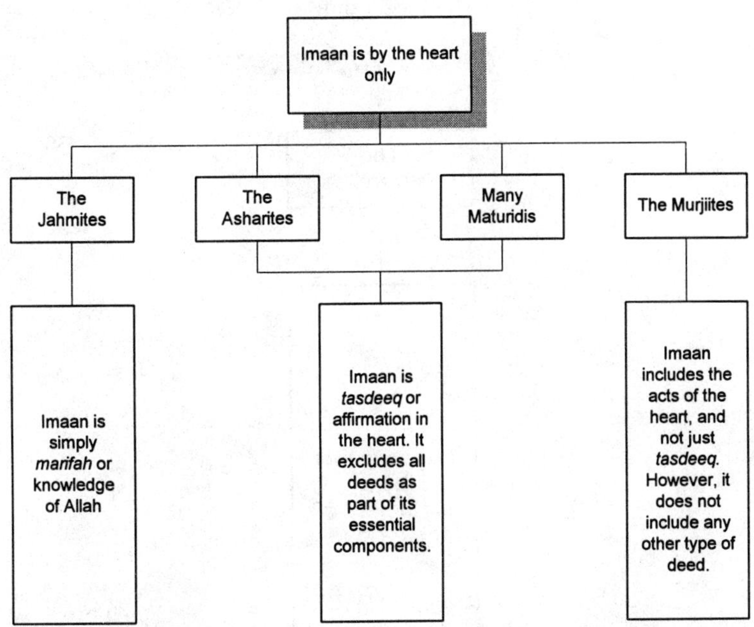

Figure 1c. The Components of *Imaan* as Viewed by Different Sects

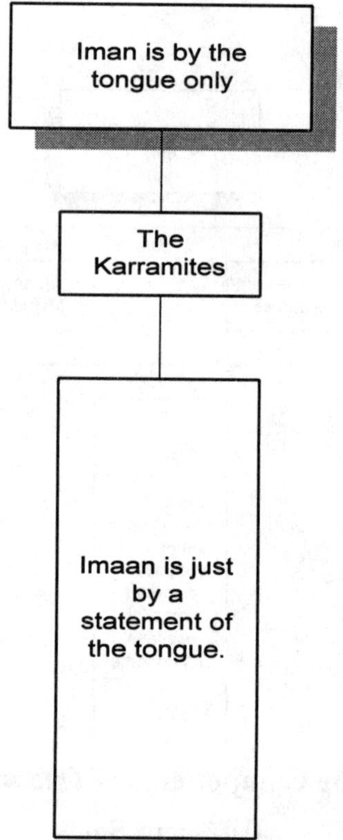

Figure 1d. The Components of *Imaan* as Viewed by Different Sects

The view of the *ahl al-Sunnah wa al-Jamaah*: According to this view, the locus of *imaan* is the heart, tongue and physical actions. *Imaan* increases and decreases. Deeds form a part of *imaan*. Some such deeds are essential, others are required and yet others are recommended. This does not preclude the possibility that true believers commit sins. Such sins, even major sins if they are less than *kufr* and *shirk*, do not take the person out of the fold of Islam. In the Hereafter, the sinner may be punished in the Hell-fire or be forgiven by Allah. However, all people who have even the slightest amount of *imaan* in their hearts will eventually be rescued from Hell and entered into Paradise. This is the belief that was passed on from the Prophet (peace be upon him) to his Companions and their followers. It is the only view that takes into consideration of the different relevant pieces of evidence from the Quran and sunnah.

Ibn Abu al-Izz wrote,

> [The Prophet (peace be upon him)] has made it absolutely clear that a person is definitely not a *mu`min* (a believer) if it is claimed that he believes in the Prophet (peace be on him) but he does not profess it with his tongue, even though he can, nor does he offer *salat*, nor fasts, nor loves Allah and His Prophet (peace be on him), nor fears Him. If, he also hates the Prophet (peace be on him) and fights against him [then he obviously cannot be called a believer]. He has also made it clear that our happiness and position in the hereafter depends upon our statement of the testimony of faith and our sincerely believing in Allah's unity and acting accordingly. For instance, he said, "*Imaan* has more than seventy parts, the highest is the confession that there is no god except Allah, and the lowest is removing a harmful object from the road."[1] "Modesty is part of *Imaan*."[2] "The most perfect *mu`min* (believer) is the one who is best in character."[3] "Simplicity in dress is part of *Imaan*."[1]

[1]The wording of the hadith in hadith collections is a little different. The hadith in Muslim and al-Bukhari begins with, "*Imaan* has more than sixty parts (*bid wa sittun shu'bah*)." Abu Dawud, al-Tirmidhi and Ibn Majah record, "*Imaan* is more than sixty or seventy chapters (*bid wa sittun aw sab'un bab*)." The reporter of this hadith was not sure whether the Prophet (peace be on him) said, "more than sixty" or "more than seventy".

[2]This is the ending of the hadith mentioned in the previous note.

[3]Recorded by Al-Tirmidhi, Abu Dawud, Ahmad, al-Darimi and Ibn Hibban. It is an authentic hadith according to al-Albani. See al-Albani's footnotes to Ali ibn Abu al-Izz, *Sharh al-Aqeedah al-Tahawiya*, (Beirut: al-Maktab al-Islami, 1984), p. 339. Hereinafter, this work will simply be referred to as "al-Albani, footnotes to *Sharh*."

> If *Imaan* has different parts and each part is called *Imaan*, it follows that *Salat* is *Imaan*, Zakah and *hajj* are *Imaan*, virtues such as modesty, trust, fear, and submission, even removing an obstacle from the way, are part of *Imaan*. Some of these parts are so basic, like the two *Shahaadah*, that if you lose them you lose *Imaan* completely; others are so marginal, such as removing an obstacle from the road, that if you lose them you do not lose *Imaan*. In between the two, we have numerous parts of varying importance, some next only to the *Shahaadah*, and others only a little more important than removing an obstacle from the way. As the parts of *Imaan* are *Imaan*, similarly the parts of *kufr* are *kufr*. To judge according to the rules revealed by Allah is part of *Imaan*, and to judge against them is *kufr*.[2]

The view of the Khawaarij: According to this view, the locus of *imaan* is the heart, tongue and physical actions. But in this view, if anyone falls short in his deeds (such as failing to perform an obligatory deed or actually performing a major sin), he becomes a disbeliever, falls outside of the fold of Islam and will be in Hell forever. This view clearly contradicts the Quran and sunnah. For example, Allah has prescribed a punishment for the person who commits adultery. That punishment is not the same as the punishment for apostasy. This is because the one who commits such a sin does not, by that act in itself, remove himself from the fold of Islam.

---

[1]Recorded by Ibn Majah. The words in Abu Dawud are, "Do you hear? Do you hear? Verily, simplicity in dress (*al-badhadhah*) is part of *Imaan*." This is a *hasan* hadith. See al-Albani, footnotes to *Sharh*, p. 340.

[2] Ibn Abu al-Izz, vol. 2, pp. 471-475. The translation used here is a pre-publication copy of Muhammad Abdul Haq Ansari, *Sharh al-Aqeedah al-Tahawiyah* (Fairfax, VA: Institute of Islamic and Arabic Sciences in America, forthcoming). For the sake of the page numbering, the published version from Muassasat al-Risaalah will be the work referred to.

The view of the Mutazilah: According to this view, the locus of *imaan* is the heart, tongue and physical actions. They supposedly took a position between the above two positions. They stated that a great sinner is neither a believer or a disbeliever; he falls somewhere in between the two. At the same time, though, they say that such a person will be in the Hell-fire forever. In order to come to this conclusion, they have to reject numerous authentic and conformed reports from the Prophet (peace be upon him) that believers who commit such sins will be rescued from the Hell-fire.

The view of the Murjiites of the jurists: According to this view, the locus of *imaan* is the heart and the tongue, and it excludes physical deeds. The deeds of the heart are included but not the physical acts that a person performs. Acts are only the fruit of faith and do not make up one of the essential components of faith. *Imaan* is, in essence, *tasdeeq* or affirmation in the heart. Therefore, it is as one level and cannot possibly increase or decrease. This view also contradicts the Quran and sunnah. The Quran and sunnah clearly demonstrate that *imaan* increases and decreases. Furthermore, numerous hadith also demonstrate that acts do form a part of *imaan*.

The view of the majority of the Maturidis: According to this view, the locus of *imaan* is the heart and the tongue, and it excludes physical deeds. They also say that *imaan* neither increases or decreases, since it is *tasdeeq* or affirmation in the heart. They differ from the Murjiah in that they say that the deeds of the heart are also not included as part of *imaan*, only the statements or beliefs in the heart. Some of them even exclude the statement of the tongue as part of *imaan*, arguing that it is only a sign of *imaan* and not a component of *imaan*.

The view of the Asharites and many Maturidis: According to this view, the locus of *imaan* is the heart only. *Imaan* is only *tasdeeq* or affirmation in the heart. *Imaan* does not increase or decrease. They exclude all deeds,

deeds of the heart as well as of the body. A person is a perfect and complete believer even if he does not perform any corresponding deeds, as long as *tasdeeq* is in his heart. They even exclude statement of the tongue and argue that a person does not have to make the testimony of faith— so he will be considered a disbeliever in this world while he is a believer in his heart. This view also contradicts the Quran and sunnah in many aspects. *Imaan* being only *tasdeeq* would imply, for example, that Abu Talib was a believer and should be in Paradise. However, this is not what the Prophet (peace be upon him) stated about him.

The view of many of the Mujiites: According to this view, the locus of *imaan* is the heart only. *Imaan* does not increase or decrease. Many of them do include the deeds of the heart and not just *tasdeeq*. At the same time, they exclude all other deeds, including statement of the tongue.

The view of the Jahmites: According to this view, the locus of *imaan* is the heart only. However, it is not *tasdeeq* (belief, affirmation) but it is simply *marifah* or having knowledge of Allah. Most scholars have declared the Jahmites to be outside of the fold of Islam due to such beliefs. Commenting on the Jahmites, ibn Abu al-Izz wrote,

> Al-Jahm ibn Safwan and Abu l-Husayn al-Salihi, a leading Libertarian (Qadari), believe that *Imaan* is a kind of knowledge in the heart... [This] implies that the Pharaoh and his people were believers since they knew that Moses and Aaron, peace and blessings of Allah be on them, were true prophets even though they denied them. This is clear from what Moses said to the Pharaoh, "You know very well that these things have been sent down by none but the Lord of the heavens and the earth as eye-opening evidence" (*al-Israa* 102). The People of the Book knew that Muhammad (peace be on him) was the Prophet just as they knew their own sons, but they were not believers in him. In fact, they were his deniers and opponents. Abu Talib too

> would be among his believers according to the view, for he is reported to have said [in lines of poetry], "I know that the religion of Muhammad, is the best of all the religions of mankind. Were I not to be scolded and abused, I would have confessed it openly."
>
> Actually even Iblis, also, would be a perfect believer according to al-Jahm's view. He did not plead ignorance of Allah. He knew Him well as he said, "My Lord, give me then respite till the Day the dead are raised" (*al-Hijr* 36), "My Lord, because you have put me in the wrong ..." (*al-Hijr* 39), and "Then, by Your Power, I will put them all in the wrong" (*Saad* 82). For al-Jahm, *kufr* is ignorance of Allah. No one, however, is more ignorant of Allah than him, for he reduces Allah to a Being as such and strips Him of all His attributes. There can be no greater ignorance than this. He is therefore a disbeliever (*kaafir*) according to his own testimony.[1]

The view of the Karramites: According to this view, the locus of *imaan* is the tongue only. In other words, a person who states the testimony of faith is considered a complete and true believer regardless of what is in his heart. Ibn Abu al-Izz said about them,

> According to their view, the hypocrites are perfect believers. Nevertheless, they believe that the hypocrites will suffer the punishment which Allah has promised for them. Thus they contradict themselves.[2]

With respect to the views of the Asharites, Maturidis and Murjiites, it is very important to realize that *Imaan* is not simply faith or belief in something, which is

---

[1] Ibn Abu al-Izz, vol. 2, pp. 459-462.
[2] Ibn Abu al-Izz, vol. 2, p. 460.

the opposite of disbelieving in something.[1] That is not the correct concept of *Imaan* whatsoever, as is clear from the verses of the Quran and sunnah. On this point, ibn Abu al-Izz wrote,

> *Imaan* is not in contrast to *takdhib* (to deny) but *tasdeeq* (to affirm, to believe) is. *Imaan*, however, is in contrast to *kufr*, which is not necessarily just *takdhib*. If I say, "I know that you are truthful (*sadiq*), but I will not follow you, rather I will oppose you and hate you," I will be guilty of a greater *kufr*. Hence it is clear that *Imaan* is not simply *tasdeeq*, nor is *kufr* simply *takdhib*. *Kufr* is sometimes *takdhib* but sometimes more than that, where it includes opposition and hostility. On the other hand, *Imaan* is not only *tasdeeq*; it is more than that, wherein it includes assent (*muwafaqah*), love (*muwalat*) and submission (*inqiyaad*). *Tasdiq* does not give the whole meaning of *Imaan*; and *islam* (submission) is only a part of *Imaan*.
>
> If, however, *tașdeeq* is regarded as a synonym [of *Imaan*], then it should be taken in a wider sense which includes action also. For this wider meaning of the term one can refer to a hadith of the Prophet (peace be on him), "The eyes fornicate, and their fornication is to look; and the ears fornicate, and their fornication is to hear... and the private parts confirm (*yusaddiqu*) it or deny (*yukadhdhibu*) it."[2] Hasan al-Basri, may Allah bless him, said, "*Imaan* is neither formal conformity nor vain expectation; it is what settles in the heart and is confirmed by

---

[1] Ibn Taimiya states that it is very easy to affirm the existence of something and then to hate that thing. For example, people affirm the existence of disbelief and devils while they hate disbelief and devils. This affirmation obviously cannot be considered equivalent to *imaan*. See ibn Taimiya, *Majmoo*, vol. 7, p. 541.

[2] Recorded by Al-Bukhari and Muslim.

action."[1] If it is *tasdeeq*, it is a particular kind of *tasdeeq*...

Ibn Uthaimin has also emphasized the fact that *imaan* is not simply composed of "belief" in the heart, in the sense that one affirms that there is no one worthy of worship but Allah. Instead, along with that "belief" other components must be present for it to be the correct form of *imaan* that is acceptable to Allah. He wrote,

> *Imaan* is the affirmation that requires acceptance and submission. If a person believes in something without acceptance and submission, that is not *imaan*. The evidence for that is that the polytheists [Arabs] believed in Allah's existence and believed in Allah as the Creator, Sustainer, Giver of Life, Bringer of Death and the Manager of the Universe's Affairs. Furthermore, one of them even accepted the messengership of the Prophet Muhammad (peace be upon him) but he was not a believer. That person was Abu Talib, the uncle of the Prophet (peace be upon him)..[2] But that [belief in the Prophet (peace be upon him)] will not avail him whatsoever because he did not accept and submit to what the Prophet (peace be upon him) brought.[3]

The Components of *Imaan*

As just noted, a thorough study of the Quran and sunnah shows that *Imaan* has certain components. Ibn al-Qayyim once wrote that *Imaan* is a compound of the following components: (1) having the knowledge of what

[1]Recorded by Ibn Abi Shaybah, *al-Musannnaf*, vol. 11, p. 22.

[2] Ibn Uthaimin then goes on to quote some lines of poetry from Abu Talib in which he expressed his belief in the Prophet Muhammad (peace be upon him).

[3] Muhammad ibn Uhtaimin, *Sharh Hadith Jibreel Alaihi al-Salaam* (Dar al-Thuraya, 1415 A.H.), pp. 4-5.

the Prophet (peace be upon him) taught; (2) having complete and firm belief in what the Prophet (peace be upon him) brought; (3) verbally professing one's belief in what he brought; (4) yielding or submitting to what he brought out of love and humility; (5) acting in accord with what the Prophet (peace be upon him) brought, both outwardly and inwardly, implementing it and calling to its path according to one's ability.[1]

These components were summed up by the earliest scholars in their saying, "*Imaan* is statement and action."[2] Statement here includes both statement of the heart (affirmation) and statement of the tongue (verbal profession). Action includes both the actions of the heart (willingness to submit, love and so forth) and actions of the body (such as prayer and so forth).[3]

For the sake of clarity, over time, these two components were broken down into the three following essential components of *Imaan* that have also been stated by many scholars: (1) Belief in the heart; (2) Profession by the tongue; (3) Performance of deeds by the physical parts of the body.[4]

Each one of these three components shall be discussed separately. The third component shall be dealt with in some detail in the next section entitled, "The Relationship Between *Imaan* and Deeds".

(1) Belief in the Heart. The heart is the locus of *Imaan* or its foundation. If what is in the heart is not sound

---

[1] Ibn al-Qayyim, *al-Fawaid*, p. 107. (As quoted in Al-Misri, p. 41.)

[2] Abu Zura and Abu Haatim, two of al-Bukhari's most important teachers, narrated that the scholars that they had met from Hijaz, Iraq, Greater Syria and Yemen all said, "*Imaan* is statement and action, it increases and decreases." See al-Laalakai, vol. 1, p. 176.

[3] Cf., Ahmad ibn Taimiya, *Majmoo Fatawaa Shaikh al-Islaam ibn Taimiya* (collected by Abdul Rahmaan Qaasim and his son Muhammad, no publication information given), vol. 7, p. 672; al-Hawaali, vol. 1, pp. 221-236.

[4] Al-Hawaali convincingly argues that the statement, "*Imaan* is statement and action," is the preferred statement. See al-Hawaali, *Fikr*, vol. 1, pp. 227-228. However, for ease of presentation, the later division into three components will be followed here.

and proper, then nothing else will be sound and proper. The first component of *Imaan* being belief in the heart has two aspects.

The first aspect is what the scholars call the "statement of the heart". It is made up of recognition, knowledge and affirmation. For example, one recognizes that there is none worthy of worship except Allah, one has knowledge of that and one affirms that. Obviously, if one does not meet this necessary condition of faith, one cannot truthfully claim to have *Imaan*.

The second aspect is what the scholars call the "actions of the heart". This aspect is made up of commitment, voluntary submission and acceptance (*al-iltizaam*, *al-inqiyaad* and *al-tasleem*). There are also other necessary components in the heart. These include love for Allah, awe for Allah, trust in Allah, fear of Allah and hope in Allah. Al-Misri stated, "The Pious Forefathers and leaders of the Muslims agreed that these follow the first essential aspect and are necessary consequences thereof. A person is not a believer unless he possesses both of them."[1] This is so because, as was already alluded to, simple affirmation of belief in Allah and His Messenger without the minimum requirements of love, awe and submission does not make one a believer.

Actually, the first aspect should directly lead to the second aspect— unless one's heart is diseased and refuses to follow the truth. This was pointed out by ibn Taimiya. He stated that if a heart has the knowledge and recognition of the truth then, if it is free from diseases such as envy, arrogance, following of doubts and misconceptions, following of desires and lusts, it will fill with love for the truth and will submit to the truth. This is because the hearts are endowed with a love for truth and seeking it. Therefore,

---

[1] Al-Misri, p. 26.

there is nothing more beloved to a pure and sound heart than Allah.[1]

In reality, the first aspect of recognizing and admitting the existence or truth of Allah is something that readily comes about. It is, in fact, ingrained in the nature of man. It is the second aspect of this first component, the actions of the heart, that needs to be stressed and implied properly. In fact, in general, when Allah sent messengers to mankind, their main message and dispute with their people was not the recognition or acceptance of Allah's existence but it was with respect to submitting to Allah and following His commands. The truth of the first proposition was clear and could not be denied. Allah has made it clear in many verses of the Quran that the main problem for disbelievers is not a recognition of the truth but a hatred for it. Allah has said,

فَإِنَّهُمْ لَا يُكَذِّبُونَكَ وَلَٰكِنَّ

ٱلظَّٰلِمِينَ بِـَٔايَٰتِ ٱللَّهِ يَجْحَدُونَ

"It is not you [O Muhammad] that they deny, but it is the signs of Allah that the wrongdoers deny" (*al-Anaam* 33). In another verse, Allah says,

بَلْ جَآءَهُم بِٱلْحَقِّ وَأَكْثَرُهُمْ

لِلْحَقِّ كَٰرِهُونَ

"Nay, he brought them the Truth but most of them are averse to the Truth" (*al-Muminoon* 70).

Thus, the difficult aspect for the disbelievers is that of having love for the truth, seeking the truth and submitting to it. That is, they must free themselves from all the things that act as barriers to their required submission to the truth. This includes arrogance, pride, envy, ego, seeking

[1] Ibn Taimiya (*al-Imaan al-Ausit*), p. 79 as quoted in al-Misri, p. 28.

after the fleeting pleasures of this world, love for power, control and dominance, nationalistic pride and customs, lust and so forth. In general, the truth of *tauheed* is clear to all of them; however, they do not want to submit and accept it— the diseases of the heart can become so strong in a person that he no longer recognizes the truth or he completely refuses to recognize it whatsoever. This is one of the major aspects that distinguishes a believer from a non-believer. It is not simply a matter of knowing that Allah exists or recognizing that fact.

It is this component of *Imaan*, "belief in the heart", that is the most important. It is the foundation and driving force behind the other components of *Imaan*. When it comes to the components of faith, one is never excused from fulfilling this component while, under different circumstances, one may be excused for not fulfilling the other components. Hence, if a person really wants to be certain that he has true *Imaan* and he seeks to protect himself from losing that *Imaan*, he must concentrate on these components and follow the steps that will strengthen them in himself. The essential components are the recognizing of the truth, desiring the truth and having love for the truth in one's heart. This is combined with hatred for falsehood and disbelief. Note what Allah stated while describing the true believers,

وَلَٰكِنَّ ٱللَّهَ حَبَّبَ إِلَيْكُمُ ٱلْإِيمَٰنَ وَزَيَّنَهُۥ فِى قُلُوبِكُمْ وَكَرَّهَ إِلَيْكُمُ
ٱلْكُفْرَ وَٱلْفُسُوقَ وَٱلْعِصْيَانَ ۚ أُو۟لَٰٓئِكَ هُمُ ٱلرَّٰشِدُونَ

"But Allah has endeared the faith to you and has beautified it in your hearts and has made disbelief, wickedness and disobedience hateful to you. These! They are the rightly guided ones" (*al-Hujuraat* 7).

It must once again be noted that the word *tasdeeq* ("affirmation, belief") when used in the definition of faith does not simply refer to the abstract or theoretical concept of believing in something rationally. Instead, it means the belief in something that drives one to accept it, submit to it and implement it. This is what is meant by *tasdeeq* being the foundation or essential definition of faith.[1]

(2) Profession by the Tongue. The second necessary component of *Imaan* is profession of one's faith by the tongue.[2] Al-Misri stated, "It is inconceivable that the belief in the heart is completely realized— both statement and deeds of the heart— without the faith being realized with the profession of the tongue."[3]

This profession of the tongue plays a two fold role. It is first a statement of a fact. One is testifying that he recognizes the truthfulness of that statement of faith. This would be analogous to a person giving testimony in a court of law. All he is really stating is that those are the facts that he believes to be true. Second, though, it is statement of commitment to that fact. It is an admission by the person that he intends to adhere to the requirements and guidance of what he has testified to.

In an important passage in *Kitaab al-Imaan*, ibn Taimiya has written,

> The Arabs do not have any such thing in their language as affirmation or denial unless it be in meaning and wording or wording that points to meaning. One will not find in Arabic speech the statement, "Mr. X believed in Mr. Y," or "denied him" if he knew only in his heart that so and so was true or false. [Such a statement would only be made if the person actually] spoke it. Whoever does not affirm his belief in someone else with his speech, if he has the ability to do so, is not called, according to the Arabs, a believer. Therefore, the Pious Forefathers of this Nation, of the Companions and those who followed them in goodness, agree on this

---

[1] See Hakimi, vol. 2, pp. 19-20.
[2] Obviously, this only applies to those who have the physical means to do so.
[3] Al-Misri, p. 33.

> point. The one who believes in his heart but does not verbally state his belief is not treated in either this life or the Hereafter as a believer in any way. Allah has not declared such a person to be a believer in the Messenger simply because of the knowledge and belief in his heart. He is only considered a believer if he confirms it by his speech. Therefore, the outward speech is an essential aspect of the faith and, according to the early and later scholars, one will not be saved except with that speech. The Muslims have agreed that the one who does not make the profession of faith although he has the ability to do so is a disbeliever. He is a disbeliever both inwardly and outwardly according to the Pious Forefathers and Imams of this Nation.[1]

However, the simple pronouncement of the words in and of themselves is not what is sought. Obviously, the hypocrites did such and they were by no means true believers. The pronouncement of the words must be accompanied by a sincere attempt to implement the following aspects: (1) the correct belief in the Lordship of Allah and its related aspects; (2) the abandonment of and freedom from any kind of association of partners with Allah; and (3) the following and implementation of the laws of Islam. If this is not what the person means by his profession of faith, then such a profession will not avail the person whatsoever.[2] Hence, before a person makes the testimony of faith, he must be taught and explained that this is what he is testifying to. The testimony does not have to be in the Arabic language or with specific terms but it must

---

[1] See ibn Taimiya, *al-Imaan*, p. 126. Also see Mahmood al-Aini, *Umdah al-Qaari Sharh Sahih al-Bukhari* (Beirut: Dar al-Turath al-Arabi, n.d.), vol. 1, p. 110 where he reiterates the same sentiment.

[2] Al-Misri, p. 35.

be very clear as to the exact meaning and purport of what the person is saying.[1]

The Relationship Between *Imaan* and Deeds

The third component mentioned above as an essential component of *Imaan* is "performance of deeds by the body". Deeds form a primary part of the concept of *Imaan*.[2] The concept or word *Imaan* incorporates in its meaning the deeds that are to be performed in accordance with *Imaan*.

Some scholars get stuck on the linguistic meaning of *Imaan* as being *tasdeeq* (belief) and, therefore, they divorce actions from the essential aspects of *Imaan*.[3] However, such a view is not the view of the early scholars of Islam. In *Kitaab al-Umm*, al-Shafi'i wrote, "There was a consensus of the Companions and the Followers after them and those we have met that *Imaan* is statement, action and intention. None of them are sufficient in themselves without the others."[4] The Maliki jurist Ibn Abdul Barr also said,

> The scholars of fiqh and hadith have agreed that *Imaan* is statement and action. And there is no action without intention. Faith, in their view, increases by acts of obedience [to Allah] and decreases by acts of disobedience. Every act of obedience is a part of faith in their view... As for

---

[1] In a hadith, some people embraced Islam by saying, *Saba`na*, meaning they had entered the faith of those who were called *Sabi`iya*, which was a term of the people of Ignorance for the Muslims.

[2] As noted above, there are a group of scholars that divorce faith from deeds and state that the latter is not an essential component for the former. Their views, although in many aspects simply a question of semantics, do not seem to be the strongest views and will not be covered in detail here.

[3] Al-Hawaali (*Fikr*, vol. 2, pp. 445-475) describes the process— influenced by Greek logic— that led early heretical groups to the conclusion that *imaan* is *tasdeeq* and only *tasdeeq*.

[4] Quoted in ibn Taimiya, *al-Imaan*, p. 197.

> the remaining jurists of personal reasoning (*ahl al-ra`i*) [other than Abu Hanifa] and the scholars of the reports from the Hijaz, Iraq, Greater Syria and Egypt, including Malik ibn Anas, al-Laith ibn Saad, Sufyan al-Thauri, al-Auzai, al-Shafi'i, Ahmad ibn Hanbal, Ishaq ibn Rahawaih, Abu Ubaid al-Qasim ibn Salaam, Dawud ibn Ali, al-Tabari and those who follow their path, they all say that *Imaan* is statement and action. [They say that it is] statement with the tongue, which is profession of the faith, belief in the heart and deeds of the body. All of that [must be] with purity towards Allah by a sincere intention. They also say that every act of obedience to Allah, whether obligatory or voluntary, is a part of *Imaan*.[1]

Sahl ibn Abdullah al-Tustari, one of the early ascetics, was once asked, "What is *Imaan*?" and he answered, "[It is] statement, action, intention and [following the way of the] sunnah. This is because if *Imaan* is only a statement without action then it is disbelief. If it is statement and action without [proper] intention, it is hypocrisy. If it is statement, action and intention without [following the way of the] sunnah, it is heresy."[2] Similar statements have also been recorded from Ali ibn Abu Talib, al-Hasan al-Basri, al-Auzai, Sufyan al-Thauri and Saeed ibn Jubair.[3]

The heart is the driving force behind all actions. Therefore, if the heart is filled with *Imaan*— with the love

---

[1] See Muhammad al-Magharaawi, *Fath al-Barr fi al-Tarteeb al-Fiqhi li-Tambeed ibn Abdul Barr* (Riyadh: Majmuat al-Tahaf al-Nafais al-Dauliya, 1996), vol. 1, p. 432 and p. 436.

[2] Quoted by ibn Taimiya, *al-Imaan*, p. 43. Sahl ibn Abdullah al-Tustari was one of the early ascetics in Islam. It is their path that the later Sufis claim to follow. However, as can be seen from this quote, many of the later Sufis clearly have left the path of the early ascetics due to the lack of adherence to the *Shariah* and their following of practices and beliefs that have no foundation in the sunnah. Sahl ibn Abdullah has clearly stated that such acts, even if they are accompanied with "good intentions" are nothing but heresies and do not form part of *Imaan*.

[3] See Baadi, vol. 2, p. 462, fn. 3.

of Allah, fear of Allah, hope in Allah— it will drive the body to perform acts of obedience and keep away from forbidden, and even doubtful or questionable, acts. Hence, in reality, there is no such thing as true or strong *Imaan* being in the heart and that not being reflected in the deeds. Such is simply not possible. Ibn Taimiya's view on this point is clearly expressed in his words,

> It is inconceivable that there be a man who is a believer with confirmed belief in his heart that Allah has obligated him to pray, give zakat, fast and perform the pilgrimage and he lives his whole life without making one prostration to Allah or never fasting any month of Ramadhan, never paying zakat for the sake of Allah and never making the pilgrimage to His house. This is impossible. This would only happen if the person has hypocrisy and opposition to Islam[1] in his heart. It would not happen with a true faith. For this reason, Allah describes those who refused to prostrate as unbelievers...[2]

In the same discussion, ibn Taimiya makes another very important point: This *imaan* must be reflected in the ritual acts, such as the prayer and fasting, because Allah has made such acts obligatory. It is not sufficient that the person is honest in his speech, fulfills his trust and so forth. These are not sufficient as long as the person does not have the *imaan* that leads him to the ritual acts. Ibn Taimiya comes to this conclusion because even the polytheists, Jews and Christians believe in and perform those acts. Therefore, a person cannot be considered a believer in Allah and His Messenger if he is not performing any of the rites that were specifically made obligatory in the message of the Prophet Muhammad (peace be upon him).[3]

---

[1] The word ibn Taimiya used as *zandiqah*, which implies that a person outwardly shows that he is a Muslim while inwardly he hates and opposes Islam.
[2] Ibn Taimiya, *Majmoo*, vol. 7, p. 611.
[3] Ibn Taimiya, *Majmoo*, vol. 7, p. 621.

The relation between true faith and acts may be one reason why Allah so often describes the believers by the acts they perform. If the true *Imaan* really exists in the heart, the corresponding good deeds must follow. It is simply inconceivable that the inner aspects are at a level of great faith and the external deeds do not demonstrate that *Imaan* whatsoever.

This is why a believer must always be a "submitter" or Muslim. The belief in his heart drives him to submit externally. On this point, al-Khattabi wrote,

> A Muslim could be a *mumin*[1] some of the time. He also may not be a *mumin* during some times. However, a *mumin* is a Muslim at all times. This is because the root of Islam is submission and enactment. The root of *Imaan* is belief and affirmation. A person could be outwardly submitting while he is not submitting internally. But he could not be believing on the inside while not submitting externally. Therefore, every *mumin* is a Muslim and not every Muslim is a *mumin*.[2]

Similarly, ibn Taimiya wrote,

> If the belief is truly in the heart, the deeds will not delay in following it whatsoever. The complete recognition of Allah and proper love cannot be in the heart if it does not have an overriding effect on the outward deeds. For this reason, Allah has denied faith for those who do not fulfill its necessary consequences. The absence of the necessary consequences is a denial of the necessitating factor. For example, Allah says, "And had they believed in Allah and in the Prophet and in what has been revealed to him, never would they have taken them [the disbelievers] as patrons" (*al-*

---

[1] A Muslim is one who submits outwardly to Allah while a *mumin* is a believer who has real faith in his heart.

[2] Quoted in al-Husain al-Baghawi, *Sharh al-Sunnah* (Beirut: Muassasat al-Risaalah, 1983) p. 11.

> *Maaidah* 81). And, "You will not find any people who believe in Allah and the Last Day making friendship with those who oppose Allah and His Messenger" (*al-Mujaadilah* 22). The external and internal must go together. The external acts cannot be sound and upright unless the internal aspects are sound and upright. If the internal aspects are upright, then the external deeds must also be upright.[1]

However, the question here is somewhat tricky. There is no question that deeds form part of *Imaan* in the sense that true *Imaan* leads to actions and there is a direct relationship between the dynamic growth or stagnation of *Imaan* and deeds. However, according to the *Ahl al-Sunnah wa al-Jamaah*, as can be clearly proven from the Quran and sunnah, a person does not leave the realm of Islam simply due to a sin that he commits. Therefore, what exactly is the relationship between these different components? Ibn Abu al-Izz has offered one answer to this perplexing question:

> It has also been pointed that *qawl* ("statement") is of two kinds: *qawl* of the heart which is faith (*i'tiqad*), and *qawl* of the tongue which is uttering the testimony of Islam. Similarly *'amal* (action) is of two kinds: actions of the heart, which are intention and sincerity, and actions of the body. When all four of these disappear, *Imaan* disappears completely. When faith (*tasdeeq*) of the heart disappears, the other three do not avail the person; *tasdeeq* is the condition of their authenticity and significance. If there is *tasdeeq* in the heart but the others are no longer there, this is the case where the dispute arises [whether such a person is still a believer or not].

---

[1] Ibn Taimiya, *Majmu*, vol. 18, p. 272. Also see Abdul Razaaq Maash, *Al-Jahl bi-Masail al-Itiqaad wa Hukmuhu* (Riyadh: Dar al-Watn, 1996), pp. 63-75.

There is no doubt that the non-submission of the body implies lack of submission on the part of the heart. For if the heart submits, the body also surrenders and obeys; but if, on the other hand, the heart does not submit there will be no assent (*tasdeeq*) that would manifest in obedience. The Prophet (peace be on him) said, "There is a lump of flesh in the body. When it is sound, the whole body is sound; but when it goes wrong, the whole body goes wrong as a result. Lo! it is the heart."[1] This means that one whose heart is good, his body [and actions] shall definitely be good. The opposite is not true.[2] However, the point is that when a part of *Imaan* is lost, the whole *Imaan* is lost only in the sense that it does not remain intact, but not in the sense that it disappears completely. It is only impaired [not completely gone].

Faith is like intelligence in that it differs from person to person. Although everyone has a core of intelligence which qualifies him as a rational being and distinguishes him from a lunatic, some people are definitely more intelligent than others. It is also obvious that the faith which produces actions of the heart and the body is more complete than the faith which does not produce them. Similarly, the knowledge upon which one acts is more complete than the knowledge upon which one does not act. That which cannot produce anything is plainly weaker than that which can produce something. The Prophet said, "One who is told about something is not equal to one who sees it."[3] When Moses was told that his people were worshipping a heifer he did not cast the stone tablets down. He

---

[1]Part of a hadith in al-Bukhari and Muslim.

[2] Hypocrites may do outward acts of piety but, in general, they will also display signs of their false piety.

[3] Recorded by Ibn Hibban and al-Tabarani. With a different wording the hadith has been reported in Ahmad, Ibn Hibban and al-Hakim. It is an authentic hadith according to al-Albani, footnotes to *Sharh*, p. 335.

threw them only when he actually saw them worshipping the calf. The reason was not that he doubted the information Allah gave him. The reason was that the importance of a thing informed, no matter how reliable is the informer, is often not realized to the extent it is when it is seen. Ibrahim, peace and blessings of Allah be upon him, said, "My Lord! Show me how you give life to the dead? (Allah) said: Do you not believe? He said: Yea, but to satisfy my own heart" (*al-Baqara* 260).

In fact, faith in the faith formula (*kalimah*), "there is no god except Allah", varies in its radiance from heart to heart. There are, in fact, innumerable degrees of faith's radiance which are known only to Allah. In some hearts it is as bright as the sun, in others it is like stars, in some like a big lamp, in some like a glowing candle, and in some like a flickering light. That is why, on the Day of Judgment, the light of the believers will shine according to the strength of their faith in Allah's unity, and the nobility of their practices. As the light of the *kalimah* increases, doubts and disbelief burn away till one reaches a stage where all uncertainties and vacillations are completely destroyed. This is the stage of the true believer in *tawheed* where the heights of his faith are fully secured against the assault of all miscreants. He who knows this would know the meaning of the Prophet s words, "Allah has barred him from the Fire who says, 'There is no god except Allah , and by it seeks no one's pleasure but Allah's,"[1] or "No one will enter the Fire who says, 'There is no god except Allah.'"[2]

---

[1]Part of a long hadith recorded by al-Bukhari and Muslim.

[2]Muslim has the hadith on the authority of 'Ubadah that the Prophet (peace be on him) said, "One who witnesses that there is no god other than Allah, and that Muhammad is His messenger, Allah will not let him enter the Fire." Muslim and al-Bukhari have the hadith on the authority of Anas that the Prophet (peace be on

There is no doubt that the one who has firm sincerity in his heart, that cannot be overridden by desires or doubts, will not commit sins. If one is not afflicted by desires and doubts, or one of them, one would not commit sins. However, at the time of committing a sin, his heart is occupied with the sin and it loses its sincerity and remembrance of a threatened punishment. Therefore, he sins.[1]

Imaan Increases and Decreases

Although historically speaking there has been some dispute over this question, it is very clear from the Quran that a person's *Imaan* increases and decreases.[2] For example, Allah says,

وَإِذَا تُلِيَتْ عَلَيْهِمْ

ءَايَـٰتُهُۥ زَادَتْهُمْ إِيمَـٰنًا

"And when His verses are recited to them they [the verses] increase their faith" (*al-Anfal* 2).

وَيَزِيدُ ٱللَّهُ ٱلَّذِينَ ٱهْتَدَوْا۟ هُدًى

---

him) said, "Allah will not allow the person to enter into the Fire who has testified that there is no god but Allah and Muhammad is His Messenger." However, these hadith should not be taken alone, without taking into consideration what other texts state; various verses of the Quran and a number of the Prophet's hadith state that the sinners among the faithful will be punished for a time in the Fire and then released. They should be qualified and interpreted to mean that those who witness to God's unity and Muhammad's prophecy and act righteously will not enter the Fire.

[1] Ibn Abu al-Izz, vol. 2, pp. 460-462.

[2] Those scholars who equated *imaan* with *tasdeeq* (affirmation, belief) argued that there is no such thing as affirmation going up or down. There argument has two flaws to it. First, *imaan* is not equivalent to *tasdeeq*. Second, *tasdeeq* itself can vary, as shall be noted shortly in a reference from ibn Taimiya.

"And Allah increases in guidance those who seek guidance (*Maryam* 76).

وَيَزْدَادَ ٱلَّذِينَ ءَامَنُوٓاْ إِيمَـٰنًا

"That the Believers may increase in faith" (*al-Mudaththir* 31).

هُوَ ٱلَّذِىٓ أَنزَلَ ٱلسَّكِينَةَ فِى قُلُوبِ ٱلْمُؤْمِنِينَ لِيَزْدَادُوٓاْ إِيمَـٰنًا مَّعَ إِيمَـٰنِهِمْ

"It is He who sent down tranquillity into the hearts of the Believers, in order that faith be added to their faith" (*al-Fath* 4).

ٱلَّذِينَ قَالَ لَهُمُ ٱلنَّاسُ إِنَّ ٱلنَّاسَ قَدْ جَمَعُواْ لَكُمْ فَٱخْشَوْهُمْ فَزَادَهُمْ إِيمَـٰنًا وَقَالُواْ حَسْبُنَا ٱللَّهُ وَنِعْمَ ٱلْوَكِيلُ

"Those to whom people said: 'A great army is gathering against you, hence you should fear it, but such only increased their faith and they said: 'For us Allah is sufficient'; He is the Perfect Disposer of affairs" (*ali-Imran* 173).

Commenting on these verses, ibn Abu al-Izz wrote,

> Obviously, one cannot say that the increase mentioned in the last verse and the other verses means increase in the objects of faith [or aspects that one must believe in]. Is there anything in the statement, "A great army is gathering against you," which pertains to some additional aspect that one must believe in? Did the tranquillity that Allah sent down in the hearts add to the objects of faith? Allah sent down to their hearts calmness upon their return from Hudaibiyah in order to increase their tranquillity and conviction. This is supported by the verses, "They (the hypocrites) were that day nearer

> to not having faith than to faith" (*ali-Imraan* 167) and the verse, "Whenever there comes down a *surah* some of them say: 'Which of you has had his faith increased by it? Yes, those who believe— their faith is increased and they do rejoice. But as for those in whose hearts is disease, it only adds wickedness to their wickedness, and they die while they are disbelievers" (*al-Tauba* 124-125). [The former emphasizes the weakening of the faith and the latter its enhancement.][1]

There is no question that there are differences in the outward deeds of mankind. This is a reflection and an aspect of the increase and decrease in *Imaan*. One must not believe, though, that such is the only fluctuation of *Imaan*. Actually, all of the aspects of faith are exposed to this possibility, including— or especially— the deeds of the heart. Even the level of "belief" in the heart or certainty can change in one person and certainly is different from one person to the next. Indeed, one's love for Allah, fear of Allah, trust in Allah and other aspects of the heart are probably the most prone to change and fluctuation.

Perhaps every individual has experienced this fact described in the verses above. At times, a person is very aware of Allah and of his fear and love for Him. This strong feeling in the person's heart brings tranquillity and warmth to the person and it also keeps him from committing sins. Not only that, it drives him to sacrifice and work harder for the sake of Allah. He becomes very anxious to get up late at night for prayer, for example, or give freely for the sake of Allah. However, at other times, perhaps when the affairs of this world are engulfing him, his remembrance and attachment to Allah is not that great. He does not feel that great feeling of *Imaan* in his heart. His behavior and actions are not of the same quality as they are at other times. When he encounters this stage, when he

---

[1] Ibn Abu al-Izz, vol. 2, p. 479.

thinks about getting up at night for prayer or giving charity for the sake of Allah, his soul becomes too tired or not willing to sacrifice. This is nothing but the fluctuations of *Imaan* in the person's heart.

There may be times when a person is at a very high level of *Imaan* and remembrance of Allah. When he mixes with worldly events, his family and friends, he may not be at that same level. This type of occurrence even happened to Abu Bakr, who was known as *al-Sideeq*. A hadith in *Sahih Muslim* states that Abu Bakr asked Handhalah, another Companion, how he was doing. He answered that he was committing hypocrisy. He explained that by saying that when they are with the Prophet (peace be upon him) and reminded of Heaven and Hell, they are as if they are seeing Heaven and Hell. Then when they retreat to their families, they forget much of what they felt earlier. Abu Bakr stated that he also experienced the same. This is something natural. The person should learn to appreciate those times when he was at his highest level of faith and seek to maintain them for as long as possible.

Even the level of affirmation and knowledge in the heart varies from person to person and time to time in one person. Ibn Taimiya states that the affirmation in the heart of the person who simply knows the general aspects of the teaching of the Prophet Muhammad (peace be upon him) will not be the same as that of the person who knows the details of the Prophet's life and teachings. Similarly, the one who knows more about Allah's names and attributes, the life of the Hereafter and so forth will be at a different level of affirmation and knowledge than the one who is ignorant of such matters.[1]

Ibn Taimiya also argues that the faith of a person who knows the proofs for his beliefs and recognizes the

[1] Ibn Taimiya, *Majmoo*, vol. 7, p. 564.

falsehood of other beliefs will be stronger and greater than the one who is unaware of these aspects.[1]

Ibn Taimiya concludes that there is nothing more variable in the heart of man than faith. He says that people should be able to recognize this fact when they consider one of the components of *imaan*, which is love. People recognize their own different levels of love. Love sometimes simply implies a desire to be with or close to one's beloved. However, it can reach the level where one cannot live without being in the presence of one's beloved.[2] Similarly *imaan*, of which love for Allah is one component, can be extremely variable.

This question of *imaan* increasing or decreasing is not simply a theoretical question over which the scholars of the past differed. If a person feels that he has *imaan* and *imaan* is a fixed attribute, he will not strive for increasing his *imaan* and he will not fear or notice a decrease in his *imaan*. This approach in itself can be very dangerous to his *imaan* as the person may not recognize the signs that his *imaan* is decreasing.

Complete *Imaan* and Lacking *Imaan*

Allah says in the Quran,

﴿قَالَتِ ٱلْأَعْرَابُ ءَامَنَّا ۖ قُل لَّمْ تُؤْمِنُوا۟ وَلَـٰكِن قُولُوٓا۟ أَسْلَمْنَا وَلَمَّا يَدْخُلِ ٱلْإِيمَـٰنُ فِى قُلُوبِكُمْ ۖ وَإِن تُطِيعُوا۟ ٱللَّهَ وَرَسُولَهُۥ لَا يَلِتْكُم مِّنْ أَعْمَـٰلِكُمْ شَيْـًٔا ۚ إِنَّ ٱللَّهَ غَفُورٌ رَّحِيمٌ

"The bedouins say, 'We believe.' Say [to them], 'You believe not but say, "We have submitted [in Islam]," for faith has not yet entered your hearts.' But if you obey Allah

---

[1] Ibn Taimiya, *Majmoo*, vol. 7, pp. 565-566.
[2] Ibn Taimiya, *Majmoo*, vol. 7, pp. 566-567.

and His Messenger, He will not decrease anything in reward for your deeds. Verily, Allah is Oft-Forgiving, Most Merciful" (*al-Hujuraat* 14). In this verse, Allah is distinguishing between *Imaan* and Islam. However, it is clear that the bedouins were not hypocrites, void of any belief in their hearts whatsoever. If that were the case, the remainder of the verse would not make any sense because such people who are completely void of faith shall not be rewarded for their obedience to Allah and His Messenger. What is being described is a case where the true and complete *Imaan* is not yet present in their hearts. However, they are not outside of the fold of Islam although they are not deserving of being called true or complete believers.

Al-Bukhari and Muslim both record the following hadith (this being Muslim's wording):

عَنْ سَعْدٍ أَنَّهُ أَعْطَى رَسُولُ اللَّهِ صَلَّى اللَّهُ عَلَيْهِ وَسَلَّمَ رَهْطًا وَأَنَا جَالِسٌ فِيهِمْ قَالَ فَتَرَكَ رَسُولُ اللَّهِ صَلَّى اللَّهُ عَلَيْهِ وَسَلَّمَ مِنْهُمْ رَجُلاً لَمْ يُعْطِهِ وَهُوَ أَعْجَبُهُمْ إِلَيَّ فَقُمْتُ إِلَى رَسُول اللَّهِ صَلَّى اللَّهُ عَلَيْهِ وَسَلَّمَ فَسَارَرْتُهُ فَقُلْتُ يَا رَسُولَ اللَّهِ مَا لَكَ عَنْ فُلان وَاللَّهِ إِنِّي لَأَرَاهُ مُؤْمِنًا قَالَ أَوْ مُسْلِمًا فَسَكَتُّ قَلِيلاً ثُمَّ غَلَبَنِي مَا أَعْلَمُ مِنْهُ فَقُلْتُ يَا رَسُولَ اللَّهِ مَا لَكَ عَنْ فُلان فَوَاللَّهِ إِنِّي لَأَرَاهُ مُؤْمِنًا قَالَ أَوْ مُسْلِمًا فَسَكَتُّ قَلِيلاً ثُمَّ غَلَبَنِي مَا أَعْلَمُ مِنْهُ فَقُلْتُ يَا رَسُولَ اللَّهِ مَا لَكَ عَنْ فُلان فَوَاللَّهِ إِنِّي لَأَرَاهُ مُؤْمِنًا قَالَ أَوْ مُسْلِمًا قَالَ إِنِّي لَأُعْطِي الرَّجُلَ وَغَيْرُهُ أَحَبُّ إِلَيَّ مِنْهُ خَشْيَةَ أَنْ يُكَبَّ فِي النَّارِ عَلَى وَجْهِهِ

Saad reported: The Messenger of Allah (peace be upon him) bestowed [some gifts] upon a group of people and I was sitting among them. The Messenger of Allah (peace be upon him) left out a person and did not give him anything. I thought that he was the best of the group. So I stood up before the Prophet (peace be upon him) and said, "O Messenger of Allah (peace be upon him), what about so and so. By Allah, I find him to be a believer." The Messenger of Allah (peace be upon him) answered, "He may be [just] a Muslim." I kept quiet for a short while but then I could not restrain myself and again said to the Messenger of Allah (peace be upon him), "O Messenger of Allah (peace be upon him), what about so and so? By Allah, I find him to be a believer." He said, "He may be [just] a Muslim." I remained quiet for a while and then what I knew about that man made me speak again, "O Messenger of Allah (peace be upon him), what about so and so? By Allah, I find him to be a believer." The Messenger of Allah (peace be upon him) answered, "He may be [just] a Muslim. I often bestow something upon a person whereas someone else is dearer to me than he, because of the fear that he may fall headlong into the Fire."

In this hadith one also finds the Messenger of Allah (peace be upon him) differentiating between a true or complete believer and a Muslim. What can be derived from the above is that for a person to be called an absolute, complete or true believer, he must fulfill the conditions and obligations of *Imaan*. If he is lacking in them, then he is not deserving of being called a believer. But he has not left the fold of Islam. Instead, he has moved from the lofty level of being called a "believer" to the level of being a "Muslim".

This is a very important point to understand as, when misunderstood, this point leads to a great deal of confusion. In fact, it leads to more than just confusion— it leads to Muslims calling other Muslims disbelievers. A disbeliever is one who completely leaves the fold of Islam. A Muslim is one who is in the fold of Islam by performing the outward deeds of Islam. However, a Muslim may not perform all of the required aspects of faith, especially those deeds of the heart, to be called a believer in an absolute sense. A believer, in an absolute sense, on the other hand, is one who submits completely— that is, fulfills the requirements of Islam— but, in addition to that, fulfills all of the characteristics and requirements of a true believer. Hence, he is termed a believer. Therefore, every true believer must first be a true Muslim. However, not every Muslim is necessarily a true and complete believer in an absolute sense.

This point must be kept in mind when one reads hadith like the following:

لا يُؤْمِنُ أَحَدُكُمْ حَتَّى يُحِبَّ لِأَخِيهِ مَا يُحِبُّ لِنَفْسِهِ

"None of you truly believes until he loves for his brother what he loves for himself." (Recorded by al-Bukhari and Muslim.) In other words, no one is a true and complete believer— meeting all the requirements and necessary components of *Imaan*— until he loves for his brother what he loves for himself. This is one of the necessary components of being a true and complete believer.[1]

Another hadith states,

لا يَزْنِي الزَّانِي حِينَ يَزْنِي وَهُوَ مُؤْمِنٌ وَلا يَسْرِقُ السَّارِقُ حِينَ يَسْرِقُ وَهُوَ مُؤْمِنٌ وَلا يَشْرَبُ الْخَمْرَ حِينَ يَشْرَبُهَا وَهُوَ مُؤْمِنٌ

[1] The different sects have gone to different extremes in interpreting hadith of that nature or hadith which describe people who perform specific acts as, "not being from among us." The correct interpretation is that given in the text above. The Murjiah, on one hand, understand these texts to mean the person is not similar to the others or he is not from the best of the people while his *imaan* is still complete and not lacking in any fashion. The Khawarij and Mutazilah understand these texts to mean that the person leaves Islam completely or will be in the Hell-fire forever. Cf., ibn Taimiya, *Majmoo*, vol. 7, p. 525.

"A fornicator while committing illegal sexual intercourse is not a [true] believer. A thief while committing theft is not a [true] believer. A drinker while drinking alcohol is not a [true] believer." (Recorded by al-Bukhari and Muslim.) A similar hadith states,

إِذَا زَنَى الْعَبْدُ خَرَجَ مِنْهُ الإِيمَانُ فَكَانَ فَوْقَ رَأْسِهِ كَالظُّلَّةِ فَإِذَا خَرَجَ مِنْ ذَلِكَ الْعَمَلِ عَادَ إِلَيْهِ الْإِيمَانُ

"When a person commits illegal sexual intercourse, *Imaan* leaves him and remains above his head like an awning. When he discontinues this [illegal] behavior, *Imaan* comes back to him." (Recorded by al-Tirmidhi.[1]) Ibn Taimiya was asked about the meaning of this hadith and whether it should be taken at face value. He wrote,

> During the time of the Messenger of Allah (peace be upon him), some people committed adultery, stole and drank alcohol. The Prophet (peace be upon him) did not declare them to be disbelievers nor did he cut off the relations between them and the Muslims. Instead, he flogged this one and cut the hand of the other. At the same time, he also sought forgiveness for them...
>
> Some say that such people's *Imaan* is still complete without any shortcoming... That statement goes against the Quran, sunnah and consensus of the earlier scholars and those who followed them... The opinion of the *Ahl al-Sunnah wa al-Jamaah* is that the term believer is not completely removed from them nor is it given to them uncategorically. We say [regarding a person who performs such deeds]: He is a believer who has a deficiency in his faith. Or, he is a believer with respect to his faith and a

---

[1] Al-Hakim and Abu Dawud have something very similar. The hadith is graded *sahih* by al-Albani. See al-Albani, *Sahih al-Jami*, vol. 1, p. 162.

faasiq (evildoer) with respect to the great sin he performed. Or, one says that he is not a true believer or he does not fulfill his faith sincerely...

[Someone asked:] Did any Imam take this hadith at face value? This question is not clear. If one means by that statement that the apparent meaning of the hadith is that a fornicator is a disbeliever, then none of the Imams understood this hadith in that sense. However, that is not the apparent meaning of the hadith anyway. The Prophet's words, "*Imaan* leaves him and is above his head like an awning," indicates that *Imaan* did not depart from him completely. Certainly, an awning shades its companion and is directly connected to it...

The correct view is that the exact essence of *tasdeeq* (belief and assent) that distinguishes him from a disbeliever is not non-existent. However, if that level of *tasdeeq* had remained at its previous level, the person would believe and affirm that Allah has forbidden that great sin and has threatened a great punishment for it. [He also would know] that Allah sees the doer and witnesses him; also, Allah, in His Greatness, Esteem, Exaltedness and Pride despises that act. Therefore, when he commits that act, one of three aspects must be true: (1) His belief is confused and muddled, thinking that the threat of punishment is not exactly as it states... (2) He has become heedless or neglectful that the act is forbidden, of the greatness of his Lord and the harshness of His punishment. (3) Or his desires have completely overtaken him and overpowered the effects of *Imaan*... [His *Imaan*] has become like the rational thought of a person who is sleeping or drunk. [That is, it has no influence over him whatsoever.]...

It is known that the *Imaan* that is the real *Imaan* no longer resides in him as it had resided. It is not

> apparent and residing in his heart... [His case is similar to the soul while one is asleep. In some aspects, the person is dead while sleeping [while with respect to other aspects he is still alive.]
>
> Similarly, the fornicator, thief and drinker have not lost the *Imaan* that can keep them from being forever in the Hell-fire. Therefore, intercession and forgiveness is still hoped for him. He still has the right to get married and inheritance [since he has not left the fold of Islam]...[1]

There is one more level that goes beyond "believer" and this is *muhsin*, the one characterized by *ihsaan* (excellence in his worship of Allah). Every *muhsin* must meet all of the conditions of a Muslim and a believer. Hence, every *muhsin* is a Muslim and a believer. However, not every believer is a *muhsin*. Being a *muhsin* is a stage higher than that of being a *mumin* or *muslim*.

These different levels of *Imaan*, Islam and *Ihsan* bring up some very important questions. These questions are related to the fact that disbelievers will be in the Hell-fire forever while believers may either be punished first in Hell and then rescued from Hell and entered into Paradise or they may go directly to Paradise without first being punished in Hell. Therefore, it is logical to ask the following:[2]

(1) What is the minimum level or foundation of *Imaan* that will prevent one from being among the disbelievers in the Hell-Fire forever?

(2) What is the level of *Imaan* that one must fulfill to be saved from ever being punished in the Hell-fire?

---

[1] Ibn Taimiya, *Majmoo*, vol. 7, pp. 670-676. In general, this interpretation is that of the vast majority of scholars. See Muhammad al-Mubaarakfoori, *Tuhfah al-Ahwadhi bi-Sharh Jaami al-Tirmidhi* (Beirut: Dar al-Fikr, n.d.), vol. 7, pp. 375-377.

[2] See al-Misri, p. 55.

(3) What is the level of *Imaan* that will raise one to the highest ranks in Paradise?

These questions shall be dealt with separately.

(1) What is the minimum level of *Imaan* that will prevent one from being among the disbelievers in the Hell-Fire forever? The minimum which forms the basics or foundations of faith that is obligatory upon every Muslim at all times is where the person has met the minimum requirement of *tasdeeq* (belief, assent) and *inqiyaad* (submission, yielding). These are composed of:

(a) Belief in everything that one knows to be from the Messenger of Allah (peace be upon him) as well as the readiness to believe in all new information that one receives from the Messenger of Allah (peace be upon him). That is, one accepts, admits and realizes the he must believe in everything that is authentically reported from the Messenger of Allah (peace be upon him). This includes everything that the person knows at the present moment as well as anything that the person may learn in the future.[1]

(b) Adherence to everything that one knows to be from the Messenger of Allah (peace be upon him) as well as the readiness to adhere to all new information that one receives from the Messenger of Allah (peace be upon him) that one previously did not know. What this means is that every Muslim must have the willingness, desire and recognition that he is obligated to adhere to everything that he knows has come from the Prophet (peace be upon him) as well as have the willingness and desire to adhere to anything that he shall learn in the future. Although a Muslim may not actually adhere to everything of the Quran and sunnah, the essential aspect is that he believes and understands that it is obligatory upon him to adhere to everything found in the Quran and sunnah. This is the absolute minimum that is required of a person.

[1] This would include believing in all of the aspects that shall be described shortly under the different articles of faith mentioned in this hadith of Gabriel.

This touches upon a very important concept, especially for new converts to Islam. Belief in Islam is based on overwhelming proof and evidence for the authenticity of the Quran and the veracity of the Prophet (peace be upon him). Belief does not mean that each believer has established or verified every aspect of the Quran or sunnah. Indeed, there are many aspects that mankind may have no knowledge of. Similarly, there are many aspects that disbelievers may, in their ignorance, believe that the opposite is true, fairer or more beneficial.[1] The unquestionable truth of the Quran and the Prophet (peace be upon him) is sufficient for the person to realize that everything that comes from them is true. This is the correct *Imaan* that every new Muslim must understand. Hence, whenever he now reads something in the Quran or authentic hadith that he previously did not know, he is willing to accept it and apply it because he knows full well the truthfulness of the Quran and the Prophet (peace be upon him).

This is what ibn Taimiya refers to as *al-Imaan al-Mujmal* or the general and unspecified faith. If someone only fulfills these minimum requirements, he is not deserving of the honorable title of "believer" or "true believer". However, if he fulfills these two aspects— and does not contradict them or negate them by any belief, statement or action— then he will have saved himself from *kufr* (disbelief) and from being in the Hell-fire forever. In other words, by simply fulfilling these conditions, he remains within the fold of Islam and that is the key to being rescued from the Hell-fire.

This minimum level can be thought of as the level of Islam, as Allah has referred to in reference to the bedouins. Although there is some submission and acceptance of the Quran and sunnah, the people of this

---

[1] For example, a person may not see the wisdom, justice or propriety of the male and female shares of the inheritance being different.

level lack the characteristics of true believers whose faith is strong in their hearts. Therefore, they will be lacking with respect to deeds like *jihad* and sacrificing for the sake of Allah. Furthermore, they might be quite lax with respect to performing major sins and acts of that nature. They have not reached the level where Allah and His Messenger are more beloved to them than anything else. They do not love for their brother Muslim what they love for themselves. They do not fear Allah alone and they do not put their trust only in Allah. All of these are obligatory aspects of being a true believer. However, at the same time, these people are not hypocrites and they may not even be evildoers. They are not deserving of the honorific title of "believers," but they are, instead, "muslims" (those who submit and do have some level of faith).

Ibn Taimiya talks about those who convert to Islam or those who were born in Muslim families but who have not taken the time to thoroughly learn about Islam. These people, he says, obey Allah and His Messenger concerning the basics of Islam. Hence, they are within the fold of Islam. However, real faith takes time to enter into their hearts. It comes gradually, as the person's knowledge, understanding and certainty increases.[1] This was probably the case with the bedouins described above in the verse from *Surah al-Hujurat*. Allah has stated their case in a very beautiful manner that indicates that true *Imaan* will come to them but at the time of the revelation of those verses, it simply was not there.[2]

This is an important point. It should make the person realize, especially the new convert, that there are greater levels of *Imaan* waiting for him if he sincerely turns to Allah and seeks His guidance. This true *Imaan*, Allah willing, will come about as the Muslim understands the

---

[1] Ibn Taimiya, *al-Imaan*, p. 257.

[2] Salaah Al-Khalidi, *Fi Dhilaal al-Imaan* (al-Zurqa, Jordan: Maktabah al-Manaar, 1987), p. 42.

Quran better, as he associates more with pious and knowledgeable people, and as he obeys Allah more and as he implements the sunnah more in his life. Allah willing, his *Imaan* will continue to grow until he becomes a true and complete believer that Allah praises throughout the Quran. He then will taste the sweetness of *Imaan*. On the other hand, if he is content with little faith and little submission to Allah, he may block off all the means to increase his *Imaan* and come closer to Allah.

Hence, one should not be satisfied with being at the level of only "Islam". This level implies that one is not doing a great deal to please Allah. He is not working for Allah's love, mercy and forgiveness. Indeed, it may mean that he is exposing himself to Allah's displeasure and punishment in the Hereafter. One second of Allah's punishment in the Hell-fire will be much greater than any sort of punishment that anyone could possibly receive in this world, although humans complain a lot about their suffering in this world. On the Day of Judgment, everyone will quickly realize that Allah's pleasure will mean more to him than everything that this world contains.

(2) What is the level of *Imaan* that one must fulfill to be saved from ever being punished in the Hell-fire? If a person goes beyond the minimum requirements of faith and fulfills all of the necessary as well as obligatory (minimum) aspects of the faith, then he has moved from the lower levels of *Imaan* to a higher level. This is the level in which he fulfills all of the obligatory aspects of *Imaan*. This is where he fulfills the description of the true believers as given in the Quran and sunnah.

If a person fulfills the obligations upon him with respect to faith and submission to Allah and avoids the forbidden acts, then he will never enter the Hell-fire; he deserves to be called a believer in an absolute sense. He is the one who fulfills the description of the true believers as found in the Quran. For example, he is the one who embodies the following characteristics:

إِنَّمَا ٱلْمُؤْمِنُونَ ٱلَّذِينَ إِذَا ذُكِرَ ٱللَّهُ وَجِلَتْ قُلُوبُهُمْ وَإِذَا تُلِيَتْ عَلَيْهِمْ ءَايَـٰتُهُۥ زَادَتْهُمْ إِيمَـٰنًا وَعَلَىٰ رَبِّهِمْ يَتَوَكَّلُونَ ﴿٢﴾ ٱلَّذِينَ يُقِيمُونَ ٱلصَّلَوٰةَ وَمِمَّا رَزَقْنَـٰهُمْ يُنفِقُونَ

"The [true] believers are only those who, when Allah is mentioned, feel a fear in their hearts and when His verses are recited to them, they increase their faith. And they put their trust in their Lord. Those who establish the prayer and spend out of what We have provided them" (*al-Anfal* 2-3). In the following verses, Allah says about the people who have those characteristics:

أُوْلَـٰٓئِكَ هُمُ ٱلْمُؤْمِنُونَ حَقًّا ۚ لَّهُمْ دَرَجَـٰتٌ عِندَ رَبِّهِمْ وَمَغْفِرَةٌ وَرِزْقٌ كَرِيمٌ

"Certainly, it is they are who are the true believers. For them are grades of dignity with their Lord, and Forgiveness and a generous provision" (*al-Anfal* 4).

(3) What is the level of *Imaan* that will raise one to the highest ranks in Paradise? These are the people of complete *Imaan*. They not only possess the necessary as well as the obligatory components of *Imaan*, but they go on beyond that. They perform much more than the essential or required deeds. They also perform voluntary or supererogatory deeds. They perform them as a result of their greater extreme *Imaan*— in other words, their greater love of, fear of and hope in Allah. They, therefore, excel in their worship of Allah.[1]

Ibn Taimiya stated, "The People of the Sunnah and Hadith state that all good deeds, obligatory as well as recommended, are part and parcel of *Imaan*. That is, they

[1] Perhaps one could describe the first level as that of Islam, the second level as that of *Imaan* and the third level as that of *Ihsaan*.

form part of the *Imaan* that is completed by performing the beloved recommended deeds, even though they are not from the obligatory aspects of *Imaan*. They differentiate between *Imaan* and the *Imaan* that is complete through recommended aspects... The word 'complete' [or 'perfected'] may mean complete in the sense that the obligatory parts are fulfilled or complete in the sense that the extra or recommended parts are fulfilled."[1]

The Prophet (peace be upon him) stated,

الإِيمَانُ بِضْعٌ وَسَبْعُونَ أَوْ بِضْعٌ وَسِتُّونَ شُعْبَةً فَأَفْضَلُهَا قَوْلُ لا إِلَهَ إِلاَّ اللَّهُ وَأَدْنَاهَا إِمَاطَةُ الأَذَى عَنِ الطَّرِيقِ وَالْحَيَاءُ شُعْبَةٌ مِنَ الإِيمَانِ

"*Imaan* is composed of seventy some-odd— or sixty some-odd[2]— branches. The greatest aspect is the statement, 'There is none worthy of worship except Allah,' and the lowest aspect is removing something harmful from the road. And modesty is a branch of faith."[3] Obviously, the one who is driven by his faith to remove something harmful from the road for the sake of Allah has gone beyond the minimum or obligatory aspects of faith. Because of his faith in Allah, he will stop and remove something harmful from the road. The only thing driving him to do that is his *Imaan*.

In sum, ibn Taimiya argues that *Imaan* is composed of:

(1) Essentials or foundation without which *Imaan* is missing in totality: If one fails to fulfill any one of these, he is outside of the fold of Islam and will remain in the Hell-fire forever.

---

[1] Ibn Taimiya, *al-Imaan*, p. 186.
[2] The doubt is from one of the narrators.
[3] Recorded by Muslim.

(2) Obligatory aspects: If one fails to fulfill any one of them, he may be deserving of punishment in the Hereafter. However, the person who fails only in these aspects will not be in the Hell-fire forever. Instead, he will be rescued by the mercy of Allah and entered into Paradise. If one performs all of these obligatory aspects, one will be entered, by the grace and mercy of Allah, directly into Paradise without first suffering any punishment for what was lacking in his *Imaan*.

(3) Recommended or beloved acts: These are the acts that will distinguish the People of Paradise from one another. These are the acts that will determine the various degrees of reward and positions of Paradise that are described in the Quran and hadith.

Ibn Taimiya then quoted the following verse of the Quran as referring to these three categories of "Muslims-*mumin*s-those who excel":

ثُمَّ أَوْرَثْنَا ٱلْكِتَـٰبَ ٱلَّذِينَ ٱصْطَفَيْنَا مِنْ عِبَادِنَا ۖ فَمِنْهُمْ ظَالِمٌ
لِّنَفْسِهِۦ وَمِنْهُم مُّقْتَصِدٌ وَمِنْهُمْ سَابِقٌۢ بِٱلْخَيْرَٰتِ بِإِذْنِ ٱللَّهِ ۚ ذَٰلِكَ
هُوَ ٱلْفَضْلُ ٱلْكَبِيرُ

"Then We gave the Book for inheritance to such of Our slaves whom We chose [the followers of Muhammad]. Then of them are some who wrong themselves, and of them are some who follow a middle course, and of them are some who are, by Allah's leave, foremost in good deeds. That [inheritance of the Quran]— that is indeed a great Grace" (*Faatir* 32).

Entering Paradise is Tied to Being a Believer

Ibn Taimiya also points out that the promise of Paradise is always tied to being a believer or having faith. There are no verses, for example, that promise Paradise for the "Muslims". There are only promises given to the believers uncategorically or those who have faith and perform good deeds.[1] For example, Allah has said,

وَعَدَ ٱللَّهُ ٱلْمُؤْمِنِينَ وَٱلْمُؤْمِنَٰتِ جَنَّٰتٍ تَجْرِى مِن تَحْتِهَا ٱلْأَنْهَٰرُ خَٰلِدِينَ فِيهَا وَمَسَٰكِنَ طَيِّبَةً فِى جَنَّٰتِ عَدْنٍ ۚ وَرِضْوَٰنٌ مِّنَ ٱللَّهِ أَكْبَرُ ۚ ذَٰلِكَ هُوَ ٱلْفَوْزُ ٱلْعَظِيمُ

"Allah has promised to the believers, men and women, gardens through which rivers flow to dwell therein forever, and beautiful mansions in Gardens of Paradise. But the greatest bliss is the Good Pleasure of Allah. That is the supreme success" (*al-Tauba* 72). An example of the second type includes,

وَبَشِّرِ ٱلَّذِينَ ءَامَنُوا۟ وَعَمِلُوا۟ ٱلصَّٰلِحَٰتِ أَنَّ لَهُمْ جَنَّٰتٍ تَجْرِى مِن تَحْتِهَا ٱلْأَنْهَٰرُ ۖ

"And give glad tidings to those who believe and do good deeds that for them will be Gardens through which rivers flow..." (*al-Baqara* 25).

Imaan, Islam and *Ihsan*

Some people are very much confused by the use of the words *Imaan* and Islam. Are *Imaan* and Islam synonymous, implying one and the same thing?[2] Does one actually imply the other or not? If the answer is yes, how is it that *Imaan* is often differentiated from Islam, as in the

---

[1] Ibn Taimiya, *al-Imaan*, p. 226.

[2] This was the view of many of the early scholars, including Imam al-Bukhari. However, as can be seen from the hadith al-Bukhari presents in his *Sahih*, it must be understood to mean that when they are mentioned separately, they refer to one and the same thing.

case of the hadith of Gabriel. The solution to this question is quite simple and boils down to the following points:

(1) If *Imaan* is mentioned by itself, not in conjunction with Islam, then the reference to *Imaan* includes all of the outward acts of submission that are considered exclusively part of Islam. That is, if the word *Imaan* is used by itself, its meaning encompasses or also indicates the acts of Islam.[1]

(2) If the word *Imaan* is used in conjunction with Islam, then, *Imaan* is only a reference to the acts and beliefs of the heart and not the outward acts that form the definition of Islam.[2]

(3) Similarly, if Islam is mentioned by itself, not in conjunction with *Imaan*, then it also includes *Imaan* as part of its meaning; that is, for example, a "Muslim" is one who has at least the minimum requirements of *Imaan*.

(4) If Islam is used in conjunction with *Imaan*, then Islam is a reference to the outward acts of submission to Allah while *Imaan* is in reference to the acts of the heart and the beliefs of the person.[3]

(5) Similarly, the word *Ihsan* encompasses both Islam and *Imaan* when it is used alone. However, when used in conjunction with Islam and *Imaan*, as in this hadith of Gabriel, it has a special and distinct meaning from both Islam and *Imaan*.

Ibn Abu al-Izz has a very lengthy and detailed discussion proving the above points. Here is a greatly abridged translation of what he wrote:

---

[1] For example, Allah says, "Only those are believers who have believed in Allah and His Messenger, and have never since doubted" (*al-Hujurat* 15). Here, the believers not only have faith in their hearts but they, by necessity, also submit to the outward laws of Islam.

[2] For example, Allah says, "The male Muslims and the female Muslims and the male believers and the female believers..." (*al-Ahzaab* 35).

[3] Obviously (2) and (4) are essentially the same. For the sake of completeness or word order both have been explicitly mentioned.

It has been said that *'amal* (action) has been often mentioned in conjunction with *Imaan*— this implies that action is not included in the connotation of *Imaan*. The first thing that should be noted in this connection is that *Imaan* is mentioned [in the texts] in two ways. Sometimes it is mentioned alone, and neither any particular act nor *islam* is mentioned along with it; and sometimes it is mentioned in association with a religious act or *islam*. In the first case, *Imaan* necessarily includes action. For instance, "Believers are those who, when Allah is mentioned, feel a tremor in the heart" (*al-Araaf* 2), or "Only those are believers who have believed in Allah and His Messenger, and have never since doubted" (*al-Hujuraat* 15), "They only are true believers who believe in Allah and His Messenger" (*al-Noor* 62)...

In the second case where any righteous action is associated with *Imaan*, the implication is that *Imaan* is different from action even though their predicate is one. However, the difference is of varying degrees...[1]

It has been recorded in the *Sahih* that the Prophet (peace be on him) said to the delegation from the 'Abd al-Qays tribe visiting him, "I enjoin upon you to believe in none other than Allah. Do you know what does faith in Allah mean? It is to testify that there is no god besides Allah, the one and the only God, without a partner. It is to establish *salah*, pay zakah and hand over (to us) a fifth of the booty."[2] Obviously the Prophet (peace be on him) did not mean by that that these acts could be called *Imaan* in Allah without having faith in the heart. On several occasions he emphasized the necessity of

[1]Ibn Taymiyah has discussed the various forms of difference in *Majmu al-Fatawa*, vol. 7, pp. 172-181.
[2]Recorded by Al-Bukhari and Muslim.

faith in the heart. It is, therefore, certain that *Imaan* is these acts along with faith in the heart. What greater proof than the hadith of the Prophet (peace be on him) can there be to show that actions are included as part of faith? He defined *Imaan* in terms of actions and did not mention conviction (*tasdeeq*) of the heart, that is because it is well known that actions have no value if rejection is in the heart...

To conclude: When Islam and *Imaan* are mentioned together [in the same sentence] it is different from the case when one is mentioned without the other. Islam is to *Imaan* like the two testimonies— witnessing to Muhammad's Prophecy in relation to witnessing to Allah's unity— are to each other. In essence these two testimonies are two different things although the idea and the effects of the one are associated with the idea and the effects of the other, as if they were one thing. The same is the case with islam and *Imaan*. No one can have *Imaan* without *islam*, nor *islam* without *Imaan*. One has to have *islam* to some extent in order to prove his *Imaan*, just as one has to have *Imaan* in order to authenticate one's *islam*.[1]

An Example: Belief in the Unseen

Before moving on to discuss what a Muslim is supposed to believe, an important conclusion from the above discussion must be explicitly stated: True and complete *Imaan* requires the person to act in accordance with what he has *Imaan* in. For example, the true *Imaan* in *al-ghaib* (the unseen) means that the person believes truly in his heart in the unseen and that this belief in his heart has some affect on his life and his actions.

[1] Ibn Abu al-Izz, vol. 2, pp. 483-487.

Belief, therefore, is not simply a theoretical or intellectual aspect in the heart that does not affect the person— although historically some have argued that such is correct linguistically speaking. For example, someone may believe that smoking is harmful and wrong by accepting the facts showing smoking to be harmful as true but he continues to smoke and he does not let what he recognizes to be true guide his actions. In other words, he does not submit to the truth he sees nor does he implement what it implies. Hence, his recognition of the facts is not the same thing as "belief" or *imaan*. *Imaan* necessitates that one has the willingness to submit to or enact what one recognizes to be true.

In the case of *Imaan*, if that *Imaan* is strong and healthy at that moment, then it will put the feeling of hatred in the person's heart for that act that he believes to be wrong or harmful. It will keep the person from wanting to commit that harmful act. It will, therefore, rule his life and it will guide him to what he should do. If it is weak and can be overcome by other forces in the heart, it may not have that effect.

Therefore, true belief or *imaan* in *al-ghaib* means that one acts in accordance with that belief. When, for example, he says that he believes in the angels, it means that he knows that the angels are present and that they are actually recording his deeds. This should affect him in that he will not perform those deeds that he does not want those angels to see and record.

The Articles of Faith

"He [the Messenger of Allah (peace be upon him)] said, 'It is to believe in Allah'"

Belief in Allah is the cornerstone of Islamic faith. All of the other Islamic beliefs revolve around belief in Allah. It is a must that a Muslim have the correct beliefs about Allah. If a person's beliefs about Allah are not correct, then his whole faith may be ruined. For this reason Muslim scholars delineated and explained the correct beliefs concerning Allah in some detail.

The importance of the correct belief in Allah, termed *tauheed*[1], was demonstrated by ibn Abu al-Izz al-Hanafi. He stated that, "Most of the Quran, rather all of it, refers to *tauheed*." He concluded this by showing that all of the Quran, in essence:

(1) Discusses Allah's names, attributes and actions, and this is part of *tauheed* in knowledge and affirmation.

(2) Calls people to Allah's worship alone, without ascribing any partners to Him and leaving everything that is worshipped other than Him, and this is *tauheed* of intention and action.

[1] Sometimes spelled in English *tawheed*, *tauhid*, or *tawhid*.

(3) Commands, forbids and requires obedience to Him, and this is all part of the rights or implications of *tauheed* and its completion.
(4) States how Allah honors those who believe in *tauheed* and how He treats them in this world and what He honors them with in the Hereafter; all of this is the reward for *tauheed*.
(5) Discusses those who have associated partners with Allah and whom He has punished in this life or would punish in the next, this is the just reward of those who abandon *tauheed*.
Ibn Abu al-Izz concludes,

> Thus the entire Quran is about *tauheed*, its consequences and the reward for it. [It also discusses the negation of *tauheed* or] *shirk*,[1] those who commit it and the punishment they will suffer for it. [The opening verses of the first chapter of the Quran], "Praise be to Allah, the Lord of the Worlds" is *tauheed*; "the Most-Compassionate, the Most-Merciful" is *tauheed*; "Master of the Day of Judgment" is *tauheed*; "You only do we worship and in You only do we seek help" is *tauheed*; "Guide us to the Straight Path" is *tauheed* as it is a request to be guided to the path of the people of *tawhid*, those whom Allah has blessed, "Not those who have earned the wrath of Allah nor those who have gone astray" or, in other words, those who have forsaken *tauheed*.[2]

The term *tauheed*, meaning "making something one," or "asserting oneness", is not a term from the Quran or sunnah. However, it became the main term used to cover the aspects of belief in Allah, dating back to the time of ibn Abbas. In order to clarify matters, the scholars divided the

---

[1] ***Shirk*** is the associating of partners with Allah.
[2] Ibn Abu al-Izz, vol. 1, p. 42-43. Virtually the same statements may also be found in Muhammad ibn al-Qayyim, *Madaarij al-Salikeen* (Beirut: Dar al-Kitaab al-Arabi, 1972), vol. 3, p. 450.

discussion of *tauheed* into different branches, each branch covering or explaining one aspect of the complete and correct belief in Allah. There is nothing sacred about these divisions or their terminology, although they have been accepted and passed on by scholars for centuries. However, what is of critical importance is the concept or belief that is being explained. Many of the deviant sects used the term *tauheed* or different types of *tauheed* but what they meant by it was not what is clear from the Quran and sunnah. Therefore, the most important point is that the understanding of the concept or the belief itself be correct according to the Quran and sunnah.

The Division of *Tauheed* Into Three Categories

A popular way of discussing *tauheed* is to divide it into three categories.[1] These three categories are *tauheed al-rububiyah*, *tauheed al-uluhiyah*[2] and *tauheed al-asma wa al-sifaat*. For quick reference, Figure 2 is a graphical representation of this way of viewing or considering *tauheed*. Each of these three essential components of *tauheed* shall be discussed separately.

[1] The dividing of *tauheed* into three categories may be found in a number of works in English. Perhaps, the best discussion is Bilal Philips, *The Fundamentals of Tawheed* (Riyadh: Tawheed Publications, 1990), pp. 1-42. In this work, an attempt will be made to emphasize some points that are not found or discussed in detail in the available English literature.

[2] In particular, this category is sometimes given a slightly different name, such as *tauheed al-ibada*.

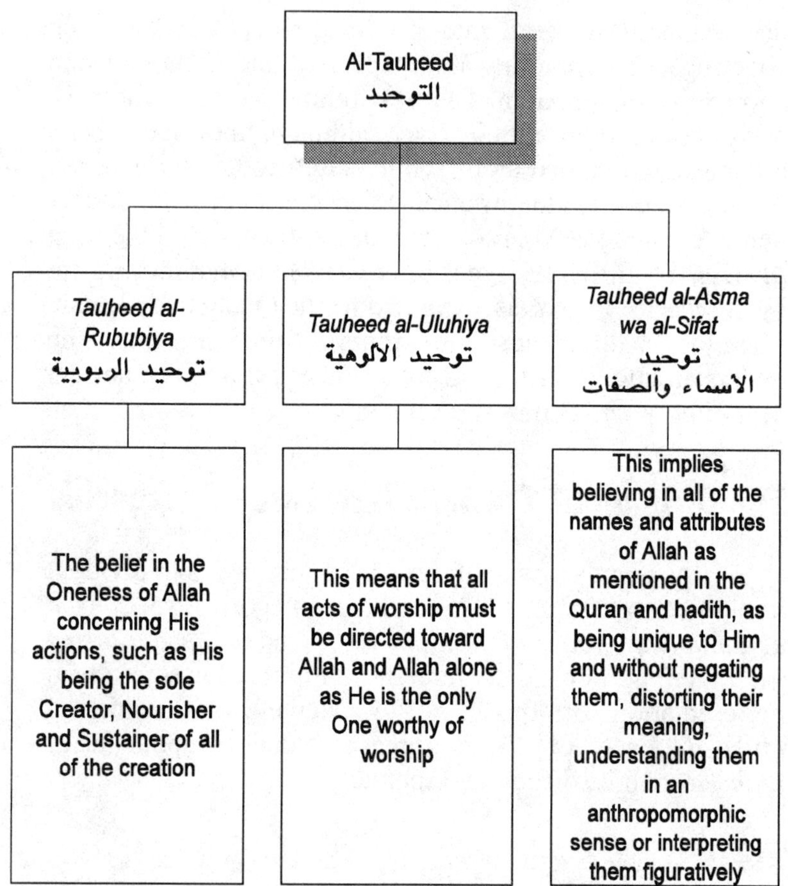

Figure 2. Graphical Representation of the Division of *Tauheed* into Three Categories

(1) *Tauheed al-Rububiyah*: In essence, this is belief in the uniqueness of Allah with respect to His actions. This is the belief in the Oneness of Allah with respect to His Lordship. He alone is the Lord (*al-Rabb*). He is One without Partner in His Dominion and His Actions.

He is the Only Creator, Owner, Nourisher, Maintainer[1] and Sustainer of this creation. All creation has been created by Him and Him alone.

According to ibn Uthaimin, all of mankind except the most arrogant and haughty accepts and recognizes this aspect of *tauheed*, namely, that there is no Lord and Creator but the One Lord and Creator.[2] This is so because this belief is ingrained in the nature of mankind. Mankind recognizes and realizes that this creation must have had a Creator. Mankind also realizes that this Creator must only be One. It is clear from numerous verses of the Quran that even the polytheistic Arabs knew and recognized that the true and only Creator was above and beyond the idols that they used to worship. For example, Allah says in the Quran,

قُل لِّمَنِ ٱلْأَرْضُ وَمَن فِيهَآ إِن كُنتُمْ تَعْلَمُونَ ﴿٨٤﴾ سَيَقُولُونَ
لِلَّهِ ۚ قُلْ أَفَلَا تَذَكَّرُونَ ﴿٨٥﴾ قُلْ مَن رَّبُّ ٱلسَّمَـٰوَٰتِ ٱلسَّبْعِ وَرَبُّ
ٱلْعَرْشِ ٱلْعَظِيمِ ﴿٨٦﴾ سَيَقُولُونَ لِلَّهِ ۚ قُلْ أَفَلَا تَتَّقُونَ ﴿٨٧﴾ قُلْ مَنۢ بِيَدِهِۦ
مَلَكُوتُ كُلِّ شَىْءٍ وَهُوَ يُجِيرُ وَلَا يُجَارُ عَلَيْهِ إِن كُنتُمْ تَعْلَمُونَ
﴿٨٨﴾ سَيَقُولُونَ لِلَّهِ ۚ قُلْ فَأَنَّىٰ تُسْحَرُونَ ﴿٨٩﴾

"Say, 'Whose is the earth and whosoever is therein, if you know?' They will say, 'It is Allah's.' Say, 'Will you not then remember.' Say, 'Who is [the] Lord of the seven heavens, and [the] Lord of the Great Throne?' They will say, 'Allah.' Say, 'Will you not then fear Allah.' Say, 'In whose hand is the sovereignty of everything? And He protects [all], while against whom there is no protector.'

---

[1] It is true that there can be other creators, owners and maintainers in this world. However, their abilities to create, own and maintain are limited and not absolute. Absoluteness in these realms belongs only to Allah. Cf., ibn Uthaimin, *Sharh Hadith*, pp. 11-14.

[2] Muhammad ibn Uthaimin, *Sharh Usool al-Imaan* (Fairfax, VA: Institute of Islamic and Arabic Sciences in America, 1410 A.H.), p. 19.

They will say, '[All that belongs to] Allah.' Say, 'How then you are deceived and turn away from the Truth?'" (*al-Muminoon* 84-89).

However, this belief concerning Allah also necessitates or implies the following aspects: Everything that occurs in this creation is by the Decree, Permission and Will of Allah. Sustenance and provisions are from Allah and Allah alone. Life and death are in the Hand of Allah alone. All blessings come from Allah. Guidance and misguidance are by the Will and Permission of Allah. Legislation or prescribing a way of life is the right of Allah alone. Allah alone has knowledge of the unseen. No one has any rights over Allah unless Allah Himself has laid down such upon Himself.

(2) *Tauheed al-Uluhiyah*: This the oneness of Allah with respect to Him being the only one who is an *ilaah* (God, object of adoration and worship). This is the actualization of *tauheed* as found in the actions of the humans or servants of Allah. This is the meaning of the testimony of faith, "There is none worthy of worship except Allah." This is the reason for which the messengers were sent and the books were revealed. This is the "trial" or test that mankind is facing in this world. Allah has said,

وَمَا خَلَقْتُ ٱلْجِنَّ وَٱلْإِنسَ إِلَّا لِيَعْبُدُونِ

"I have not created jinn and mankind except that they should worship and serve Me" (*al-Dhaariyaat* 56). Allah also says,

﴿وَقَضَىٰ رَبُّكَ أَلَّا تَعْبُدُوٓا۟ إِلَّآ إِيَّاهُ

"And your Lord has decreed that you worship none but Him" (*al-Israa* 23).

This branch of *tauheed* is the real goal or essence of the teachings of all of the messengers and prophets. The first type of *tauheed*, *tauheed al-rububiyah*, is necessary and essential. In reality, there has been very little dispute or controversy over that first type of *tauheed*. Many people would accept the basic concept that the Lord and Creator is One Lord and Creator only. However, this belief must lead to this second form of *tauheed* wherein one directs all of his acts of worship towards Allah and Allah alone. This is why so many Messengers are quoted in the Quran as telling their people,

يَـٰقَوْمِ ٱعْبُدُوا۟ ٱللَّهَ مَا لَكُم مِّنْ إِلَـٰهٍ غَيْرُهُۥٓ

"O my people, worship Allah as you have no other God besides Him" (*al-Araaf* 59, 65, 83, 85; *Hood* 50, 61, 84; *al-Muminoon* 23 and 32).

Many authors have given definitions for this type of *tauheed*. Al-Qaisi, for example, defined it in the following manner,

> This is the knowledge, belief and recognition that Allah has the position of God over all of His creation. This category of *tauheed*— which is called *tauheed al-uluhiyah* or *tauheed al-'ibada*— requires that one single out Allah alone for all acts of worship. It is the singling out of Allah and the specifying of Him as the object of all acts of worship, external and internal, statements and actions. It is the denial of the worship of anything other than Allah, whatever that other thing or being might be. It is the negation of any partner with Allah in any form whatsoever and refusal to turn any act of worship to anyone other than Him.
>
> The concept of worship which must be devoted solely to Allah covers everything that is beloved

> and pleasing to Allah, whether it be acts or statements, both inward or outward, including purity of intention, love, fear, hope, awe, turning to [Him alone], putting one's trust [only in Allah], seeking aid and assistance, seeking a means of approach...[1]

He goes on to mention many acts of worship, including the obvious ones, such as prayer, prostration, fasting, animal sacrifice, pilgrimage and so forth. All of these must be done solely for the sake of Allah. They must also be done in the manner that is prescribed by Allah and that is pleasing to Him. To perform any of these acts for anyone other than Allah negates and destroys one's fulfillment and implementation of *tauheed.*

Al-Saadi's definition sheds some further light on this concept. He wrote that *tauheed al-uluhiya*

> Is to know and recognize with knowledge and certainty that Allah is the only God and the only one truly deserving of worship. [It is also to verify that] the attributes of Godhood and its meaning are not found in any of [Allah's] creatures. No one is then deserving of worship except Allah. If the person recognizes that and recognizes it correctly, he will reserve all of his external and internal acts of servitude and worship for Allah alone. He will fulfill the external acts of Islam, such as prayer,… jihad, ordering good and eradicating evil, being dutiful to parents, keeping the ties of kinship, fulfilling the rights of Allah and the rights of His creatures… He will not have any goal in life other than pleasing His Lord and attaining His rewards. In his affairs, he will be following the Messenger of Allah (peace be upon him). His beliefs will be whatever is proven in the Quran and sunnah. His deeds and actions will be what Allah and His

---

[1] Marwaan al-Qaisi, *Maalim al-Tauheed* (Beirut: al-Maktab al-Islami, 1990), pp. 61-62.

> Messenger legislated. His character and manners will be in imitation of His prophet, in his guidance, behavior and all of his affairs.[1]

This aspect of *tauheed* comprises both the actions of the heart as well as the deeds of the physical body. There are two aspects in particular that must be combined in the worship of Allah. Al-Saadi stated,

> The spirit and actuality of worship is by the realization of love and submission to Allah. Complete love and full submission to Allah is the reality of worship. If the act of worship is missing both or one of those components, it is not truly an act of worship. For the reality of worship is found in submission and yielding to Allah. And that will only occur if there is complete and full love [for Allah] which dominates all other expressions of love.[2]

Jaafar Shaikh Idris has aptly described the process that should come about through the correct belief in Allah and how that should lead to the acts of the heart which are essential aspects of *tauheed*. Idris wrote,

> When faith enters a person's heart, it causes therein certain mental states, which result in certain apparent actions, both of which are the proof of true faith. Foremost among those mental states is the feeling of gratitude towards God, which could be said to be the essence of *ibada* (worshipping or serving God).

---

[1] Abdul Rahman Al-Saadi, *Al-Fatawa al-Saadiyah* (Riyadh: Manshooraat al-Muassasat al-Saeediyah, n.d), pp. 10-11. The definition al-Saadi gave highlights the fact that ***tauheed al-uluhiyah*** is composed of ***tauheed al-ikhlaas*** (where one acts solely and purely for Allah's pleasure), ***tauheed al-sidq*** (where one acts sincerely and honestly according to this belief) and ***tauheed al-tareeq*** (where the path that one follows is one, that established by the Prophet Muhammad (peace be upon him)). For more on these concepts, see Muhammad al-Hammad, ***Tauheed al-Uloohiyah*** (Dar ibn Khuzaima, 1414 A.H.), pp. 22-24.

[2] Quoted in al-Hammad, p. 26.

> This feeling of gratitude is so important that a nonbeliever is called *kaafir* which means, "one who denies a truth" and also "one who is ungrateful". One can understand why this is so when one reads in the Quran that the main motive for denying the existence of God is that of unjustified pride. Such a proud person feels that it does not become him to be created or governed by a being whom he must thus acknowledge to be greater than himself and to whom he must be grateful. "Those who dispute concerning the signs of God without any authority come to them, in their hearts is only pride that they shall never attain" (*Ghaafir* 56).
>
> With the feeling of gratitude goes that of love: "There are some people who take to themselves [for worship] others apart from God loving them as they should love God; But those who believe love God more ardently than they love anything else" (*al-Baqara* 165).
>
> A believer loves and is grateful to God for His bounties, but being aware of the fact that his good deeds, whether mental or physical, are far from being commensurate with Divine favors, he is always anxious lest because of his sins God should withhold from him some of these favors or punish him in the Hereafter. He therefore fears Him, surrenders himself to Him, and serves Him with great humility.[1]

There is thus no real worship unless the heart is filled with the feeling of love and glorification for Allah. Along with this flows the other necessity components of having hope in Allah and fear of Allah in the heart. Fear of Allah comes about when one truly glorifies and exalts

---

[1] Jaafar Sheikh Idris, *The Pillars of Faith* (Riyadh: Presidency of Islamic Research, Ifta and Propagation, 1984), pp. 9-10.

Allah.[1] Hope in Allah flows from a complete and true love of Allah. All of these components must be present and in a proper balance. If they are not present at all or if they are not properly balanced, one's worship becomes distorted and incorrect.[2]

Allah says about some of His true and pious servants,

إِنَّهُمْ كَانُوا۟ يُسَـٰرِعُونَ

فِى ٱلْخَيْرَٰتِ وَيَدْعُونَنَا رَغَبًا وَرَهَبًا ۖ وَكَانُوا۟ لَنَا خَـٰشِعِينَ

"Verily, they used to hasten to do good deeds. They used to call upon Us with hope and fear. They also would humble themselves before us" (*al-Anbiyaa* 90). In reference to the pious and devoted servants Jesus, Uzair and the angels, Allah has said,

وَيَرْجُونَ رَحْمَتَهُۥ وَيَخَافُونَ عَذَابَهُۥٓ ۚ

"They hope for His mercy and fear His torment" (*al-Israa* 57).[3]

This category of *tauheed* is the key to a "real life", a life that is sound and proper. Ibn Taimiya wrote,

> You must know that a human's[4] need for Allah—that he worship Him and not associate any partner

---

[1] Sometimes a person or object is feared but that fear is not combined with complete love. Hence, that fear does not constitute a false form of worship.

[2] There are numerous statements from early scholars stressing the proper balance of the different components of *imaan* in the heart. For example, it is said about fear and hope, "They are like two wings of a bird. The believer flies towards Allah by his two wings of hope and fear. If they are balanced, he flies properly. If one of them is missing, he has a shortcoming. If they are both missing, the bird is on the edge of death." (Quoted in al-Hammad, p. 41.)

[3] Cf., al-Hammad, pp. 34-41.

[4] The word ibn Taimiya used was *abd* (servant or slave); however, its inference is every human being.

with Him— is a need concerning which there is no comparison that one can make an analogy to. In some matters, it resembles the need of the body for food and drink. However, there are many differences between the two.

The reality of a human being is in his heart and soul. These cannot be prosperous except through [their relation] with Allah, concerning whom there is no other god. There is[, for example,] no tranquillity in this world except in His remembrance. Verily, man is heading toward his Lord and he shall meet Him. He must definitely meet Him. There is no true goodness for him except in meeting Him.[??] If the human experiences any pleasure or happiness other than in Allah, that joy and happiness will not endure. It will move from one nature to another or from one person to another. The person will enjoy it at one time or only some of the time. In fact, sometimes the thing he enjoys and gets pleasure from does not bring him pleasure or enjoyment. Sometimes it even hurts him when it comes to him. And he is even more harmed by that. But his God is definitely always with him under every circumstance and at all times. Wherever he is, He is with him [by His knowledge and aid]...

If someone worships anything other than Allah— even if he loves it and attains some love in this world and some form of pleasure from that— [that false worship] will destroy the person in a way greater than the harmful displeasure that comes to a person who ate poison...

You must know that if anyone loves something other than for the sake of Allah, then that beloved

---

[1] This is because the soul, by its ingrained nature, yearns for its meeting with its Creator.

> thing will definitely be a cause of harm and punishment.... If somebody loves something other than for the sake of Allah, that thing will harm him whether it is with him or he is without it...[1]

In order for any deed to be accepted by Allah, it must be done in accordance with this aspect of *tauheed.* In other words, if a person is fulfilling and understanding this form of *tauheed* properly, this, by necessity, implies that he is accepting and applying the other forms of *tauheed.* Therefore, his deeds may then be accepted by Allah.[2] Allah says,

فَمَن كَانَ يَرْجُواْ لِقَآءَ رَبِّهِۦ فَلْيَعْمَلْ عَمَلًا صَـٰلِحًا وَلَا يُشْرِكْ بِعِبَادَةِ رَبِّهِۦٓ أَحَدًا

"So whoever hopes for the meeting with his Lord, let him work righteousness and not associate anyone [with Allah] in the worship of his Lord" (*al-Kahf* 110).

One of the acts that must be done solely towards Allah is prayer or supplication. The Prophet (peace be upon him) has said,

الدعاء هو العبادة

"Supplication is the [essence of] worship."[3] When a person prays or supplicates to another, he is showing his trust and reliance in that other. He is demonstrating his need for the one he is praying to. He is demonstrating his trust in that

---

[1] Ibn Taimiya, *Majmoo*, vol. 1, pp. 24-29.
[2] Cf., al-Hammad, *Tauheed al-Uloohiyah*, p. 18.
[3] Recorded by Abu Dawud, al-Nasai, al-Tirmidhi and others. Graded *sahih* by al-Albani. Al-Albani, *Sahih al-Jami al-Sagheer*, vol. 1, p. 641. An excellent discussion of the relationship between supplications and *tauheed* may be found in Jailaan al-Uroosi, *Al-Duaa wa Manzalatuhu min al-Aqeedah al-Islaamiyah* (Riyadh: Maktabah al-Rushdi, 1996), vol. 1, pp. 237-307.

person or being's ability to know, understand and fulfill his need. This kind of feeling in the heart that is reflected in supplication must be directed towards Allah only. That is why the Prophet (peace be upon him) called supplication the essence of worship. Hence, anyone who prays or supplicates to anyone other than Allah is associating partners with Allah or, in other words, committing *shirk*. This is the antithesis of *Imaan* and *tauheed*.

This type of *tauheed* is actually a necessary consequence or result of the correct belief in *tauheed al-rububiyah*. If one realizes that there is no *rabb* (Lord) except Allah, then one will realize that none is worthy or deserving of worship except Allah. If none other than Allah is worthy of worship, then why would anyone worship somebody or something other than Allah?

On this aspect of *tauheed*, ibn Abu al-Izz al-Hanafi wrote,

> The Quran abounds with statements and parables concerning this type of *tawhid*. It first affirms the *tawhid al-rububiyah*, that there is no Creator other than Allah. This conviction necessitates that no one should be worshipped except Allah. It takes the first proposition [that Allah is lord] as evidence for the second proposition [that Allah is the only one worthy of worship]. The Arabs believed in the first proposition and disputed the second. Allah then made it clear to them: Since you know that there is no Creator except Allah, and that He is the One who can give a person what benefits him or keep away from him what harms him, and He has no partner in those acts, then how can you worship others besides Him and associate partners with Him in His Godhead? For example, Allah says in the Quran, "Say: Praise be to Allah and peace on His servants whom He has chosen [for His message]. Who is better: God or the false gods they associate with Him? Or who has created the heavens and the earth, and who sends you down rain from the sky

with which He brings forth beautiful gardens? It is not in your power to cause the growth of the trees in them. Can there be another god besides Allah? Yet they are a people who assign equals [to Him]" (*al-Naml* 59-60). At the end of other similar verses, Allah states, "Can there be another god besides Allah?" (*al-Anbiya* 61, 63 and 64). This is a question with a clearly implied negative answer. They accepted the notion that no one but Allah does such things. Allah used that as a proof against them. It does not mean to ask if there is another god besides Allah, as some have claimed. Such a meaning is inconsistent with the context of the verses and the fact that the people actually used to take other gods alongside Allah. As Allah says, "Can you possibly bear witness that besides Allah there is another god? Say: I witness it not" (*al-Anaam* 19). And they used to say [about the Prophet], "Does he make all the gods one? That it is truly a strange thing" (*Saad* 5). But they would never say that there was another god [with Allah] that would "make the earth a fixed abode, place rivers in its fold, and place firm hills therein" (*al-Nahl* 61). They accepted the fact that only Allah did all of those things. Therefore Allah says, "O people, adore your Guardian-Lord who created you and those who went before you that you may learn to be righteous" (*al-Baqara* 21) and "Say: Think, if Allah took away your hearing and your sight and sealed up your hearts, who, a god other than Allah, could restore them to you" (*al-Anaam* 46). And there are other similar verses.[1]

(3) *Tauheed al-Asma wa al-Sifat*: The third aspect of *tauheed*, in this way of viewing *tauheed*, is recognizing and affirming the Oneness of Allah with respect to His names and attributes. One must affirm that these attributes are perfect and complete in Allah alone. These attributes

[1] Ibn Abu al-Izz, vol. 1, pp. 37-38.

are unique to Allah. No one else can attain any of these attributes.

Throughout the history of Islam, this is another aspect of *tauheed* concerning which many sects deviated. Shuaib al-Arnaut describes the different views that developed in the following passage,

> There is no doubt that the topic of Allah's attributes must be considered as one of the greatest and most important topics of the foundations of faith. The views of the Islamicists have differed on this issue. Some of them followed the approach of complete denial of the attributes. Others accepted Allah's names in general but denied the attributes. Some of them accepted both the names and attributes but, at the same time, rejected or gave interpretations for some of them, turning away from their apparent meanings [of the texts found in the Quran and sunnah]. Some of them took the approach that it is obligatory to believe in all of the names and attributes that are mentioned in the Book of Allah and the authentic sunnah. They took them and passed them on according to their plain, apparent meaning. They deny any understanding of their modality (*kaifiyah*) and deny any kind of similarity [of those attributes to any other than Allah]. The people of this last opinion are those who are called the *salaf* [pious predecessors] and *ahl al-sunnah*.[1]

---

[1] Shuaib al-Arnaut, introduction to Zain al-Din al-Maqdisi, *Aqaweel al-Thiqaat fi Taweel al-Asma wa al-Sifaat wa al-Ayaat al-Muhkamaat wa al-Mushtabihaat* (Beirut: Muassassat al-Risalah, 1985), p. 6. One of the earliest examples of a person asking about these attributes and seeking an explanation for them comes from the time of Malik. A man came to him and said, "O Abu Abdullah [Imam Malik], [about the verse,] 'Allah rose over the Throne,' how is this rising?" Malik's reply was, "The modality of His act is not known. But His rising over the Throne is not unknown. Belief in it is obligatory. Asking about it is an innovation. And I suspect that you are a heretic." This narration from Malik, with various wordings, can be found in numerous works. For a discussion of its chains and meanings, see Baadi, vol. 1, pp. 226-231.

Al-Arnaut wrote that passage in the introduction to Zain al-Din al-Maqdisi's *Aqaweel al-Thiqaat fi Taweel al-Asma wa al-Sifaat wa al-Ayaat al-Muhkimaat wa al-Mushtabihaat*. This book quotes the earliest scholars to prove that the view of the attributes of Allah which is known as the *salafi* view is the correct view according to the Quran and sunnah. Unfortunately, there developed the idea that the view of the later scholars was the "wiser" or "stronger" approach. Those "later scholars" did not believe in these attributes at what could be called "face value" and instead reinterpreted them and gave them new meanings. In his introduction to al-Maqdisi's work, again, Arnaut states, referring to this belief,

> I am certain that the one who reads this book [al-Maqdisi's book] attentively and sincerely will have his heart and mind filled with the conviction of the correctness of the approach of the *salaf* concerning the attributes of Allah. It is the best, strongest and most guided approach. He [the reader] will reject, with pleasure and conviction, what has been written in the books of the later scholars that the approach of the *salaf* is safer but the approach of the later scholars is wiser and more intelligent. [The reader] will clearly state that the view [of the later scholars] is incorrect and goes against the guidance of the sunnah and the Book. The correct statement based on the Prophetic sunnah and Book of Allah is that the way of the *salaf* is more intelligent, wisest and safest.[1]

The correct belief concerning this topic that has been passed on from the time of the Prophet (peace be upon him) and his Companions was aptly summarized by al-Saadi when he wrote,

> As for belief in Allah, it includes: belief in whatever attributes Allah has described Himself

---

[1] Al-Arnaut, introduction to al-Maqdisi, p. 8.

with in His book and whatever attributes His Messenger (peace be upon him) has attributed to Him. [The belief in those attributes are] without any distortion or negation, and without stating how or what manner the attributes are. In fact, the belief is that there is nothing similar to Allah and, at the same time, He is the All-Hearing, the All-Seeing. Therefore, what He has attributed to Himself is not denied nor are such descriptions distorted from their proper meanings. In addition, the names of Allah are neither denied, nor is their manner described, nor are they depicted in a way that makes His attributes similar to the attributes of any of His creation. This is because there is no one and nothing similar or comparable to Him. He has no associate or partner. One cannot make an analogy between Him and His creation, glorified and most High be He.

With respect to belief in what Allah has been attributed with of attributes and names, there must be a combination of affirmation and negation. The *ahl al-Sunnah wa al-Jamaah* do not allow any straying from what the Messengers preached, as that is the Straight Path. Included in this very important principle are all the statements from the Quran and the Sunnah detailing Allah's names, attributes, actions and what should be negated of Him. Included among this is the belief in Allah's settling Himself over the Throne[1], His descending to the lowest heaven, the believers seeing Him in the Hereafter— as the confirmed, continuous reports have stated. Also included under this principle is that Allah is close and responds to the supplications. What is mentioned in the Quran and

---

[1] As al-Baihaqi pointed out, this belief, which is clearly and plainly indicated in the Quran and sunnah refutes the Jahamiyah view that Allah is everywhere and in everything. See Abu Bakr al-Baihaqi, *al-Itiqaad ala Madhhab al-Salaf Ahl al-Sunnah wa al-Jamaah* (Beirut: Dar al-Kutub al-Arabi, 1984), p. 55.

> sunnah concerning His closeness and "being with" the believers does not contradict what is stated concerning His transcendence and His being above the Creation. For, Glory be to Him, there is nothing at all similar to Him with respect to any of His characteristics.[1]

In one verse, Allah has pointed out that both nothing is similar to Him whatsoever and, at the same time, He has attributes, such as hearing and seeing. Allah has stated,

لَيْسَ كَمِثْلِهِۦ شَىْءٌ ۖ وَهُوَ ٱلسَّمِيعُ ٱلْبَصِيرُ

"There is nothing similar to Him and He is the All-Hearing, the All-Seeing" (*al-Shoora* 11). Hence, there is a complete denial of anthropomorphism while affirming Allah's attributes of hearing and seeing.[2]

This aspect of *tauheed* is very important and should not be underestimated. As Ahmad Salaam points out, the people before the coming of the Prophet (peace be upon him) accepted the idea of Allah alone being the only Creator of the Universe. However, they associated partners with Allah in different forms of worship. Therefore, Islam came to purify this concept of Allah being the Lord or *Rabb* and gave it its proper understanding. By doing so, then they would worship Allah alone properly. But the way to achieve that, or the beginning point, is to have the

---

[1] Quoted from Abdullah al-Jarullah, ***Bahjah al-Naadhireen fima Yuslih al-Dunya wa al-Deen*** (1984), pp. 7-8.

[2] Ibn Taimiya (as well as his student ibn al-Qayyim) was a staunch opponent of anthropomorphism. His writings clearly state that Allah's attributes are unique to Him and are not the same as the attributes of humans. However, some people have actually accused him of anthropomorphism. These accusations are based on blatantly false reports concerning ibn Taimiya, extreme ignorance or a biased hatred for this scholar who opposed many heresies. For more on this point and a refutation of such accusations, see Salaah Ahmad, ***Dawah Shaikh al-Islaam ibn Taimiya wa Atharuhaa ala al-Harakaat al-Islaamiyah al-Muasirah*** (Kuwait: Dar ibn al-Atheer, 1996), vol. 2, pp. 375-388.

knowledge and correct understanding of Allah's names and attributes. If one has knowledge of and a correct understanding of Allah's names and attributes, then one would never turn to anyone else or direct any form of worship to anyone other than Allah. Hence, a correct and detailed understanding of Allah's names and attributes is truly the foundation for the correct fulfillment of the other types of *tauheed.*[1] He further states that *tauheed al-rububiyah* is like a tree. Its root, then, is *tauheed al-asma wa al-sifaat*. In other words, *tauheed al-rububiyah* stands on a foundation, which is *tauheed al-asma wa al-sifaat*. If that root or foundation is not found, the tree itself may be diseased and weak.[2]

However, given that parable, the real fruit of *tauheed al-asma wa al-sifaat*, once again, is *tauheed al-uluhiyah*. The more that one knows about Allah and His attributes, the more one will love Allah, fear Allah and have hope in Allah. Definitely, the more one knows about Allah, the more one will love Allah and desire to please Allah and have Allah pleased with him. Hence, the correct understanding of the names and attributes of Allah is very important and very beneficial. Those people who stray on this issue have harmed themselves greatly and lost a great fortune.

The Division of *Tauheed* Into Two Categories

The division of *tauheed* into three categories is a very common presentation of the concept of *tauheed*. Another important presentation of it is to divide it into two categories.[3] It is important to note at the outset that the two

---

[1] Ahmad Salaam, *Muqaddimah fi Fiqh Usool al-Dawah* (Beirut: Dar ibn Hazm, 1990), p. 97.

[2] Salaam, p. 100.

[3] This is the approach found in Hakimi, vol. 1, *passim*; Abdul Majeed al-Shaadhili, *Hadd al-Islaam wa Haqiqat al-Imaan* (Makkah: Umm al-Qura University, 1983),

ways are simply two presentations of exactly the same concepts and ideas. In essence, there is no difference between them. However, one approach may be easier for some to understand and grasp than the other— and the correct understanding is the goal of both presentations.

Another common way to view *tauheed* is to divide it into two categories. These two categories may, in essence, be referred to as "*tauheed* in theory" and "*tauheed* in practice".[1] One's beliefs about Allah must be correct. That is, at the theoretical or rational level, one must know what to believe about Allah. These aspects are clearly presented and explained in the Quran and sunnah. However, *tauheed* is not simply a theoretical matter, a matter of "dry" belief or academic discussion. It is something that is supposed to be put into practice in the life of a Muslim. Hence, *tauheed* goes beyond the simple matter of, "What do I believe about Allah," to the question, "What are the ramifications that this belief must have on my life and actions?" This is the other essential half of *tauheed*: how one relates to Allah and implements that belief in Allah.

Ibn Abu al-Izz mentioned this conceptualization of *tauheed* when he stated,

> The *tauheed* which the prophets preached and the heavenly books taught are of two kinds: *tauheed* in knowledge and recognition and *tauheed* in will and intention. The first is to affirm that God is unique in His essence, attributes, name and acts; that there is nothing like Him in any respect; and that He is as He has said about Himself or as His Prophet (peace be on him) has said about Him. The Quran has expounded this type of *tauheed* in the clearest fashion, as may be found in the beginning of *surah*

---

passim; ibn al-Qayyim, *Madaaraj*, vol. 3, pp. 445-451. The further subdivisions that will be discussed are mostly from al-Shaadhili.

[1] These are the author's terminology but they fairly reflect what is meant by the concepts.

al-Hadid (chapter 57), *Taha* (chapter 20), end of *al-Hashr* (chapter 59), beginning of *Alif Lam Mim Tanzeel* (chapter 32), beginning of *ali 'Imran* (chapter 3), all of *al-Ikhlas* (chapter 112) and so on.

The second type of *tauheed*, *tauheed* in actions and intention, is described in *al-Kafirun* (chapter 109), in the verse, "Say: O People of the Book, let us agree to a statement that is fair and just between you and us..." (3:64), in the first and last parts of *Tanzil al-Kitaab* (chapter 39), in the beginning, middle and end of *Yunus* (chapter 10), in the beginning and ending of *al-Araaf* (chapter 7) and the whole of *al-Anaam* (chapter 6).[1]

Figure 3 is a graphical representation of this conceptualization of *tauheed*. The two basic or general categories are quite basic and simple to understand. To understand them fully, they have been divided into separate subsections. In this way of discussing *tauheed*, specific emphasis is given to some issues that are grouped together under the three categories of *tauheed* mentioned earlier.

[1] ibn Abu-l-Izz, vol. 1, p. 42. Again, virtually the same words may be found in ibn al-Qayyim, *Madaarij*, vol. 3, p. 449.

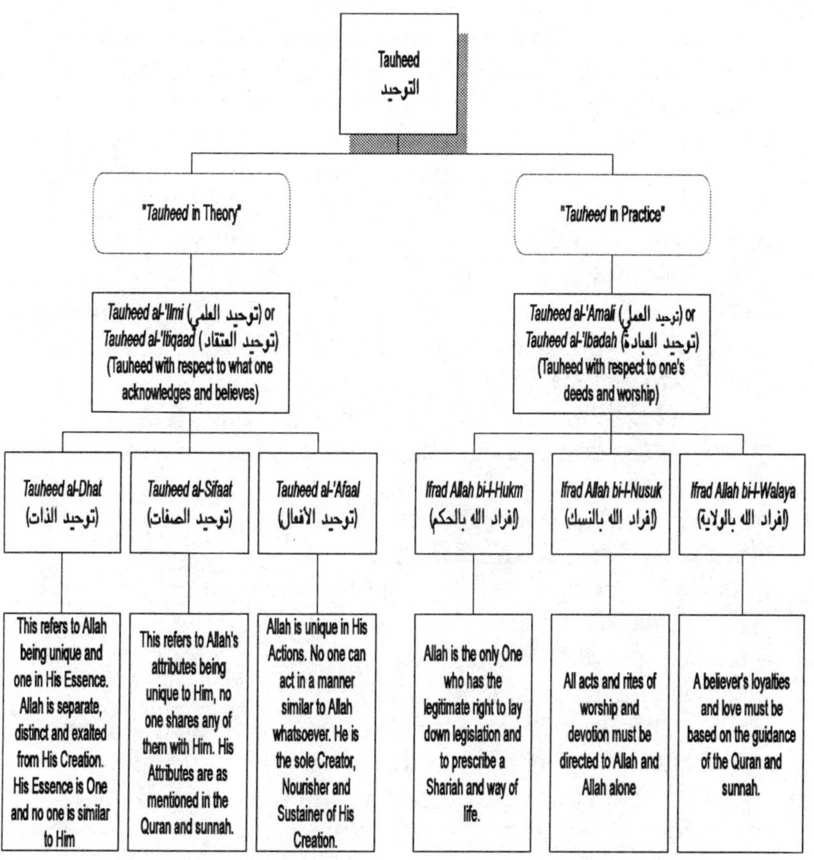

Figure 3. Graphical Representation of the Division of *Tauheed* into Two Categories

(1) "*Tauheed* in Theory": This category of *tauheed* is actually known by many names, including *tauheed al-'ilmi al-khabari al-'itiqaadi* (*tauheed* with respect to what one knows and believes to be true), *tauheed al-'itiqaad* (*tauheed* with respect to what one believes) and *tauheed al-marafah wa al-ithbaat* (*tauheed* with respect to what one recognizes and affirms of Allah). This category of *tauheed* can also be divided into three subcategories: *tauheed al-dhat* (the Oneness of Allah with respect to His being and essence, that He is separate and distinct from His creation); *tauheed al-sifaat* (the Oneness of Allah with respect to His attributes, which are unique unto Him alone); *tauheed al-afaal* (the Oneness of Allah with respect to His actions, being the sole Creator and Nourisher of the Universe). These are shown and defined in Figure 3.

In essence, the topics covered under this branch of *tauheed* are the same as those discussed under *tauheed al-rububiyah* and *tauheed al-asma wa al-sifaat*.

(2) "*Tauheed* in Practice": This branch of *tauheed* is also known by other names, including *tauheed al-talab wa al-qasd* (*tauheed* with respect to one's goal and purpose; that is, one's goal and purpose is to worship Allah alone), *tauheed al-'ibadah* (*tauheed* with respect to one's *ibaadah* or acts of worship; that is, one worships Allah and Allah alone) and *tauheed al-'amali* (*tauheed* with respect to one's deeds; that is, one only performs the deeds that are pleasing and acceptable to Allah).

This branch of *tauheed* is often divided into three subcategories. Each of these subcategories form an essential and necessary aspect of implementing *tauheed* in one's life. These three can be characterized in the following statements: (a) *Ifraad Allah bi-l-Nusk* (making Allah the only object of one's ritual acts of worship); (b) *Ifraad Allah bi-l-Hukm* (submitting oneself only to the commands and revelation coming from Allah); and (c) *Ifraad Allah bi-l-Walaayah* (submitting one's loyalties and love to the commands and guidance of the revelation of Allah). Each of these three shall be discussed separately.

(a) *Ifraad Allah bi-l-Nusk* (making Allah the only object of one's ritual acts of worship): Every rite of worship must be done solely for the sake of Allah, according to His commands and seeking His pleasure. Allah says in the Quran,

قُلْ إِنَّ صَلَاتِي وَنُسُكِي وَمَحْيَايَ وَمَمَاتِي لِلَّهِ رَبِّ ٱلْعَٰلَمِينَ

"Say: Verily, my prayer, my sacrifice, my living and my dying are for Allah, the Lord of the Worlds" (*al-Anaam* 162). Another verse states,

وَمِنْ ءَايَٰتِهِ ٱلَّيْلُ وَٱلنَّهَارُ وَٱلشَّمْسُ وَٱلْقَمَرُ ۚ لَا تَسْجُدُوا۟ لِلشَّمْسِ وَلَا لِلْقَمَرِ
وَٱسْجُدُوا۟ لِلَّهِ ٱلَّذِى خَلَقَهُنَّ إِن كُنتُمْ إِيَّاهُ تَعْبُدُونَ

"And from among His signs are the night and the day, and the sun and the moon. Prostrate not to the sun nor to the moon, but prostrate to Allah Who created them, if you (really) worship Him" (*Fussilat* 37). Indeed, this is the essence of the verse that every Muslim recites in every one of his prayers:

إِيَّاكَ نَعْبُدُ وَإِيَّاكَ نَسْتَعِينُ

"You only do we worship and in You only do we seek help" (*al-Faatiha* 4).

As was alluded to earlier, any rite of worship, be it prayer, fasting, pilgrimage, sacrificing an animal, vowing and so forth, must be done only for the sake of Allah. Similarly, all supplications and prayers must be directed toward Allah. If someone does any of these acts for someone other than Allah, even if he theoretically upholds the oneness of Allah, he is negating his *tauheed* by, in practice, not fulfilling what he believes theoretically.

This category also covers the acts of worship of the heart, which were mentioned earlier. These include putting one's trust only in Allah, having fear and devotion only for Allah and so forth.

(b) *Ifraad Allah bi-l-Hukm* (submitting oneself only to the commands and revelation coming from Allah): In order for one's *tauheed* to be correct, one must reject and deny any form of *taaghoot*, false god or false object of worship and submission. Allah says in the Quran,

وَلَقَدْ بَعَثْنَا فِى كُلِّ أُمَّةٍ رَّسُولًا أَنِ ٱعْبُدُوا۟ ٱللَّهَ وَٱجْتَنِبُوا۟ ٱلطَّٰغُوتَ

"And verily, We have sent among every nation a Messenger proclaiming, 'Worship Allah [alone] and avoid all false deities (*al-taaghoot*)" (*al-Nahl* 36). Muhammad ibn Abdul Wahab has divided *taghoots* into five categories:

(1) The devil who is calling to the worship of anything other than Allah.

(2) The tyrannical ruler who has changed the laws of Allah.

(3) The one who rules in accordance with something other than what Allah has revealed.

(4) The one who claims knowledge of the Unseen.

(5) The one who is worshipped instead of Allah while he himself is pleased with such worship.[1]

Allah has made it clear that judging and ruling in accord with what He has revealed is an essential obligation upon the believers. In fact, it is one of the main purposes for which the Book was revealed. Allah has said,

كَانَ ٱلنَّاسُ أُمَّةً وَٰحِدَةً فَبَعَثَ ٱللَّهُ ٱلنَّبِيِّـۧنَ مُبَشِّرِينَ وَمُنذِرِينَ وَأَنزَلَ مَعَهُمُ ٱلْكِتَٰبَ بِٱلْحَقِّ لِيَحْكُمَ بَيْنَ ٱلنَّاسِ فِيمَا ٱخْتَلَفُوا۟ فِيهِ

"Mankind was one community and Allah sent prophets with glad tidings and warnings, and with them He sent the

[1] Muhammad ibn Abdul Wahab, *Mualafaat al-Shaikh al-Imam Muhammad ibn Abdul Wahaab* (Maktaba ibn Taimiya, n.d.), vol. 1 pp. 376-378. The same passage may be found in Saleh ibn Muhammad al-Sa'uwi, *Majmuat al-Manaahil al-'Idhaab feema ala al-Abd li-Rabb al-Arbaab* (no city or publisher given, 1414 A.H.), vol. 1, pp. 24-25.

Scripture in truth to judge between people in matters wherein they differed" (*al-Baqara* 213). Another verse states,

إِنَّآ أَنزَلۡنَآ إِلَيۡكَ ٱلۡكِتَٰبَ بِٱلۡحَقِّ لِتَحۡكُمَ بَيۡنَ ٱلنَّاسِ
بِمَآ أَرَىٰكَ ٱللَّهُۚ

"Surely, We have sent down to you (O Muhammad) the Book in truth that you might judge between men by that which Allah has shown you" (*al-Nisaa* 105). Judging by the Book of Allah is a characteristic of the believers while judging by anything else— any form of false god or lawgiver— is a characteristic of pure hypocrites and disbelievers. Allah has said,

وَيَقُولُونَ ءَامَنَّا بِٱللَّهِ وَبِٱلرَّسُولِ وَأَطَعۡنَا ثُمَّ يَتَوَلَّىٰ فَرِيقٞ مِّنۡهُم مِّنۢ بَعۡدِ
ذَٰلِكَۚ وَمَآ أُوْلَٰٓئِكَ بِٱلۡمُؤۡمِنِينَ ﴿٤٧﴾ وَإِذَا دُعُوٓاْ إِلَى ٱللَّهِ وَرَسُولِهِۦ لِيَحۡكُمَ
بَيۡنَهُمۡ إِذَا فَرِيقٞ مِّنۡهُم مُّعۡرِضُونَ ﴿٤٨﴾ وَإِن يَكُن لَّهُمُ ٱلۡحَقُّ يَأۡتُوٓاْ إِلَيۡهِ
مُذۡعِنِينَ ﴿٤٩﴾ أَفِي قُلُوبِهِم مَّرَضٌ أَمِ ٱرۡتَابُوٓاْ أَمۡ يَخَافُونَ أَن يَحِيفَ ٱللَّهُ
عَلَيۡهِمۡ وَرَسُولُهُۥۚ بَلۡ أُوْلَٰٓئِكَ هُمُ ٱلظَّٰلِمُونَ ﴿٥٠﴾ إِنَّمَا كَانَ قَوۡلَ ٱلۡمُؤۡمِنِينَ
إِذَا دُعُوٓاْ إِلَى ٱللَّهِ وَرَسُولِهِۦ لِيَحۡكُمَ بَيۡنَهُمۡ أَن يَقُولُواْ سَمِعۡنَا وَأَطَعۡنَاۚ

"They [the hypocrites] say, 'We have believed in Allah and in the Messenger and we obey,' then a party of them turn away thereafter, such are not believers. When they are called to Allah and His Messenger to judge between them, lo, a party of them refuse [to come] and turn away. But if the right is with them, they come to him willingly with submission. Is there a disease in their hearts? Or do they doubt or fear lest Allah and His Messenger should wrong them in judgment? Nay, it is they themselves who are the wrongdoers. The only saying of the faithful believers when they are called to Allah and His Messenger to judge between them is that they say, 'We hear and we obey'" (*al-Noor* 47-51).

Ruling in accord with what Allah has revealed is the same as singling out Allah for obedience. One owes his complete and total obedience only to Allah. This obedience is, in essence, a form of worship. Allah has said,

إِنِ ٱلْحُكْمُ إِلَّا لِلَّهِ ۚ أَمَرَ أَلَّا تَعْبُدُوٓا۟ إِلَّآ إِيَّاهُ ۚ ذَٰلِكَ ٱلدِّينُ ٱلْقَيِّمُ

"The dominion [of rule and judgment] is for none but Allah. He has commanded that you worship none but Him, that is the [true] straight religion" (*Yusuf* 40). Another verse states,

ٱتَّخَذُوٓا۟ أَحْبَارَهُمْ وَرُهْبَٰنَهُمْ أَرْبَابًا مِّن دُونِ ٱللَّهِ وَٱلْمَسِيحَ ٱبْنَ مَرْيَمَ وَمَآ أُمِرُوٓا۟ إِلَّا لِيَعْبُدُوٓا۟ إِلَٰهًا وَٰحِدًا ۖ لَّآ إِلَٰهَ إِلَّا هُوَ ۚ سُبْحَٰنَهُۥ عَمَّا يُشْرِكُونَ

"They [the Jews and Christians] took their rabbis and their monks to be their lords besides Allah and [they also took] Messiah, son of Mary [as Lord], but they were commanded to worship none but One God. There is no God but He. Praise and glory be to Him, from having the partners they associate [with Him]" (*al-Tauba* 31). The manner in which they took their rabbis and monks as lords besides Allah is that they would allow them to decree for them what was permissible and what was forbidden instead of relying only on what Allah had revealed for such laws.

Ibn Taimiya once wrote,

> Islam requires complete submission to Allah alone. Whoever submits to Him and someone else has associated a partner with Allah (*shirk*). Whoever does not submit to Him has haughtily refused to worship Him. The one who commits *shirk* as well

> as the one who haughtily refuses to worship Him is a disbeliever. Submission to Him alone encompasses worshipping Him alone and obeying Him alone.[1]

In his commentary on the Quran, al-Shanqiti wrote, "Associating partners with Allah with respect to His rule and associating partners with Him in worship are one and the same thing. There is no difference between them whatsoever. Whoever follows a system or way of life other than Allah's or a legal system other than Allah's... is like one who worships an idol or prostrates to a false god. There is no difference between the two of them in any respect whatsoever. They are one and the same thing. They are both associating partners with Allah."[2]

Al-Abdul-Lateef demonstrates that refusal to rule according to what Allah has revealed violates every aspect of *tauheed.*[3] As was just mentioned, *tauheed al-ibada* implies that Allah alone is obeyed and has absolute authority in one's life. If one follows or obeys anything else, despite what Allah has revealed, he is giving a share of his servitude to that other source of law rather than to Allah alone.

Refusing to submit to and implement Allah's *shariah* also violates *tauheed al-Rububiyah. Tauheed al-Rububiyah* implies that Allah is the Complete Owner and Master of the Universe. He is in charge and has the right to control and direct everything in the Universe. Everything in this Universe either must or should take place according to His Command and Decree.[4] This is why Allah has used the

---

[1] Ibn Taimiya, *Majmu*, vol. 3, p. 91.

[2] Quoted in Abdul Rahman al-Sudais, *al-Haakimiyah fi Tafseer Adhwa al-Bayaan* (Riyadh: Dar Taiba, 1412 A.H.) p. 53.

[3] Al-Abdul-Lateef, p. 296.

[4] Natural phenomena must and does act according to Allah's law. However, if Allah has given man "free choice" concerning a matter, then man should act in accordance with what Allah has commanded.

word *arbab* (plural of *rabb* or Lord) in the verse just quoted,

ٱتَّخَذُوٓا۟ أَحْبَارَهُمْ وَرُهْبَٰنَهُمْ أَرْبَابًا مِّن دُونِ ٱللَّهِ وَٱلْمَسِيحَ ٱبْنَ مَرْيَمَ

وَمَآ أُمِرُوٓا۟ إِلَّا لِيَعْبُدُوٓا۟ إِلَٰهًا وَٰحِدًا ۖ لَّآ إِلَٰهَ إِلَّا هُوَ ۚ سُبْحَٰنَهُۥ عَمَّا يُشْرِكُونَ

"They [the Jews and Christians] took their rabbis and their monks to be their lords besides Allah and [they also took] Messiah, son of Mary [as Lord], while they were commanded to worship none but One God. There is no God but He. Praise and glory be to Him, from having the partners they associate [with Him]" (*al-Tauba* 31).

Furthermore, الحَكَم (*al-Hakam*, "the Judge and the Decider"[1]) is considered one of the names of Allah. Belief in this name of Allah requires that one take all matters to Allah's revelation and ruling. As Allah says,

وَلَا يُشْرِكُ فِى حُكْمِهِۦٓ أَحَدًا

"And He shares not His Rule or Legislation with anyone" (*al-Kahf* 26).

Al-Abdul-Lateef also talks about another aspect of *tauheed*, which is called *tauheed al-itibaa'* (*tauheed* concerning following). This aspect of *tauheed* means that the only one who is to be followed and completely obeyed is the one whom Allah sent for that purpose, the Messenger of Allah (peace be upon him). Hence, not following his way and, instead, choosing to follow another's way or law violates this aspect of *tauheed*.[2] Muhammad ibn Ibrahim wrote, "Anyone who rules in accord with something other than what the Messenger of Allah (peace be upon him)

---

[1] Allah is the One who judges between His servants with justice, fairness and equity. He wrongs no soul even the slightest amount. Similarly, His decrees and laws are the most just. For a complete discussion of the meaning of this name, see Muhammad al-Hamood, *Al-Nahaj al-Asma fi Sharh Asma Allah al-Husna* (Kuwait: Maktaba al-Imam al-Dhahabi, 1992), vol. 1, pp. 225-240.

[2] Cf., Al-Abdul-Lateef, pp. 296-302.

brought is ruling by a *taaghut* (false god) and taking it as the decider of his affairs."[1]

(c) ***Ifraad Allah bi-l-Walaayah* (submitting one's loyalties and love to the commands and guidance of the revelation of Allah):** Having loyalty for the sake of Allah and basing one's love and hatred on guidance from Allah is an essential condition for one's faith to be sound and correct.[2] Allah says in the Quran,

---

[1] Muhammad ibn Ibrahim Ali-Shaikh, *Tahkeem al-Qawaaneen* (no city or publisher given, 1411 A.H.), p. 9. This brings up another very important point. What about the rulers who do not apply the guidance of Allah in their lands? Are they all considered unbelievers because of this act? Many people, on both sides of this question, have made mistakes concerning this point. Allah says in the Quran, "Whoever does not rule by what Allah has revealed are unbelievers" (*al-Maida* 44). Ibn Abbas, in interpreting this verse, was asked about the rulers of his time who did not always apply the Islamic law to everything. He answered that what they are doing does fall under this verse but it is a *kufr* that is less than the great *kufr*. That is, it does not mean that they are no longer to be considered Muslims. Actually, there are different types of rulers— some of them are clearly unbelievers while others cannot be considered such. If a ruler openly performs the practices of Islam and he believes that it is obligatory upon him to apply the *shariah* yet he does not do so completely for some reason, then this is what ibn Abbas was describing when he said, "*Kufr* that is less than *kufr*." Such a ruler is not to be considered a non-Muslim although he may be considered a *faasiq* or evildoer. In fact, that ruler is very much similar to a person who knows that he must obey Allah yet due to some reason, for example, desire or lust, he commits an act of disobedience towards Allah. Such a person, due to that sin alone, does not become a disbeliever. Other rulers openly deny Islam and say that they prefer some other form of government and economy, like socialism or capitalism. This verse also applies to them as these people prefer some other guidance to the guidance of Allah. This is clearly the greater *kufr* without any doubt or dispute about it. There are other rulers who do not deny Islam openly yet they do not believe that it is obligatory upon them to enforce the *shariah* or they may oppose or refuse to apply the *shariah* because they do not believe in its implementation. This is also a type of *kufr*, the greater kind, and the person becomes a non-Muslim even if he prays and fasts and performs some of the other rites of Islam. Finally, there are those who claim that they want Islam while in reality they do not want to apply the *shariah* and they may even have a hatred in their heart for Islam. This person is clearly a hypocrite and hypocrisy is a type of *kufr*. An excellent discussion of this topic may be found in Abdul Aziz Kaamil, *al-Hukum wa al-Tahaakum fi Khitaab al-Wahi* (Riyadh: Dar Taiba, 1995), vol. 1, pp. 253-264.

[2] It is extremely important to note that, like ruling not in accord with what Allah has revealed, there are different levels of not making loyalty for the sake of Allah. Such loyalty for what is displeasing to Allah may reach the level that the person falls out

تَرَىٰ كَثِيرًا مِّنْهُمْ يَتَوَلَّوْنَ ٱلَّذِينَ كَفَرُوا۟ ۚ لَبِئْسَ مَا قَدَّمَتْ لَهُمْ أَنفُسُهُمْ أَن
سَخِطَ ٱللَّهُ عَلَيْهِمْ وَفِى ٱلْعَذَابِ هُمْ خَٰلِدُونَ ﴿٨٠﴾ وَلَوْ كَانُوا۟ يُؤْمِنُونَ
بِٱللَّهِ وَٱلنَّبِىِّ وَمَآ أُنزِلَ إِلَيْهِ مَا ٱتَّخَذُوهُمْ أَوْلِيَآءَ وَلَٰكِنَّ كَثِيرًا مِّنْهُمْ
فَٰسِقُونَ

"You see many of them taking the disbelievers as their *auliyaa* [friends and protectors]. Evil indeed is that which their ownselves have sent forward before them. For that reason, Allah's wrath fell upon them and in torment they will abide. And had they believed in Allah and in the Prophet and in what was revealed to him, they would not have taken them [the disbelievers] as *auliyaa*, but many of them are disobedient to Allah" (*al-Maida* 80-81). According to ibn Taimiya, the last statement, "and had they believed," is a conditional statement implying that those who do such an act do not have any faith whatsoever.[1]

Allah also says,

إِنَّمَا وَلِيُّكُمُ ٱللَّهُ وَرَسُولُهُۥ وَٱلَّذِينَ ءَامَنُوا۟ ٱلَّذِينَ يُقِيمُونَ ٱلصَّلَوٰةَ
وَيُؤْتُونَ ٱلزَّكَوٰةَ وَهُمْ رَٰكِعُونَ ﴿٥٥﴾ وَمَن يَتَوَلَّ ٱللَّهَ وَرَسُولَهُۥ وَٱلَّذِينَ
ءَامَنُوا۟ فَإِنَّ حِزْبَ ٱللَّهِ هُمُ ٱلْغَٰلِبُونَ ﴿٥٦﴾ يَٰٓأَيُّهَا ٱلَّذِينَ ءَامَنُوا۟ لَا تَتَّخِذُوا۟
ٱلَّذِينَ ٱتَّخَذُوا۟ دِينَكُمْ هُزُوًا وَلَعِبًا مِّنَ ٱلَّذِينَ أُوتُوا۟ ٱلْكِتَٰبَ مِن قَبْلِكُمْ
وَٱلْكُفَّارَ أَوْلِيَآءَ ۚ وَٱتَّقُوا۟ ٱللَّهَ إِن كُنتُم مُّؤْمِنِينَ

"Verily, your Protector and Helper is Allah, His Messenger, and the believers— those who establish the prayer, and give zakat, and they bow down [in submission]. And whosoever

---

of the fold of Islam. (This is what some scholars refer to as *al-tawali*.) However, at other times, the act may be a sinful act but does not take the person out of the fold of Islam.

[1] Ibn Taimiya, *Kitaab al-Imaan*, p. 14.

takes Allah, His Messenger and those who believe as Protectors, then the party of Allah will be the victorious. O you who believe! Take not for *auliyaa* [protectors and helpers] those who take your religion for a mockery and fun from among those who received the Scripture [Jews and Christians] before you, nor from among the disbelievers. And fear Allah if you indeed are true believers" (*al-Maida* 55-57).

In another verse, Allah states,

﴿يَـٰٓأَيُّهَا ٱلَّذِينَ ءَامَنُوا۟ لَا تَتَّخِذُوا۟ ٱلْيَهُودَ وَٱلنَّصَـٰرَىٰٓ أَوْلِيَآءَ بَعْضُهُمْ
أَوْلِيَآءُ بَعْضٍ ۚ وَمَن يَتَوَلَّهُم مِّنكُمْ فَإِنَّهُۥ مِنْهُمْ ۗ إِنَّ ٱللَّهَ لَا يَهْدِى ٱلْقَوْمَ
ٱلظَّـٰلِمِينَ ﴿٥١﴾

"O believers! Take not the Jews and the Christians as friends and protectors. They are but friends and protectors to one another. And if any among you take them as *auliyaa* [loyal friends and protectors], then surely he is one of them" (*al-Maida* 51).

Concerning this topic as a whole, Hamad ibn Ateeq once wrote that there is nothing more stressed and there is nothing that has more evidence provided for it, after the obligation of *tauheed*, than the topic of opposing and not having loyalty for the disbelievers.[1]

Every Muslim must realize that part of the essential meaning of the word *ilah* ("God") is the one who is adored, extolled and loved in the heart. A verse in the Quran states,

وَإِذْ قَالَ إِبْرَٰهِيمُ لِأَبِيهِ وَقَوْمِهِۦٓ إِنَّنِى بَرَآءٌ مِّمَّا تَعْبُدُونَ
﴿٢٦﴾ إِلَّا ٱلَّذِى فَطَرَنِى فَإِنَّهُۥ سَيَهْدِينِ ﴿٢٧﴾ وَجَعَلَهَا كَلِمَةًۢ بَاقِيَةً
فِى عَقِبِهِۦ لَعَلَّهُمْ يَرْجِعُونَ

[1] Quoted in al-Abdul-Lateef, p. 359.

"And [remember] when Abraham said to his father and to his people, 'Verily, I am innocent of what you worship, except Him Who did create me, and verily, He will guide me.' And he made it a lasting word among his offspring, that they may turn back [to Allah]" (*al-Zukhruf* 26-28). Abdul Rahman ibn Hasan pointed out that in this verse, Ibrahim says, "I am innocent of what you worship," this means that there is none worthy of worship, love and adoration— except, "Him Who did create me," who is Allah. The Prophet Abraham (peace be upon him) was stating, in different words, the testimony of faith. Hence, part of the testimony of faith is that one completely frees himself and absolves himself from anything that is worshipped besides Allah.[1] Allah has obligated the believers to be free of and dissociate themselves from any form of polytheism or polytheist. The believer is ordered to oppose their falsehood and to have dislike for them in general.

The key behind this aspect is the proper and complete love for Allah and the pure and total worship of Allah. If a person truly and correctly loves Allah, Allah will be more beloved to him than anything else. In addition, he will love whatever Allah loves and despise whatever Allah despises. In particular, he will be disgusted and have complete contempt for anything that is an affront to his Beloved, Allah. Obviously, associating partners with Allah and the worship of others while only Allah is deserving of worship is the greatest insult to and disrespect for Allah. It is part of the testimony of faith that one opposes such deviations from Allah's guidance. If the Muslim does not do so, then he does not have the correct understanding or implementation of his statement of faith, "There is none worthy of worship and adoration except Allah."

---

[1] Ibn Hasan was quoted in Mahmaas al-Jalood, ***al-Muwaalat wa al-Muaadaat fi al-Shariah al-Islamiya*** (Al-Mansurah: al-Yaqeen li-l-Nashr wa al-Tauzee', 1987), vol. 1, pp. 132-133. A similar analysis of Quranic statements being restatements of the testimony of faith may be made for ***al-Kahf*** 16 and ***ali-Imran*** 64.

Mahmaas al-Jalood wrote,

> Those who give loyalty to the disbelievers and do not oppose them are not worshipping Allah in the proper way that He is to be worshipped. In worship, they are associating others with what is exclusively His. This is because if they were worshipping Allah properly, how could they openly show approval, love and support for the enemies of Allah and the enemies of His religion, of the disbelievers, polytheists and apostates. If a Muslim obeys the disbelievers, shows love and support for them in their disbelief, supports them with wealth, weapons, manpower or advice and helps them in those matters, and cuts off his relationship with the Muslims or makes his ties with the disbelievers stronger than his ties with the Muslims, then he has violated the meaning of, "There is none worthy of worship except Allah," and apostatized from Islam. The ruling concerning him is that he has fallen into disbelief. Because, in such a case, he will be considered one of the polytheists, with respect to both legal ruling and in action. He did not fulfill the meaning of, "There is none worthy of worship except Allah," denying what it denies and affirming what it affirms, even if he says it tens of times. This is because the truthfulness of a statement is indicated by actions.[1]

An Incorrect Conceptualization of *Tauheed*

The term *tauheed* is used quite often by many sects in Islam. Everyone claims to have *tauheed*. The only true *tauheed* is that which was taught by the Prophet Muhammad (peace be upon him) to his Companions and which came down from them. In later years, philosophers

[1] al-Jalood, vol. 1, pp. 136-137.

and scholastic theologians developed their own concepts of *tauheed* which shared some aspects with the true *tauheed* but also strayed from it in many aspects.

Similarly, the Sufis developed their own concept and levels of *tauheed*. In reality, in many cases, what they claim to be *tauheed* is nothing but *shirk* (associating partners with Allah) and *kufr* (disbelief). Hence it is important to be aware of some of their misconceptions that they spread among Muslims. Concerning their views of *tauheed*, ibn Abu al-Izz wrote,

> Now that it is established that *tawhid al-uluhiyah* is what the prophets preached and what the heavenly books taught, as has been pointed out, then one should not listen to the statement of those who divide *tawhid* into [the following] three types: This first type of *tawhid*, they say, is the *tawhid* of the commoners. The second type is the *tawhid* of the elect which, they say, is the *tawhid* that is realized in mystical experience. The third is the *tawhid* of the elect of the elect (*khaasat al-khaasah*). This *tawhid*, they believe, is affirmed by the Eternal Being Himself. No one should heed these statements for the people who were most perfect in *tawhid* are the prophets (peace be on them all)…
>
> The *millah* of Abraham is *tawhid*. The religion of Muhammad is every statement, action, and belief that He brought from Allah. The 'statement of sincerity' is the testimony that there is no god but Allah. The *fitrah* of Islam is the natural disposition man has been given to love and worship only Allah without ascribing any partner to Him and submitting to Him with complete servitude, humility and reverence.
>
> This is the *tawhid* of the most elite or dear from among the chosen ones of Allah. Whoever turns away from it is the fool of all fools. Allah has

Himself said, "Who turns away from the faith of Abraham but such as debase their souls with folly? Him We chose and rendered pure in this world, and he will be in the Hereafter in the ranks of the righteous. Behold! His Lord said to him, 'Submit to me,' [and] he said, 'I submit to the Lord and Cherisher of the Universe'" (*al-Baqara* 130-131).

The second and third types of *tawhid*, which have been called the *tawhid* of the elect and of the elect of the elect, culminate in the passing away of the self (*fana*) which most Sufis strive for. It is a dangerous alley which leads to [the false concept of] union (*ittihad*). Read these lines which Shaykh al-Islam Abu Ismail al-Ansari al-Harwi, may Allah have mercy on him, composed,[1] "No one affirms the unity of the One, For whoever affirms His unity denies it. Whoever describes Him, His description of Unity is void and unacceptable to the One. The real affirmation of His unity is what the One Himself does, and whoever tries to describe Him is a heretic."

Although the author of these lines did not mean to imply union (*ittihad*), he has used vague words which an exponent of union is likely to interpret on his lines and think that the author belongs to his way of thinking. If he had used the words which the *shariah* uses and which are clear and non-misleading, it would have been more proper. Had we been required to believe in what these lines suggest, the Prophet (peace be upon him) would have mentioned it, invited people to believe in it, and explained it at length. But there is no proof that

[1]For a review and criticism of Al-Ansari's views expressed in these lines of poetry, see ibn Qayyim, *Madaarij al-Salikin*, vol. 3, p. 518. Ibn al-Qayyim makes the point that in various verses of the Quran, Allah has testified that His angels, His prophets and their followers who have knowledge affirm and expound His unity. It is not, therefore, correct for anyone to say that no one has truly affirmed God's unity and that those who have so ventured have been guilty of heresy.

> he ever distinguished between a *tawhid* of a commoner, a *tawhid* of the elect and a *tawhid* of the elect of the elect. There is absolutely no allusion to it anywhere. In fact, there is nothing even close to it.
>
> Here is the Book of Allah, the hadith of the Prophet (peace be on him), the traditions of the best people of all ages after the age of the Prophet and the works of the leading scholars. Is there any mention of *fana* in any of them? Has anyone of them talked about these stages of *tawhid*? In fact, this concept developed later when some people became excessive with respect to some parts of the religion, just as the Khawarij did earlier in Islam or the Christians did in their religion. Allah has condemned all excess in religion and has strictly prohibited them. Allah states, "O People of the Book! Commit not excesses in your religion; nor say aught of Allah except the truth" (*al-Nisaa* 171). And also, "Say: O People of the Book! Exceed not in your religion the bounds (of what is proper), trespassing beyond truth, nor follow the vain desires of people who went wrong in times gone by, who mislead many and strayed themselves from the even way" (*al-Maida* 77).[1]

A very important point that ibn Abu al-Izz makes in that passage is that the Messenger of Allah (peace be upon him) was the most knowledgeable of Allah. The best worshipper of Allah was the Prophet Muhammad (peace be upon him). The best way to submit and serve Allah is the way of the Prophet Muhammad (peace be upon him). The best and correct beliefs about Allah are those of the Prophet Muhammad (peace be upon him). If Muslims would truly reflect on this point and apply it properly, then all the

[1] Ibn Abu al-Izz, vol. 1, pp. 53-56.

innovations that have developed since the Prophet's time could be removed.

"His angels"[1]

The second article of faith mentioned by the Prophet (peace be upon him) in the narration of Umar was belief in the angels. Angels are a type of creation of Allah that is, in general, unseen by man. They have been created from light but they do have forms and bodies. They are servants of Allah and have no aspect of divinity to them whatsoever. They submit to His command completely and never stray from fulfilling His orders.

Salaam points out that if a person does not believe in angels, he then cannot believe in the coming of revelation to the Prophet Muhammad (peace be upon him). This is because it was an angel, Gabriel, that brought the Quran to the Prophet Muhammad (peace be upon him). Therefore, belief in the Quran cannot be confirmed unless one believes in the angels, as a class, and the Angel Gabriel, in particular, who brought that revelation to the Prophet (peace be upon him).[2]

According to ibn Uthaimin, proper belief in the angels comprises four matters:[3] First, one must believe in their existence. Second, one must believe in them in general but also one must believe in their names that have been explicitly stated in either the Quran or authentic sunnah. For example, one of the angels is named *Jibreel* (Gabriel).

---

[1] Due to space limitations, the discussion of the remaining articles of faith will not be as lengthy as the discussion of the belief in Allah, which may be considered the most important and essential article of faith. In particular, sometimes the evidence for different statements will not be stated but may be found in the references cited.

[2] Salaam, p. 104.

[3] Cf., Ibn Uthaimin, *Sharh Usool al-Imaan*, pp. 27-28. "Cf.," is used implying that the points are from ibn Uthaimin but the discussion and explanation is not necessarily from his writing.

He was the angel who brought the revelation to the Prophet (peace be upon him).

Third, one must believe in their attributes as stated in the Quran or sunnah. For example, it is stated in a hadith that the Prophet (peace be upon him) saw the Angel Gabriel covering the horizon and he had six hundred wings. This shows that this species of creation is a truly great and marvelous creation of Allah. It is also demonstrated, such as in this hadith currently being discussed, that an angel can appear in different forms, such as in the form of a human. This also demonstrates Allah's great power and ability to do whatever He wills.

Fourth, one must believe in the actions that they perform as mentioned in the Quran or authentic hadith. It is stated in the Quran that they worship Allah and glorify Him. It is also indicated that specific angels have been given specific responsibilities. *Jibreel* is in charge of the "life of the heart" which is a reference to the revelation that has come from Allah. *Israafeel* is responsible for blowing the trumpet that will resurrect the bodies on the Day of Judgment. Hence, he is related to the reviving of life on the Day of Resurrection. *Mikaaeel* is responsible for the rain and vegetation. These are the "sources" of life on earth. Ibn Uthaimin points out that it is perhaps the relationship between these three angels and their "life-giving" responsibilities that led the Prophet (peace be upon him) to open his late-night prayers with the following supplication, "O Allah, Lord of *Jibreel*, *Mikaaeel* and *Israafeel*, the Originator of the Heavens and the Earth, the Knower of the Unseen and Witnessed, You judge between Your slaves in that wherein they differ, guide me to the truth in the matters concerning which they have differed, by Your Leave. You guide whom You will to the Straight Path."[1]

[1] Muhammad ibn Uthaimin, *Majmuat Fatawa wa Rasail Fadheelat al-Shaikh Muhammad ibn Salih al-Uthaimin* (Riyadh: Dar al-Watn, 1413 A.H.), vol. 3, pp. 160-161.

A fifth matter that one must fulfill in his belief in the angels is to have a strong love for them due to their obedience and worship of Allah. Furthermore, they declare the Oneness of Allah and fulfill His commands. They also have strong love and loyalty for the true believers in Allah. They pray to Allah on behalf of the believers and ask Allah to forgive them. They support them in both this life and the Hereafter.

An important aspect related to belief in the angels is that everyone must believe that he has with him at all times two angels that are recording his deeds. The following verses are in reference to those angels:

إِذْ يَتَلَقَّى ٱلْمُتَلَقِّيَانِ عَنِ ٱلْيَمِينِ وَعَنِ ٱلشِّمَالِ قَعِيدٌ ﴿١٧﴾ مَّا يَلْفِظُ مِن قَوْلٍ إِلَّا لَدَيْهِ رَقِيبٌ عَتِيدٌ

"[Remember] that the two receivers [recording angels] receive [him], one sitting on the right and one on the left. Not a word does he utter, but there is a watcher by him ready [to record it]" (*Qaaf* 17-18).

Some of The Beneficial Results of Proper Belief in the Angels[1]

(1) One has knowledge of or recognizes the greatness of Allah and His Power. This great creation known as angels is an indication of the greatness of their Creator.

(2) One should thank Allah for His extreme care and concern for humans. He has created these creatures to support the believers, protect them, record their deeds and other aspects which are beneficial to the believers.

---

[1] Cf., Ibn Uthaimin, *Sharh Usool al-Imaan*, pp. 29-30.

"His books"

Belief in Allah's books is the third article of faith mentioned in this hadith. It refers to the revelations that Allah sent down to His messengers as a mercy and a guidance to lead mankind to success in this life and happiness in the Hereafter. In particular, the Quran is the final revelation. It is the uncreated speech of Allah.

Ibn Uthaimin points out that the belief in Allah's books comprises four aspects:[1] First, one must believe that those books were truly revealed from Allah. Second, one must specifically believe in the books mentioned in the Quran and sunnah. They are the Quran revealed to the Prophet Muhammad (peace be upon him), the *Taurah* revealed to the Prophet Moses (peace be upon him), the *Injeel* revealed to the Prophet Jesus (peace be upon him) and the *Zaboor* revealed to the Prophet David (peace be upon him). There is also reference in the Quran to the "pages" of Abraham and Moses. The books that the Jews and Christians possess today, which they call the Torah, Gospel and Psalms, may contain some of those original revelations but there is no question that they have been distorted. Hence, to believe in the *Torah* of Moses, for example, does not mean that a Muslim believes in the first five books of the Old Testament. The two are different books although the latter may possess some of what was in the original *Taurah*.

Third, one must also believe in everything that Allah has revealed, whether it be in the Quran or in the previous books. That is, for example, if the Quran states something, then the Muslim must believe in it. He has no choice in this matter. If he rejects any statement in it, he has negated his beliefs in the Books of Allah. Allah says,

---

[1] Cf., Ibn Uthaimin, *Sharh Usool al-Imaan*, pp. 32-33.

أَفَتُؤْمِنُونَ بِبَعْضِ ٱلْكِتَٰبِ وَتَكْفُرُونَ بِبَعْضٍ ۚ فَمَا جَزَآءُ مَن يَفْعَلُ ذَٰلِكَ مِنكُمْ إِلَّا خِزْىٌ فِى ٱلْحَيَوٰةِ ٱلدُّنْيَا ۖ وَيَوْمَ ٱلْقِيَٰمَةِ يُرَدُّونَ إِلَىٰٓ أَشَدِّ ٱلْعَذَابِ ۗ وَمَا ٱللَّهُ بِغَٰفِلٍ عَمَّا تَعْمَلُونَ

"Then do you believe in a part of the Scripture and you reject the rest? Then what is the recompense of those who do so among you, except disgrace in the life of this world. And on the Day of Resurrection they shall be consigned to the most grievous torment. And Allah is not unaware of what you do" (*al-Baqara* 85).

Fourth, one must act in accord with the unabrogated revelation, which is the Quran. One must be pleased with it and submit to it completely. This is so even if the person does not completely grasp the wisdom behind the command or statement.

All of the previous revelations of Allah have been abrogated by the final revelation, the Quran. There is no need for any Muslim to turn to the remnants of any of the earlier scriptures. Everything that he needs for his guidance is contained in the Quran and what it points to, such as the sunnah of the Prophet Muhammad (peace be upon him). Allah has stated in the Quran,

وَأَنزَلْنَآ إِلَيْكَ ٱلْكِتَٰبَ بِٱلْحَقِّ مُصَدِّقًا لِّمَا بَيْنَ يَدَيْهِ مِنَ ٱلْكِتَٰبِ وَمُهَيْمِنًا عَلَيْهِ ۖ

"And to you We have revealed the Scripture in truth, confirming whatever Scripture that came before it, and a watcher and judge over it" (*al-Maida* 48). Commenting on this verse, ibn Uthaimin says, "It is a ruler over the previous scriptures. Hence, it is not allowed to act in accord with any ruling of the rulings from the previous scriptures unless it is verified and accepted by the Quran."[1]

It is one of the greatest blessings of Allah that He sent revelations for mankind. These revelations guide man to the purpose for which he was created. This is one of the many aspects of this creation that helps a human being see and recognize the truth. Commenting on this point, Idris wrote,

> God created men so that they may serve Him. His being a servant of God constitutes the essence of man. Man cannot therefore attain to his true humanity and acquire peace of mind unless he realizes this aim for which he was created. But how can he do this? God, being merciful and just, has helped him in many ways. He granted him... an originally good nature that is inclined to know and serve its true Lord. He granted him a mind that possesses a moral sense and the ability to reason. He made the whole universe a natural book full of signs that lead a thinking person to God. But to make things more specific and to give him more detailed knowledge of his Lord, and to show him in a more detailed manner how to serve Him, God has been sending down verbal messages through His prophets chosen from among men, ever since the creation of man. Hence, the description of these messages in the Quran as guidance, light, signs, reminders, etc.[2]

In fact, not only did He send revelations for mankind but He also sent specific and different revelations according to the needs and circumstances of different people over time. This is another expression of Allah's great mercy for mankind. This process continued until the Quran was revealed, containing all the guidance that mankind needs from the time of the Prophet Muhammad

---

[1] Ibn Uthaimin, *Sharh Usool al-Imaan*, pp. 32-33.
[2] Idris, pp. 18-19.

(peace be upon him) until the Day of Judgment. Since it is meant to be a guidance for all times until the Day of Resurrection, as opposed to the earlier scriptures, Allah has protected the Quran from any tampering, mistakes or distortions. Allah has said,

إِنَّا نَحْنُ نَزَّلْنَا ٱلذِّكْرَ وَإِنَّا لَهُۥ لَحَـٰفِظُونَ

"Verily, it is We who have sent down the Reminder [the Quran] and surely We will guard it [from corruption]" (*al-Hijr* 9).

"His messengers"[1]

The next article of faith mentioned by the Prophet (peace be upon him) is belief in Allah's Messengers. A messenger is any human who was chosen by Allah to receive revelation from Him and who was commanded to pass that revelation on. The first of the messengers was Noah (*Nooh*).[2] Every people was sent messengers and these messengers came with the same fundamental teaching:

وَلَقَدْ بَعَثْنَا فِى كُلِّ أُمَّةٍ رَّسُولًا أَنِ ٱعْبُدُوا۟ ٱللَّهَ وَٱجْتَنِبُوا۟ ٱلطَّـٰغُوتَ

[1] According to al-Qaari (vol. 1, p. 57), the reason messengers are explicitly and only mentioned, as opposed to messengers and prophets, is because that the essential belief is the belief in the messengers. This is because it was the messengers who received the revelations and conveyed them to others. One could state that the prophets were the followers of the messengers. Hence, the most important aspect is to believe in the one who received and conveyed the message. Allah knows best.

[2] As for Adam, he was a prophet and not a messenger. Every messenger was a prophet but not vice-versa. For the differences between a prophet (*nabi*) and messenger (*rasool*), see the author's "Questions and Answers," *Al-Basheer* (Vol. 2, No. 1, May-June 1988), pp. 5-7.

"And verily, We have sent among every nation a Messenger proclaiming, 'Worship Allah [alone] and avoid all false deities'" (*al-Nahl* 36). The final messenger and prophet is the Prophet Muhammad (peace be upon him). Allah has said,

مَّا كَانَ مُحَمَّدٌ أَبَآ أَحَدٍ مِّن رِّجَالِكُمْ وَلَـٰكِن رَّسُولَ ٱللَّهِ وَخَاتَمَ ٱلنَّبِيِّـۧنَ

"Muhammad is not the father of any man among you, but he is the Messenger and the Seal of the Prophets" (*al-Ahzab* 40).

It is important to note that all of these messengers and prophets were simply human beings. They did not have any divine status or attribute.[1] They had no knowledge of the unseen except for that which Allah revealed to them. Their loftiest attribute is that of being a servant of Allah. Such is Allah's description of them in the Quran. Indeed, with respect to the Prophet Muhammad (peace be upon him), in reference to three of the greatest events in his life, Allah refers to him as His servant.[2]

Correct belief in the messengers comprises four aspects[3]: First, one must believe that the message of all of them is the truth from Allah. If a person today denies any single one of them who is confirmed in the Quran or authentic hadith, then he is in fact denying all of them. Allah says about the people of Noah,

كَذَّبَتْ قَوْمُ نُوحٍ ٱلْمُرْسَلِينَ

---

[1] This is obviously one of the ways by which the Christians strayed. Their raised their Prophet Jesus (peace be upon him) to a divine status while it is clear from their own book that he was simply a human being who prayed and beseeched God on a number of occasions.

[2] See *al-Furqaan* 1, *al-Isra* 1 and *al-Jinn* 119.

[3] Cf., ibn Uthaimin, ***Sharh Usool al-Imaan***, pp. 36-38.

"The people of Noah belied the messengers" (*al-Shuara* 105). However, Noah was the first messenger. This implies that, in essence, if a person denies one messenger, he is in fact denying all of them since their message is essentially one and consistent.

Therefore, the so-called followers of Jesus who refuse to follow the Prophet Muhammad (peace be upon him) are actually denying their belief in Jesus as even in their own gospels there are plenty of signs that another messenger would come, but they do not wish to recognize these signs. Allah has referred to such aspects in the following verses,

ٱلَّذِينَ ءَاتَيْنَٰهُمُ ٱلْكِتَٰبَ يَعْرِفُونَهُۥ كَمَا يَعْرِفُونَ أَبْنَآءَهُمْ ۖ وَإِنَّ فَرِيقًا مِّنْهُمْ لَيَكْتُمُونَ ٱلْحَقَّ وَهُمْ يَعْلَمُونَ

"Those [Jews and Christians] to whom We gave the Scripture recognize him as they recognize their sons. But, verily, a party of them conceal the truth while they know it" (*al-Baqara* 146).

ٱلَّذِينَ يَتَّبِعُونَ ٱلرَّسُولَ ٱلنَّبِىَّ ٱلْأُمِّىَّ ٱلَّذِى يَجِدُونَهُۥ مَكْتُوبًا عِندَهُمْ فِى ٱلتَّوْرَىٰةِ وَٱلْإِنجِيلِ

"Those who follow the Messenger, the prophet who can neither read or write, whom they find written in the Torah and the Gospel…" (*al-Araaf* 157).

Hence, the Prophet (peace be upon him) said,

وَالَّذِي نَفْسُ مُحَمَّدٍ بِيَدِهِ لا يَسْمَعُ بِي أَحَدٌ مِنْ هَذِهِ الأُمَّةِ يَهُودِيٌّ وَلا نَصْرَانِيٌّ ثُمَّ يَمُوتُ وَلَمْ يُؤْمِنْ بِالَّذِي أُرْسِلْتُ بِهِ إِلاَّ كَانَ مِنْ أَصْحَابِ النَّارِ

"By the One in whose Hand is the soul of Muhammad, there will be no Jew or Christian of this nation[1] who hears of me and then dies without believing in that with which I have been sent except that he will be one of the inhabitants of the Hell-fire." (Recorded by Muslim.)

This is one of the aspects that distinguishes Muslims from the earlier peoples. Muslims believe in all of the prophets. However, the others refused some— whether it be the Jews rejecting Jesus (peace be upon him) or the Jews and Christians rejecting the Prophet Muhammad (peace be upon him)— although, in reality, they had no grounds whatsoever to refuse the later prophet. Each messenger came with clear signs and evidence. Their rejection by the people could only be based on arrogance, ignorance or hostility to the truth.

Second, one must believe in all of the Messengers mentioned by name in the Quran or sunnah. As for those not mentioned, one must believe in them at a general level[2], knowing that Allah has sent many messengers although not all of them are mentioned by name in the Quran or hadith. Allah has stated in the Quran,

---

[1] Meaning everyone from the time of the Prophet (peace be upon him) until the Day of Judgment. They are all the Prophet's Nation because they are all obliged to believe in him and follow him.

[2] At the same time, no one can claim that a person, for example, Buddha, was a prophet because there is no evidence from the Quran and sunnah to affirm such a claim.

وَلَقَدْ أَرْسَلْنَا رُسُلًا مِّن قَبْلِكَ مِنْهُم مَّن قَصَصْنَا عَلَيْكَ وَمِنْهُم مَّن لَّمْ نَقْصُصْ عَلَيْكَ

"And indeed We have sent messengers before you. Of them, some We have related to you their story and some We have not related to you their story" (*Ghaafir* 78).

Third, one must believe in everything that they stated. They communicated their messages from Allah completely and properly. They exerted themselves to propagate Allah's message. They strove for the sake of Allah in the most complete manner. They were most knowledgeable of Allah and the best worshippers and servants of Allah.[1] The messengers "have been protected from attributing to Allah something of their own invention, judging according to their own desires, falling into major sins, and adding to or diminishing from the religion."[2]

Fourth, one must submit to, accept and act in accord with the law of the messenger who has been sent for his guidance. Allah says in the Quran,

وَمَآ أَرْسَلْنَا مِن رَّسُولٍ إِلَّا لِيُطَاعَ بِإِذْنِ ٱللَّهِ

"We sent no messenger but to be obeyed by Allah's leave" (*al-Nisaa* 64). With respect to the Prophet Muhammad (peace be upon him), Allah says in the verse after the verse quoted above,

فَلَا وَرَبِّكَ لَا يُؤْمِنُونَ حَتَّىٰ يُحَكِّمُوكَ فِيمَا شَجَرَ بَيْنَهُمْ ثُمَّ لَا يَجِدُوا۟ فِىٓ أَنفُسِهِمْ حَرَجًا مِّمَّا قَضَيْتَ وَيُسَلِّمُوا۟ تَسْلِيمًا

---

[1] Abdullah al-Muslih and Salaah al-Saawi, *Ma La Yasa'u al-Muslim Jahla* (Islamic Foundation of America, 1995), p. 59.

[2] Abdur-Rahmaan Abdul-Khaliq, *The General Prescripts of Belief in the Quran and Sunnah* (The Majliss of al-Haqq Publication Society, 1986), p. 18.

"But no, by your Lord, they can have no faith until they make you judge in all disputes between them, and find in themselves no resistance against your decisions, and accept them with full submission" (*al-Nisa* 65).

The believer should realize that the sending of messengers for the benefit and guidance of mankind is a great blessing from Allah. The knowledge that they conveyed is knowledge that is beyond the grasp of the human intellect by itself since it deals with matters of the unseen. Indeed, mankind is in more need of their guidance than they are in need of food and drink. If they are void of food and drink for any period of time, they will die, implying loss of this life. But if they are refusing Allah's guidance through the messengers, they will lose the everlasting bounties of the Hereafter.

"the Last Day"

"The Last Day" is called such because there will be no new day after it, as the people of Paradise shall be in their abode as will the people of Hell. Among its other names are "The Day of Resurrection," "The Reality," "The Event," "The Day of Judgment," and "The Overwhelming." This is the greatest day that mankind shall pass through. Indeed, it will be the gravest and most fearful day. A person's new life will be decided on that day. It will mark a new beginning for each and every soul. This new step may lead to eternal bliss or eternal damnation.[1]

Belief in the Last Day implies belief in everything that the Quran or the Prophet (peace be upon him) has stated about the events of that Day and thereafter. There are some general aspects (resurrection, judgment and reward, Paradise and Hell) that every Muslim should be aware of

---

[1] For Quranic/rational arguments for the existence of the Hereafter, see Idris, pp. 11-16.

and believe in with certainty. There are also more detailed aspects that the Quran or the Messenger of Allah (peace be upon him) mentioned. The more one has knowledge of that Day and its surrounding events, the greater the effect this belief will have on him. Hence, it is highly recommended for each individual Muslim to learn about the events that occur prior to and on the Day of Resurrection.

As recorded in *Sahih Muslim*, before the Day of Judgment and the destruction of this earth, Allah will send a wind softer than silk, coming from Yemen, that will take the souls of every individual who has even the slightest amount of faith in his heart. Therefore, the events of the end of the earth will only be lived through by the worst of people, those with no faith whatsoever.

One of the first events to occur is the sun rising from the West. At that time, all those people will declare their faith but it will be of no avail to them. Then the Horn shall be blown and all on this earth shall die. Allah says,

وَنُفِخَ فِى ٱلصُّورِ فَصَعِقَ مَن فِى ٱلسَّمَٰوَٰتِ وَمَن فِى ٱلْأَرْضِ إِلَّا مَن شَآءَ ٱللَّهُ

"And the trumpet will be blown, and all who are in the heavens and all who are on the earth will swoon away, except him whom Allah wills" (*al-Zumar* 68). This earth and heaven shall then be destroyed. After a period of forty— it is not known whether it is forty hours, days or years— a second Horn will be blown and the people will be resurrected:

وَنُفِخَ فِى ٱلصُّورِ فَإِذَا هُم مِّنَ ٱلْأَجْدَاثِ إِلَىٰ رَبِّهِمْ يَنسِلُونَ ﴿٥١﴾ قَالُوا۟ يَٰوَيْلَنَا مَنۢ بَعَثَنَا مِن مَّرْقَدِنَا ۜ هَٰذَا مَا وَعَدَ ٱلرَّحْمَٰنُ وَصَدَقَ ٱلْمُرْسَلُونَ

"And the Trumpet will be blown [the second blowing] and, behold, from the graves they will come out quickly to their Lord. They will say, 'Woe to us! Who has raised us up from our place of sleep?' [It will be said to them,] 'This is what the Most Beneficent [Allah] has promised, and the Messengers spoke the truth'" (*Ya-Seen* 51-52).

According to ibn Uthaimin,[1] belief in the last day encompasses three aspects. First is belief in the Resurrection: after the Second Blowing of the Horn, the people will be resurrected in front of Allah. They shall be naked, barefoot and uncircumcised.[2] Allah says,

كَمَا بَدَأْنَآ أَوَّلَ خَلْقٍ نُّعِيدُهُۥ

وَعْدًا عَلَيْنَآ إِنَّا كُنَّا فَٰعِلِينَ

"As We began the first creation, We shall repeat it. [It is] a promise binding on Us. Truly, We shall do it" (*al-Anbiyaa* 104).

The resurrection is going to be in the same body that the person had in this worldly life. Ibn Uthaimin has pointed out the wisdom and importance of this: "If it were a new creation, it would mean that the body that performed the sins in this world would be safe from any punishment. To come with a new body and have that body punished goes against what is just. Hence, the texts and rational argument indicate that the [person] resurrected is not a new [creation] but a return [of the old creation]."[3] He also points out that Allah has the ability to recreate the bodies even after they have disintegrated. Humans may not be able to understand how exactly that is possible— like so many other aspects that humans cannot fathom— but Allah has stated it and a believer knows full well that it is true and well within Allah's ability to do so.

The second aspect is belief in the accounting or reckoning of the deeds and the reward/punishment for those

---

[1] Cf., Ibn Uthaimin, *Sharh Usool al-Imaan*, pp. 40-41.

[2] As the Prophet (peace be upon him) stated in a hadith recorded by al-Bukhari and Muslim.

[3] Ibn Uthaimin, *Majmu*, vol. 3, p. 174.

deeds. This aspect is mentioned and stressed in numerous places in the Quran. Here are a couple of examples:

إِنَّ إِلَيْنَآ إِيَابَهُمْ ﴿٢٥﴾ ثُمَّ إِنَّ عَلَيْنَا حِسَابَهُم ﴿٢٦﴾

"Verily, to Us will be their return. Then, verily, upon Us will be their reckoning" (*al-Ghaashiya* 25-26).

وَنَضَعُ ٱلْمَوَٰزِينَ ٱلْقِسْطَ لِيَوْمِ ٱلْقِيَـٰمَةِ فَلَا تُظْلَمُ نَفْسٌ شَيْـًٔا ۖ وَإِن كَانَ
مِثْقَالَ حَبَّةٍ مِّنْ خَرْدَلٍ أَتَيْنَا بِهَا ۗ وَكَفَىٰ بِنَا حَـٰسِبِينَ

"And We shall set up balances of justice on the Day of Resurrection, then none will be dealt with unjustly in anything. And if there be the weight of a mustard seed, We will bring it. And sufficient are We as reckoners" (*al-Anbiyaa* 47).

Allah has made it clear that all deeds will be weighed on the Day of Judgment. Allah says,

وَٱلْوَزْنُ يَوْمَئِذٍ ٱلْحَقُّ ۚ فَمَن ثَقُلَتْ مَوَٰزِينُهُۥ فَأُو۟لَـٰٓئِكَ هُمُ ٱلْمُفْلِحُونَ ﴿٨﴾ وَمَنْ خَفَّتْ مَوَٰزِينُهُۥ فَأُو۟لَـٰٓئِكَ ٱلَّذِينَ خَسِرُوٓا۟ أَنفُسَهُم بِمَا كَانُوا۟
بِـَٔايَـٰتِنَا يَظْلِمُونَ

"And the weighing on that Day will be the true weighing. So as for those whose scale [of good deeds] will be heavy, they will be the successful. And as for those whose scale will be light, those are they who will lose their ownselves because they denied and rejected Our Signs" (*al-Araaf* 8-9).

Once again, some people might ask, "Actions are like what the philosophers call accidents, without weight or mass, how can they be weighed?" The answer is that Allah has the ability to weigh them. No human has any conception of the Scales themselves that will be used on that day, not to speak of the weights of particular deeds.

Allah will weigh them and He is just. Each deed will weigh exactly what it is truly worth according to Allah's scale.[1]

One should always recall that the reward Allah gives to His servants is an act of His mercy as He rewards them more than what their deeds entail. However, Allah's punishment is out of His justice and He does not punish anyone more than what he deserves.

The third essential aspect of belief in the Last Day is belief in Heaven and Hell. Heaven is the eternal abode or reward for the believers. Hell is the eternal abode of punishment for the disbelievers. The stronger opinion is that they both are in existence at this present time and they both shall exist forever. They are not simply states of mind as some non-Muslims and a few heretical Muslims believe. Allah and His Messenger made mention of them and have described them clearly and in unequivocal terms. There is absolutely no room for any Muslim to deny their existence or their descriptions.

About Heaven, for example, Allah has said,

إِنَّ ٱلَّذِينَ ءَامَنُواْ وَعَمِلُواْ ٱلصَّٰلِحَٰتِ أُوْلَٰٓئِكَ هُمْ خَيْرُ ٱلْبَرِيَّةِ ۝٧
جَزَآؤُهُمْ عِندَ رَبِّهِمْ جَنَّٰتُ عَدْنٍ تَجْرِي مِن تَحْتِهَا ٱلْأَنْهَٰرُ خَٰلِدِينَ
فِيهَآ أَبَدًا ۖ رَّضِيَ ٱللَّهُ عَنْهُمْ وَرَضُواْ عَنْهُ ۚ ذَٰلِكَ لِمَنْ خَشِيَ رَبَّهُۥ

"Verily, those who believe and do righteous deeds, they are the best of creatures. Their reward with their Lord is gardens of eternity, underneath which rivers flow, they will abide therein forever. Allah being well-pleased with them and they with Him. That is for him who fears his Lord" (*al-Bayyina* 7-8).

فَلَا تَعْلَمُ نَفْسٌ مَّآ أُخْفِيَ لَهُم مِّن قُرَّةِ أَعْيُنٍ جَزَآءًۢ بِمَا كَانُواْ يَعْمَلُونَ

---

[1] Ibn Uthaimin, *Majmu*, vol. 3, p. 179. He also discusses the question of whether there is just one scale or numerous scales.

"No person knows what joy is kept hidden for him as a reward for what they used to do" (*al-Sajdah* 17).

Concerning Hell, for example, Allah has said,

إِنَّآ أَعۡتَدۡنَا
لِلظَّٰلِمِينَ نَارًا أَحَاطَ بِهِمۡ سُرَادِقُهَاۚ وَإِن يَسۡتَغِيثُواْ يُغَاثُواْ بِمَآءٖ كَٱلۡمُهۡلِ
يَشۡوِي ٱلۡوُجُوهَۚ بِئۡسَ ٱلشَّرَابُ وَسَآءَتۡ مُرۡتَفَقًا

"Verily, We have prepared for the wrongdoers a Fire whose walls will be surrounding them. And if they ask for relief, they will be granted water like boiling oil that will scald their faces. Terrible the drink and evil a resting place" (*al-Kahf* 29).

إِنَّ ٱللَّهَ لَعَنَ ٱلۡكَٰفِرِينَ وَأَعَدَّ لَهُمۡ سَعِيرًا ﴿٦٤﴾ خَٰلِدِينَ فِيهَآ أَبَدٗاۖ لَّا
يَجِدُونَ وَلِيّٗا وَلَا نَصِيرٗا ﴿٦٥﴾ يَوۡمَ تُقَلَّبُ وُجُوهُهُمۡ فِي ٱلنَّارِ يَقُولُونَ
يَٰلَيۡتَنَآ أَطَعۡنَا ٱللَّهَ وَأَطَعۡنَا ٱلرَّسُولَا۠

"Verily, Allah has cursed the disbelievers and has prepared for them a flaming Fire. They will abide therein forever and they will find neither a protector or a helper. On the Day when their faces would be turned and rolled in all sides of the Fire, they will say, 'Oh, would that we had obeyed Allah and obeyed the Messenger'" (*al-Ahzaab* 64-66).

Aspects of the Grave

Ibn Taimiya points out that belief in the Last Day also includes belief in everything that shall occur to a person after his death and before the Day of Resurrection.[1] This includes the trial in the grave and the pleasure or punishment in the grave. The trial in the grave is mentioned

---

[1] Quoted in ibn Uthaimin, *Majmu*, vol. 3, p. 169.

in an authentic hadith recorded by al-Tirmidhi. It states that two angels, al-Munkar and al-Nakeer, come to the person and ask him: What did you use to say about this man [meaning the Prophet (peace be upon him)]? Other narrations mention two angels coming and asking three questions: Who is your Lord? What is your religion? Who is your prophet?[1]

The punishment and reward in the grave are what is referred to in the following two verses of the Quran. The first is a description of the blessings coming through the angels before the believers enter Paradise. The second is in reference to the punishment wrongdoers receive before the day of Judgment:

إِنَّ ٱلَّذِينَ قَالُوا۟ رَبُّنَا ٱللَّهُ ثُمَّ ٱسْتَقَـٰمُوا۟ تَتَنَزَّلُ عَلَيْهِمُ ٱلْمَلَـٰٓئِكَةُ أَلَّا تَخَافُوا۟
وَلَا تَحْزَنُوا۟ وَأَبْشِرُوا۟ بِٱلْجَنَّةِ ٱلَّتِى كُنتُمْ تُوعَدُونَ

"Verily, those who say our Lord is Allah and then they stand straight [along the straight path], on them the angels will descend [at the time of their death, saying,] 'Fear you not, nor grieve! But receive the glad tidings of the Paradise which you have been promised'" (*Fussilat* 30).

وَلَوْ تَرَىٰٓ إِذِ ٱلظَّـٰلِمُونَ فِى
غَمَرَٰتِ ٱلْمَوْتِ وَٱلْمَلَـٰٓئِكَةُ بَاسِطُوٓا۟ أَيْدِيهِمْ أَخْرِجُوٓا۟ أَنفُسَكُمُ ٱلْيَوْمَ
تُجْزَوْنَ عَذَابَ ٱلْهُونِ بِمَا كُنتُمْ تَقُولُونَ عَلَى ٱللَّهِ غَيْرَ ٱلْحَقِّ وَكُنتُمْ عَنْ
ءَايَـٰتِهِۦ تَسْتَكْبِرُونَ

"If you could but see when the wrongdoers are in the agonies of death, while the angels are stretching forth their hands [saying], 'Deliver your souls. This day you shall be

[1] For the texts of these hadith, see al-Albani, *Sahih al-Jami al-Sagheer*, vol. 1, p. 186 and vol. 1, p. 344.

recompensed with the torment of degradation because of what you used to utter against Allah that was not the truth. And you used to arrogantly reject His signs with disrespect'" (*al-Anaam* 93).

Many people ask the following question about the punishment in the grave: Is the punishment in the grave a punishment that afflicts the soul only or does it also afflict the body, which over time decomposes? Ibn Uthaimin has answered this question by saying,

> The punishment in the grave is first and foremost upon the soul and, perhaps, it also reaches the body. However, it being foremost upon the soul does not mean that the body does not get any of it. In fact, it must receive some of that punishment or pleasure, even if it is not direct. Know that the punishment or pleasure in the grave is the opposite of the punishment or pleasure in this world. The punishment or pleasure in this world is [first and foremost] upon the body and it then affects the soul. In the period between death and the Day of Judgment, the pleasure or punishment is upon the soul and it also has an affect upon the body.[1]

Ibn Uthaimin also addresses the following question: How can one say that the grave squeezes the body of a disbeliever, to the point that his ribs are crushed[2], while if the grave is uncovered one will find no change in the coffin or the person? Ibn Uthaimin responded by saying,

> First and foremost, the punishment of the grave is upon the soul. It is not something physically experienced by the body. If it were something physically experienced and witnessed upon the body, it would not be one of the matters of faith in

---

[1] Ibn Uthaimin, *Majmu*, vol. 3, p. 173. Of course, in Paradise and Hell, the pleasure and punishment will be both on the soul and the body.

[2] These aspects are all stated in authentic hadith of the Prophet (peace be upon him). For more details, see Umar al-Ashqar, *Al-Yaum al-Akhir: al-Qiyaamah al-Sughra* (Kuwait: Maktab al-Falaah, 1986), pp. 41-83.

> the Unseen. And there would be no benefit to such belief. However, it is from the matters of the Unseen that is related to the soul. A person may see in a dream, while he is sleeping in his bed, that he is standing, going, coming, beating someone or being beaten. He might even see, while he is sleeping in his bed, that he traveled to perform *Umra*, circumambulated the Kaaba and went between the two mounts of Safa and Marwa, shaved or trimmed his hair and then returned to his homeland. All the while, his body is in his bed and does not change at all. Therefore, the affairs of the soul are different from that of the body.[1]

There are additional detailed aspects related to the Hereafter that a believer should learn about and believe in. Due to space limitations, they cannot be discussed in detail here.[2] These matters include: (1) The Fount or Cistern of the Messenger of Allah (peace be upon him)[3]; (2) The different intercessions[4]; (3) The distribution of the books of deeds; (4) Passing over the *siraat* (bridge) over Hell[5]; and (5) The entrance into Paradise and Hell with all of its related aspects.

Importance of Proper Belief in the Last Day

The belief in and knowledge of the great events of the Last Day and the Hereafter should have some very profound effects on the individual— if he takes the time to remember and seriously think about that Day. First, it

---

[1] Ibn Uthaimin, *Majmu*, vol. 3, p. 173.

[2] Although not used as a reference here due to its detail, Salaam (pp. 120-145) has provided an excellent yet concise discussion of many of the aspects of the Hereafter

[3] For a discussion in English on this topic, see Abu Muhammad al-Hasan al-Barbahaaree, *Explanation of the Creed* (Birmingham, UK: Al-Haneef Publications, 1995), p. 36.

[4] See al-Barbahaaree, p. 37.

[5] See al-Barbahaaree, p. 38.

should make the believer rush to perform good deeds, knowing the reward that may be in store for them. The bounties of Paradise are greater than what any eye has seen or even what any mind could imagine. First and foremost, this great reward includes the pleasure of Allah and the opportunity to see Him in the Hereafter. If a person could possibly be conscious of this aspect at every moment of his life, he would be anxiously seeking and searching for any good deed he could perform.

Second, the threat of punishment should sway the person from committing any sin, no matter how "light". No sin performed in this world could be worth the punishment it could bring about in the Hereafter. Furthermore, by committing sins, the person may also be earning the displeasure of Allah, his Lord, Creator and Beloved.

Third, according to ibn Uthaimin, the reckoning and justice of the Day of Judgment should bring comfort and solace to the heart of the believer. It is normal for humans to have a hatred for injustice. In this world, it appears to occur often. Those who cheat and who are unethical many times get ahead in this world without ever suffering for what they have done. However, that is only because, on a grand scale, this world is not the final place for judgment, reward and punishment. They will not escape the evil that they are doing. The good deeds of a person will also not be in vain, as they sometimes seem to be in this world. The time will come for all those matters to be settled and to be settled in a just manner. And that time is the Day of Judgment.[1]

[1] Ibn Uthaimin, *Sharh Usool al-Imaan*, p. 46.

"and to believe in the divine decree (*al-Qadar*), [both] the good and the evil thereof."

The Restatement of "to believe in"

The first aspect that one may note is that the Messenger of Allah (peace be upon him) repeated the word, "to believe in," before mentioning divine destiny (*al-Qadar*). The Messenger of Allah (peace be upon him) did not repeat this word before any of the other articles of faith. Obviously, there must have been some reason for this. The scholars have discussed and differed concerning the reasoning behind this.

One view, expressed by al-Qaari, is that there is some "verbal distance" between the beginning of the sentence and the last article of faith. Hence, the word was repeated to state that *al-Qadar* is also something that must be believed in.[1] In this author's view, this argument does not sound very convincing.

Al-Ubayy states that it has been mentioned that the reason behind the repeating of the word, "to believe in," is that the Messenger of Allah (peace be upon him) knew that the people would later differ about *al-Qadar*.[2] Indeed, the concept of *al-Qadar* is one that has led to a great deal of division and difference of opinion in the history of Islam. Some groups openly denied its existence completely. Hence, the Messenger of Allah (peace be upon him) emphasized that it is an essential part of *imaan* to believe in *al-Qadar*.

---

[1] Al-Qaari, vol. 1, p. 58.
[2] Al-Ubayy, vol. 1, p. 67.

A third view is given by al-Mudaabaghi. He states that the governing word, "to believe in," has been repeated due to the importance of the matter of *al-Qadar*. Its importance is not in the manner just described in the second view, but because it is something concerning which only those who are truly knowledgeable of the religion of Allah realize. They alone understand its importance and the fact that one must believe in it. This is different from the other articles of faith that are, in general, known and recognized by all Muslims.[1]

Belief in *al-Qadar*

The next and final article of faith mentioned by the Prophet (peace be upon him) is belief in "divine decree" or *al-Qadar*. Idris discusses the meaning of this word and states,

> The original meaning of the word *Qadar* is specified measure or amount, whether of quantities or qualities. It has many other usages which branch out from this core. Thus *yuqad-dir* means, among other things, to measure or decide the quantity, quality, position, etc., of something before you actually make it. And it is this latter sense which interests us here.[2]

It is obligatory upon every Muslim to believe in the concept of *Qadar* or Divine Decree. In fact, this hadith of Jibreel was passed on by Abdullah ibn Umar when some people came to him telling him that there had appeared a people who were rejecting *Qadar*. The beginning of the narration in *Sahih Muslim* is as follows:

---

[1] Hasan al-Mudaabaghi, *Haashiyah*, on the margin of al-Haitami, *Fath*, p. 71. He also mentions the first view stated by al-Qaari above.
[2] Idris, p. 24.

It is narrated on the authority of Yahya ibn Yamur that the first man who discussed *Qadar* in Basra was Ma'bad al-Juhani. I [Yahya] along with Humaid ibn Abdul Rahman al-Himyari set out for pilgrimage or *Umrah* and said, "If it should so happen that we come into contact with anyone of the Companions of the Messenger of Allah (peace be upon him), we shall ask him about what is being talked about concerning *Qadar*." Unexpectedly, we came across 'Abdullah ibn 'Umar ibn al-Khattab while he was entering the mosque. I and my friend surrounded him. One of us was on his right side and the other stood on his left. I expected that my friend would authorize me to speak [for both of us]. Therefore, I said, "O Abu Abdul Rahman [Abdullah ibn Umar], there have appeared some persons in our land who recite the Quran and pursue knowledge." Then, after explaining their affairs, I said, "They claim that there is no such thing as Divine Decree and all events are new [to everyone, including Allah]." [Abdullah ibn Umar] then said, "When you happen to meet such persons, tell them that I have nothing to do with them and they have nothing to do with me. And, verily, they are in no way responsible for my belief." Abdullah ibn Umar then swore by Allah and said, "If any of them [who does not believe in Divine Decree] had with him gold equal to the bulk of the Mountain of Uhud and then he should spend it [in the way of Allah], Allah would not accept that from him unless he affirms his faith in Divine Decree."[1] He then said, "My father Umar ibn al-Khattab told

[1] Ibn Hubairah points out that this hadith demonstrates that some people may read the Quran and study a great deal of knowledge, however, they have a deficiency in their beliefs and they follow heresies. Therefore, their deeds will not be raised to Allah whatsoever and their studying of the religion will not be accepted by Allah. Their evil or false beliefs will prevent their deeds from being accepted. This is because the beliefs are the foundations of one's religion and only a practice that has the proper foundation is pleasing to Allah. See Al-Wazeer ibn Hubaira, *Al-Ifsaah an Maani al-Sihaah* (Riyadh: Dar al-Watn, 1996), vol. 1, p. 299.

me..." [He then went on to narrated the hadith of Jibreel.][1]

Ibn al-Qayyim shows that there are four "levels" or aspects of belief in *Qadàr*. If one does not believe in these four aspects, he does not have the correct or proper belief in Allah.[2]

The first level is belief in Allah's knowledge of everything, both of universals and particulars, before its existence. This is related to both, what is sometimes referred to as, the actions of Allah, such as producing rain, giving life and so forth, as well as the actions of human beings. Allah has foreknowledge of all of the deeds of the creation according to His ever-existing knowledge that He is described as having eternally. This includes His knowledge of all their affairs with respect to obedience, disobedience, sustenance and life-spans.

This aspect can be concluded from many Quranic verses, including:

﴿وَعِندَهُۥ مَفَاتِحُ ٱلْغَيْبِ لَا يَعْلَمُهَآ إِلَّا هُوَ ۚ وَيَعْلَمُ مَا فِى ٱلْبَرِّ وَٱلْبَحْرِ ۚ وَمَا

تَسْقُطُ مِن وَرَقَةٍ إِلَّا يَعْلَمُهَا وَلَا حَبَّةٍ فِى ظُلُمَٰتِ ٱلْأَرْضِ وَلَا رَطْبٍ وَلَا

يَابِسٍ إِلَّا فِى كِتَٰبٍ مُّبِينٍ

"And with Him are the keys of the Unseen. None knows them but He. And He knows whatever there is on the earth and in the sea; not a leaf falls, but he knows it. There is not a grain in the darkness of the earth nor anything fresh or dry, but is written in a Clear Record" (*al-Anaam* 59).

The second level of belief in *Qadar* is belief in Allah's recording of all things before He created the heavens and the earth. Hence, Allah not only knew and

---

[1] Siddiqui, *Sahih Muslim*, vol. 1, pp. 1-2 (with modifications).
[2] See Shams al-Din ibn al-Qayyim, *Shifa al-Aleel fi Masa`il al-Qadha wa al-Qadar wa al-Hikma wa al-Taleel* (Beirut: Dar al-Marifah, n.d.), pp. 29-65.

knows what will happen, but Allah has also recorded this information in the Preserved Table (*al-Lauh al-Mahfoodh*). Such an act is not difficult for Allah whatsoever. Allah says,

أَلَمْ تَعْلَمْ أَنَّ ٱللَّهَ يَعْلَمُ مَا فِى ٱلسَّمَآءِ وَٱلْأَرْضِ ۗ إِنَّ ذَٰلِكَ فِى كِتَـٰبٍ ۚ إِنَّ ذَٰلِكَ عَلَى ٱللَّهِ يَسِيرٌ

"Don't you know that Allah knows all that is in heaven and on earth? Verily, it is all in the Book. Verily, that is easy for Allah" (*al-Hajj* 70). Allah also says,

مَآ أَصَابَ مِن مُّصِيبَةٍ فِى ٱلْأَرْضِ وَلَا فِىٓ أَنفُسِكُمْ إِلَّا فِى كِتَـٰبٍ مِّن قَبْلِ أَن نَّبْرَأَهَآ ۚ إِنَّ ذَٰلِكَ عَلَى ٱللَّهِ يَسِيرٌ

"No calamity occurs on the earth or among yourselves but it is inscribed in the Book [of Decrees] before We bring it into existence. Verily, that is easy for Allah" (*al-Hadeed* 22). Furthermore, the Prophet (peace be upon him) said,

كَتَبَ اللَّهُ مَقَادِيرَ الْخَلائِقِ قَبْلَ أَنْ يَخْلُقَ السَّمَاوَاتِ وَالأَرْضَ بِخَمْسِينَ أَلْفَ سَنَةٍ قَالَ وَعَرْشُهُ عَلَى الْمَاءِ

"Allah recorded the measures of the creation five thousand years before He created the heavens and the earth." He also said, "And His Throne was over the water." (Recorded by Muslim.)

Ibn al-Qayyim points out that there are actually four different types of "pre-recording" or "pre-determination" of future events.[1] These four are the following: (a) The pre-existent measure by the knowledge of Allah that is recorded in the Preserved Tablet; (b) Allah's decree concerning the

[1] See ibn al-Qayyim, *Shifa*, pp. 6-24.

life of an individual while he is still a fetus in the womb of his mother. This includes the person's sustenance, lifespan, deeds and whether he will be successful or miserable. (c) A yearly determination that occurs on *Lailat al-Qadr* which measures what will occur during the year.[1] (d) A daily pre-measuring for everything that occurs. According to ibn al-Qayyim and others[2], based on some reports recorded by al-Tabarani and others, this is what the following verse is in reference to,

كُلَّ يَوْمٍ هُوَ فِي شَأْنٍ

"Every day He has a matter to bring forth" (*al-Rahmaan* 29). Allah knows best.

The third level is to believe in Allah's decreeing of everything that is in existence, and if He does not will something, it can never come into existence. Once again, this also refers to all things. It refers to Allah's actions of giving life, sustenance and so forth; and it also includes all of the acts performed by human beings. Nothing can be done unless Allah decrees it and allows it to occur. A person may intend or try, for example, to shoot and kill another person but such can only occur if Allah decrees it. The person may take all the necessary steps but if Allah does not will it to occur, it will not occur. In the case just mentioned, Allah may will the gun to jam or the shooter's hand to flinch and miss his target and so forth.

This aspect of *Qadar* may also be concluded from numerous pieces of evidence. For example, Allah says,

---

[1] ***Surah al-Dukhaan***, verses 3-4, are in reference to this recording.

[2] This last type is also mentioned in Abdul Rahman al-Mahmood, ***al-Qadha wa al-Qadar fi Dhau al-Kitaab wa al-Sunnah wa Madhaahib al-Naas feeh*** (Riyadh: Dar al-Nashr al-Dauli, 1994), p. 51; Muhammad al-Hammad, ***al-Imaan bi-l-Qadha wa al-Qadar*** (Riyadh: Dar al-Watn, 1416 A.H.), p. 71.

وَلَوْ شَآءَ ٱللَّهُ مَا ٱقْتَتَلَ ٱلَّذِينَ مِنۢ بَعْدِهِم مِّنۢ بَعْدِ مَا جَآءَتْهُمُ
ٱلْبَيِّنَٰتُ وَلَٰكِنِ ٱخْتَلَفُوا۟ فَمِنْهُم مَّنْ ءَامَنَ وَمِنْهُم مَّن كَفَرَ ۚ وَلَوْ شَآءَ ٱللَّهُ
مَا ٱقْتَتَلُوا۟ وَلَٰكِنَّ ٱللَّهَ يَفْعَلُ مَا يُرِيدُ

"If Allah had willed, succeeding generations would not have fought against each other, after clear verses of Allah had come to them. But they differed, some of them believing and others disbelieving. If Allah had willed, they would not have fought against one another, but Allah does what He likes" (*al-Baqara* 253). Allah also says,

إِنْ هُوَ إِلَّا ذِكْرٌ لِّلْعَٰلَمِينَ
﴿٢٧﴾ لِمَن شَآءَ مِنكُمْ أَن يَسْتَقِيمَ ﴿٢٨﴾ وَمَا تَشَآءُونَ إِلَّآ أَن يَشَآءَ ٱللَّهُ رَبُّ
ٱلْعَٰلَمِينَ

"Verily, this [Quran] is no less than a reminder to whomsoever among you who wills to walk straight. And you will not will such unless [it be] that Allah wills, the Lord of the Worlds" (*al-Takweer* 27-29).

Ibn Uthaimin also offers a rational argument for this aspect of belief in *Qadar*. He says that it must be accepted that Allah is the Owner, Master and Controller of this creation. Hence, it cannot be the case, as long as everything is under His Control and part of His Dominion, that something occurs in His Dominion that He does not want to happen. Therefore, everything that occurs in His creation is by His Will. Nothing could ever occur unless He willed it. Otherwise, His control and mastery over His dominion would be deficient and lacking, as things would be occurring in His dominion that either He did not will to occur or they occurred without His knowledge. These hypotheses are unacceptable.[1]

The fourth level of belief in *Qadar* is the belief in Allah's creating of everything, bringing of everything into existence and making everything be. This aspect is also demonstrated by numerous verses in the Quran, including:

تَبَارَكَ ٱلَّذِى نَزَّلَ ٱلْفُرْقَانَ عَلَىٰ عَبْدِهِۦ لِيَكُونَ لِلْعَٰلَمِينَ نَذِيرًا ﴿١﴾ ٱلَّذِى لَهُۥ مُلْكُ ٱلسَّمَٰوَٰتِ وَٱلْأَرْضِ وَلَمْ يَتَّخِذْ وَلَدًا وَلَمْ يَكُن لَّهُۥ شَرِيكٌ فِى ٱلْمُلْكِ وَخَلَقَ كُلَّ شَىْءٍ فَقَدَّرَهُۥ تَقْدِيرًا

"Blessed be He who sent down the Criterion to His slave [Muhammad] that he may be a warner to the Worlds. He to whom belongs the dominion of the heavens and the earth, and who has begotten no offspring and for whom there is no partner in the dominion. He has created everything, and has measured it exactly according to its due measurements" (*al-Furqaan* 1-2). Also,

ٱللَّهُ خَٰلِقُ كُلِّ شَىْءٍ

"Allah has created everything" (*al-Zumar* 62). Another verse states,

إِنَّا كُلَّ شَىْءٍ خَلَقْنَٰهُ بِقَدَرٍ

"Verily, We created all things with Divine Pre-ordainment" (*al-Qamar* 49). Allah also says,

وَٱللَّهُ خَلَقَكُمْ وَمَا تَعْمَلُونَ

"And Allah has created you and what you make" (*al-Saaffaat* 96).

Ibn Uthaimin has explained this point by saying,

[1] Ibn Uthaimin, *Majmuat*, vol. 3, p. 195.

Everything is a creation of Allah. Even the deeds of mankind are creations of Allah. Although they are by [man's] free choice and will, they are creations of Allah. This is because every act of a human is the result of two aspects: a definitive will [to do the act] and the complete ability [to do the act]. For example, suppose that in front of you is a stone weighing twenty pounds. I say to you, "Lift this stone," and you say, "I don't want to lift it." In this case, your lack of will has prevented you from lifting the stone. If I said a second time to you, "Lift that stone," and you said, "Yes, I will listen and do what you have said." In this case, if you wanted to lift it but you were not capable of lifting it, you would not have lifted it because you did not have the capability to do so. If I said to you a third time, "Lift that stone," and you complied and lifted it above your head, that was because you had the ability and the will to do it.

All of our deeds that we perform[1], therefore, are the result of a definitive will and complete ability. The one who created that ability and will is Allah. If Allah had made you paralyzed, you would not have the ability. If you turned your attention to some other deed, you would not have done it...

Therefore, we say: All of the actions of humans are created by Allah. This is because they are the result of definitive will and complete ability. The one who created that will and ability is Allah. The way in which Allah is the creator of that will and capability is that the will and ability are two characteristics of the one who wants something and the one who has ability but the one who created that person with that ability was Allah. The One who created the person who has specific

---

[1] This should probably say, "All of our voluntary deeds…" because there are some deeds that humans perform involuntarily and without a definitive will.

> characteristics is also the one who created those characteristics. This makes the matter clear and shows that the actions of human beings are the creation of Allah.[1]

Actually, there are a number of questions and misconceptions that have arisen surrounding the concept of *Qadar*. Due to space limitations, they cannot be dealt with in detail here. However, in a not-too-lengthy passage, Jaafar Sheikh Idris has adequately dealt with a number of such issues. He wrote,

> God decided to create man as a free agent, but He knows (and how can He not know?) before creating every man how he is going to use his free will; what, for example, his reaction would be when a Prophet clarifies God's message to him... "But if we are free to use our will," a Qadari[2] might say, "we may use it in ways that contradict God's will, and in that case we would not be right in claiming that everything is willed or decreed by God." The Quran answers this question by reminding us that it was God who willed that we shall be willful, and it is He who allows us to use our will. [He then quotes *surah al-Insaan* 29-30.] "If so," says a Qadari, "He could have prevented us from doing evil." Yes, indeed he could, "Had God willed, He would have brought them all together to the guidance; if thy Lord had willed whoever is in the earth would have believed, all of them, all together" [*Yunus*, X:99]... But He had willed that men shall be free especially in regard to matters of belief and disbelief. "Say: 'The truth is from your Lord; so let whosoever will believe, and let whosoever will disbelieve" [*al-Kahf*, XVIII:29]...

---

[1] Ibn Uthaimin, *Majmuat*, vol. 3, pp. 196-197.

[2] A Qadari is one who denies the concept of *al-Qadar* altogether.

> "If our actions are willed by God," someone might say, "then they are in fact His actions." This objection is based on a confusion. God wills what we will in the sense of granting us the will to choose and enabling us to execute that will, i.e., He creates all that makes it possible for us to do it. He does not will it in the sense of doing it, otherwise it would be quite in order to say, when we drink or eat or sleep for instance, that God performed these actions. God creates them, He does not do or perform them. Another objection, based on another confusion, is that if God allows us to do evil, then He approves of it and likes it. But to will something in the sense of allowing a person to do it is one thing; and to approve of his action and commend it is quite another...[1]

"[both] the good and the evil thereof"

After mentioning, "the good and evil thereof," other narrations mention, "the sweet and the sour thereof". Al-Mudaabaghi states that the good is obedience to Allah while the evil is disobedience. The sweet is what is beloved to the soul, such as rain, health and so forth. The sour is what is displeasing to the soul, such as illness and disease.[2]

Ibn al-Qayyim points out that what is meant by "evil" is with respect to the human beings and not with respect to Allah. The "evil" is the result of the human's act of ignorance, wrong, oppression and sin. However, it was allowed and brought into being by Allah. But no evil is to be attributed to Allah because, with respect to Allah, the act is good and full of wisdom, as it must be a result of Allah's knowledge and wisdom. Any act of that nature must, in its

---

[1] Idris, pp. 25-27.
[2] Al-Mudaabaghi, p. 71.

essence, be good and cannot be pure evil. This is supported by the Prophet's hadith,

والشر ليس عليك

"Evil is not to be attributed to You." (Recorded by Muslim.) That is because every act that occurs is the result of some wisdom and goodness and can never be pure evil. The individual himself may think it otherwise, but in reality there is wisdom and good in everything that occurs in Allah's creation.[1]

Ibn Uthaimin gives an example illustrating this point. Allah says in the Quran,

ظَهَرَ ٱلْفَسَادُ فِى ٱلْبَرِّ وَٱلْبَحْرِ بِمَا كَسَبَتْ أَيْدِى ٱلنَّاسِ لِيُذِيقَهُم بَعْضَ ٱلَّذِى عَمِلُوا۟ لَعَلَّهُمْ يَرْجِعُونَ

"Evil has appeared on land and sea because of what the hands of men have earned, that Allah may make them taste a part of that which they have done, in order that they may return [by repenting]" (*al-Room* 41). In this verse, Allah states the evil (*fasaad*) that has appeared, the cause for it and its result. The evil (*fasaad*) and the cause of it are both evil (*sharr*). However, the goal of it is good: that Allah may make them taste a part of that which they have done, in order that they may return [by repenting]. Hence, there is a wisdom and a goal behind that *fasaad*. This goal and wisdom makes the entire action something good and not a pure evil.[2]

Pure evil, on the other hand, would be one in which there was no benefit or positive result related to it. Allah's

---

[1] See Abdul Aziz al-Rasheed, *al-Tanbeehaat al-Sanniya ala al-Aqeeda al-Waasitiya* (Dar al-Rasheed li-l-Nashr wa al-Tauzee'), p. 263.

[2] Muhammad ibn Uthaimin, *Sharh al-Aqeedah al-Waasitiyah* (al-Damaam, Saudi Arabia: Dar ibn al-Jauzi, 1415 A.H.), vol. 1, pp. 191-192. Also see, in the same work, vol. 1, pp. 70-72.

wisdom and knowledge preclude the existence of acts of that nature.[1]

The Fruits of Proper Belief in *al-Qadar*[2]

(1) When a person realizes that all things are under the control and decree of Allah, he is freeing his belief from any form of *shirk* or associating partners with Allah in His Lordship. There is truly only One Creator and Master of this creation. Nothing occurs except by His will and permission. When this is firmly in the heart of the person, he then also realizes that there is none worthy of praying to, seeking assistance from, relying upon, and so forth, except that one Lord. Hence, he directs all of his acts of worship toward that One who has decreed and determined all matters. Thus, both *tauheed al-rububiyah* and *tauheed al-uluhiyah* are correctly and completely fulfilled with the proper belief in *al-Qadar*.

(2) A person will put one's reliance upon Allah. A person should follow the outward "causes and effects" that one sees in this world. However, he must realize that those "causes and effects" will not bring about any ends unless Allah so wills them to do so. Hence, a believer never puts his complete trust and reliance upon his own actions or the worldly aspects that he might have some control over. Instead, he follows whatever causes he may know of which lead to a desired end and then he puts his trust in Allah to bring about that desired end.[3]

(3) Ibn Uthaimin argues that with proper belief in *al-Qadar*, one does not become arrogant and boastful. If he

[1] Even the creation of Satan is not a pure evil. See Umar al-Ashqar, "The Wisdom behind the Creation of Satan," *al-Basheer* (Vol. 2, No. 3, Sept.-Oct. 1988), pp. 13-22.

[2] In his work on *al-Qadar*, al-Hammad (pp. 31-44) mentions twenty-five benefits or fruits of the belief in *al-Qadar*. Here, just a few examples shall be given from a number of different sources.

[3] Cf., ibn Uthaimin, *Sharh Usool al-Imaan*, p. 58.

achieves any goal that he desired, he knows that such goal only came about because Allah, in His mercy, had decreed it for him. If Allah had so wished, He could have put many obstacles in his way and prevented him from reaching his goal. Therefore, instead of becoming full of himself and arrogant upon reaching his goal, the person who truly believes in *al-Qadar* becomes very thankful to Allah for bringing about that blessing.[1]

(4) The proper belief in *al-Qadar* brings about tranquillity and peace of mind. The person realizes that everything that occurs is according to Allah's Divine Decree. Furthermore, there is a wisdom behind everything Allah does. Hence, if the person loses a beloved or something of this world, he does not go insane, despair or give up hope. Instead, he realizes that such was the will of Allah that he must accept. He must also realize that such has occurred for a purpose. It did not occur haphazardly or accidentally, without any reason behind it. Allah has said,

مَآ أَصَابَ مِن مُّصِيبَةٍ فِى ٱلْأَرْضِ وَلَا فِىٓ أَنفُسِكُمْ إِلَّا فِى كِتَـٰبٍ مِّن قَبْلِ أَن
نَّبْرَأَهَآ ۚ إِنَّ ذَٰلِكَ عَلَى ٱللَّهِ يَسِيرٌ ﴿٢٢﴾ لِّكَيْلَا تَأْسَوْا۟ عَلَىٰ مَا فَاتَكُمْ وَلَا
تَفْرَحُوا۟ بِمَآ ءَاتَىٰكُمْ ۗ وَٱللَّهُ لَا يُحِبُّ كُلَّ مُخْتَالٍ فَخُورٍ

"No calamity befalls on the earth or in yourselves but it is inscribed in the Book [of Decrees] before We bring it into existence. Verily, that is easy for Allah. In order that you may not be sad over matters that you fail to achieve, nor rejoice because of that which has been given to you. And Allah likes not prideful boasters" (*al-Hadeed* 22).[2]

(5) Belief in *al-Qadar* gives a person strength and courage. He knows that Allah has recorded his life and his sustenance for him. Such comes only from Allah and is already decreed. Hence, he need not fear struggling and

[1] Cf., ibn Uthaimin, ***Sharh Usool al-Imaan***, p. 58.
[2] Cf., ibn Uthaimin, ***Sharh Usool al-Imaan***, p. 58.

fighting for the sake of Allah as the time of his death is already recorded. He need not fear anyone when it comes to his sustenance and provision as such come only from Allah and have been already recorded for him. No human can cut off his sustenance and livelihood if Allah has decreed that he shall continue to receive provisions and sustenance from some source.[1]

---

[1] Cf., Salaam, p. 173.

The Concept of *Ihsaan*

He said, "Tell me about *al-Ihsaan* (goodness)."

The Implication of "*al*" in *al-Ihsaan*

The *al* (ال) in *al-ihsaan* implies that the matter referred to is something known and recognized by the speakers: the known *ihsaan*. *Ihsaan* and its linguistic relatives are mentioned in a number of places in the Quran.[1] For example, Allah says,

لَيْسَ عَلَى ٱلَّذِينَ ءَامَنُوا۟ وَعَمِلُوا۟ ٱلصَّٰلِحَٰتِ جُنَاحٌ فِيمَا طَعِمُوٓا۟ إِذَا مَا ٱتَّقَوا۟ وَّءَامَنُوا۟ وَعَمِلُوا۟ ٱلصَّٰلِحَٰتِ ثُمَّ ٱتَّقَوا۟ وَّءَامَنُوا۟ ثُمَّ ٱتَّقَوا۟ وَّأَحْسَنُوا۟ ۗ وَٱللَّهُ يُحِبُّ ٱلْمُحْسِنِينَ

"On those who believe and do righteous good deeds, there is no sin for what they ate [in the past], if they fear Allah

[1] Ibn Rajab points out that, like the concepts of *islaam* and *imaan*, *ihsaan* is sometimes mentioned by itself and is sometimes mentioned in conjunction with *islaam* and *imaan*. When mentioned by itself, it includes the aspects of *islaam* and *imaan*. When mentioned in conjunction with these two terms, it has its own special connotation. See Abdul Rahman ibn Rajab, *Jaami al-Uloom wa al-Hikm* (Beirut: Muassasat al-Risaalah, 1991), vol. 1, pp. 125-126.

and believe and do righteous deeds, and again fear Allah and believe, and once again fear Allah and did good deeds with *ihsaan* (perfection). And Allah loves the good-doers (*muhsineen*)" (*al-Maidah* 93). The *al* might imply that it is that concept that is being referred to. The Angel Jibreel asked about it so that the people would realize how great and important a concept it is.[1] On the other hand, others state that it is not referring to that known concept but it is referring to *ikhlaas* (purity of action).[2]

However, the first interpretation is more apparent. It implies that there are three levels in Islam: the level of *Islaam*, the level of *Imaan* and the level of *Ihsaan*, as was alluded to in the discussion on the concept of *Imaan*.

A General Conception of *Ihsaan*

The lexical meaning of *ihsaan* implies doing well, doing goodness, behaving with others in a goodly manner. It is the opposite of causing harm to someone else. In such a case, the form of the word will be followed with a preposition. However, the word also implies perfecting something or doing something in the best way. This is, perhaps, closer to what is meant by the word *ihsaan* in this particular hadith.[3] However, the two concepts are not inseparable. A person will behave towards others in the best way possible if he is truly doing that to please Allah. Hence, he excels both in his relation towards Allah— or rites of worship— as well as in his relationship to Allah's creatures, due to his knowledge that Allah is watching him.

Therefore, *ihsaan* is a very comprehensive term. It includes all types of acts of goodness to others. Its meaning is that a person spreads good instead of harm to others. He uses his wealth, knowledge, position and body to do good

---

[1] Al-Haitami, p. 79.
[2] Al-Qaari, vol. 1, p. 54.
[3] See al-Aini, vol. 1, p. 288.

to others. He gives part of his wealth in zakat and charity, and that is *ihsaan*. He spreads his knowledge and never misses an opportunity to guide others, and that is *ihsaan* with respect to his knowledge. He uses his rightful position and influence to help those that are deserving and in need of help. That is also *ihsaan*. He helps his brother get into his car or to carry something and that is an example of *ihsaan* with respect to his body.[1]

In this hadith of Jibreel, the Messenger of Allah (peace be upon him) did not give a dictionary-type definition of *ihsaan*. Instead, he explained the main motivating factor behind *ihsaan* or goodness and excellence. This is the fact that Allah is watching one's actions. If the heart is aware of that fact, the person will hope to please his Lord and fear displeasing Him. This will bring about purity in his heart. When such *ikhlaas* or purity is present in the heart, he will do what he can for Allah's sake. This also means that he will try to do everything in the best possible way. He will be concerned about the quality of his deeds and not simply their quantity or outward execution.[2]

He answered, "It is that you worship Allah as if you see Him. And even though you do not see Him, He sees you."

Perhaps the first matter that needs to be discussed is whether these two sentences embody one concept or two

[1] Cf., Ibn Uthaimin, *Majmu*, vol. 3, pp. 216-217.
[2] Salaam, p. 183.

distinct concepts. Scholars have interpreted this hadith in both ways.

The View that Two Concepts are Being Conveyed

Ibn Rajab[1], ibn Hajr[2] and others are of the view that this hadith describes two different levels of awareness at which a believer may be. One of the positions is loftier than the other. If a person cannot achieve the loftier position, he should at least seek the less loftier position. It is as if the Messenger of Allah (peace be upon him) said, "Worship Allah[3] as if you are seeing him. But if you cannot achieve that level, worship Him knowing that He sees you."

The believers and *muhsineen*[4] differ quite a bit in the levels that they reach, depending on their levels of *imaan* and *ihsaan*. The loftier position is known as *al-mushahadah* ("personal witnessing"). This is not the real seeing of Allah but a very strong feeling in the heart. This is where the realization of Allah's presence, by His knowledge and mercy, is so great that the person practically witnesses Allah in front of him. The person's thought and mind become completely attuned to the act of worship he is performing. This is the implication of the first sentence, "It is that you worship Allah as if you see Him." There is no question that if one could see Allah, this would have a

---

[1] In his commentary to *Sahih al-Bukhari*, ibn Rajab only presents this view while in his commentary to al-Nawawi's *40 Hadith*, he presents both. See Abu al-Faraj ibn Rajab al-Hanbali, *Fath al-Bari Sharh Sahih al-Bukhari* (Madina: Maktaba al-Ghuraba al-Athariya, 1996), vol. 1, pp. 211f; ibn Rajab, *Jami*, vol. 1, p. 128.

[2] Ibn Hajr, *Fath*, vol. 1, p. 164.

[3] The reader is reminded that the Islamic concept of "worship" is not simply a matter of specific rites that a person performs. Instead, it is a complete form of servitude to Allah that encompasses one's outward acts as well as the acts of the heart, as described earlier.

[4] Those characterized by the quality of *ihsaan*.

profound effect on his worship and obedience of Allah. This can be seen in the following hadith:

إِنَّ لِلَّهِ مَلائِكَةً يَطُوفُونَ فِي الطُّرُقِ يَلْتَمِسُونَ أَهْلَ الذِّكْرِ فَإِذَا وَجَدُوا قَوْمًا يَذْكُرُونَ اللَّهَ تَنَادَوْا هَلُمُّوا إِلَى حَاجَتِكُمْ قَالَ فَيَحُفُّونَهُمْ بِأَجْنِحَتِهِمْ إِلَى السَّمَاءِ الدُّنْيَا قَالَ فَيَسْأَلُهُمْ رَبُّهُمْ وَهُوَ أَعْلَمُ مِنْهُمْ مَا يَقُولُ عِبَادِي قَالُوا يَقُولُونَ يُسَبِّحُونَكَ وَيُكَبِّرُونَكَ وَيَحْمَدُونَكَ وَيُمَجِّدُونَكَ قَالَ فَيَقُولُ هَلْ رَأَوْنِي قَالَ فَيَقُولُونَ لا وَاللَّهِ مَا رَأَوْكَ قَالَ فَيَقُولُ وَكَيْفَ لَوْ رَأَوْنِي قَالَ يَقُولُونَ لَوْ رَأَوْكَ كَانُوا أَشَدَّ لَكَ عِبَادَةً وَأَشَدَّ لَكَ تَمْجِيدًا وَتَحْمِيدًا وَأَكْثَرَ لَكَ تَسْبِيحًا

"Allah has some angels who look for those who celebrate the Praises of Allah on the roads and paths. And when they find some people celebrating the Praises of Allah, they call each other, saying, 'Come to the object of your pursuit.' The angels then encircle them with their wings up to the sky of the world. Then their Lord asks them, although He is most knowledgeable of them, 'What do My slaves do?' The angels reply, 'They say, *subhanallah*, *allahu akbar* and *al-hamdulillah*.' Allah then says, 'Did they see Me?' The angels reply, 'No, by Allah, they didn't see You.' Allah says, 'How would it have been if they saw Me?' The angels reply, 'If they saw You, they would worship You more devoutly, and celebrate Your Glory more deeply, and more often declare Your freedom from any resemblance to anything...'"[1]

---

[1] Recorded by al-Bukhari. See Muhammad Muhsin Khan, trans., *Sahih al-Bukhari* (Beirut: Dar al-Arabia, 1985), vol. 8, pp. 278-279.

The effect of the feeling of the seeing of Allah on the person is that he will perform every act of obedience in the best way possible. He practically sees Allah in front of him so he knows full well— beyond a mere theoretical belief— that Allah is observing everything that he is doing. He will be extremely shy and embarrassed to do anything in a less than perfect or excellent manner. He will also be filled with the fear, awe and admiration of Allah. He will make every effort to please Allah who he "sees" in front of him. He will exert himself to perform his act of worship in the best way possible, without any deficiency.

So the person who reaches the higher level of *ihsaan* has reached a level wherein his heart practically witnesses his Lord, wherein he becomes full of pleasure when being alone with his Lord and when he remembers Allah, speaks to Allah and beseeches Him. These acts become the most beautiful and enjoyable acts in his eyes. The Prophet (peace be upon him) himself was undoubtedly at this level of worship of Allah. He one time said,

وَجُعِلَ قُرَّةُ عَيْنِي فِي الصَّلاةِ

"The sweetness of my eye has been made the prayer."[1]

If a person is not able to reach that level or if it is difficult for him, then he moves to the lower level where he worships Allah realizing full well that Allah is watching him and knows both what goes on externally and inside of the person's heart and soul. This level has been termed *al-muraqabah* ("the level of one who is being observed and watched"). This level of *ihsaan* is still quite important and beneficial. The person knows that Allah is seeing him and observing every action that he performs. This can drive a Muslim to perfect and excel in his acts of worship. Hence, this level also leads to *ihsaan* or excellence in worship.

---

[1] Recorded by al-Nasai and Ahmad. Al-Albani has called it *sahih*. See al-Albani, *Sahih al-Jami*, vol. 1, p. 599.

But this feeling cannot be considered as strong as in the first case of *al-mushahadah*. The feeling of being watched may not always be that strong in a person's heart. Even though he may theoretically know that he is being watched, he may still be lax at times. He does not experience the same feelings of awe and humility than the feeling of he who is practically seeing Allah in front of him.[1]

Thus, the presence of either level of *ihsaan* makes the person worship Allah in an excellent manner— which is what *ihsaan* would imply linguistically. Those who reach the level of *ihsaan* are far ahead of those Muslims who may know and believe— but unfortunately only at a theoretical or academic level— that Allah knows and witnesses all things. All Muslims must know and believe this. But as long as that knowledge has no real effect on their worship of Allah, they are not deserving of the title of *Muhsin*, or a person who has the quality of *ihsaan*. Yes, they legally fulfill their obligations of worship. But those acts are lacking in spirit and quality and, therefore, they do not rise to the level of *ihsaan* and excellent worship of Allah.

Ibn Uthaimin notes other aspects that differentiate between these two levels of *ihsaan*. According to him, *al-ihsaan* with respect to the worship of Allah is where the person worships Allah as if he sees Him, as is stated in this hadith. This type of worship is the worship of craving, yearning and delight. This makes the person, on his very own, very keen on performing the acts of worship. This is because he sincerely loves that act and he will seek that act of worship because he loves it so much. He will anxiously desire to get closer to Allah and will turn to Him as if he is seeing Allah. The lower level of *al-ihsaan* is one of fleeing and fear. If one does not worship Allah as if he is seeing

[1] The reader can envision the case of a guard vis-a-vis a surveillance camera. In both cases, the person knows that he is being watched. But, many times, in one case the feeling is much stronger and has a greater effect.

him, he must at least realize that Allah is seeing him. That is, he is being watched. His deeds are being accounted for. Hence, the person should fear the Watcher's punishment and displeasure. This level or drive behind worship is considered lower than the first. However, all worship is actually built upon these two aspects: extreme love and extreme submission. When love is present, the person seeks the object. When submission is present, there is fear and flight.[1] Ibn Uthaimin does not make this point, but it must be noted that those of the lower level of *ihsaan* also have this feeling. They do not see Allah yet, at the same time, they know that Allah is seeing them. Hence, they combine both of these aspects of love and submission and that is one of the reasons why their worship of Allah is so excellent.

If this understanding of the hadith is accepted, then, as was mentioned by al-Qastilaani, al-Ubayy and al-Shanqiti[2], there are three levels for the Muslim with respect to *ihsaan*.[3] The lowest level is where the Muslim fulfills all of the minimum requirements of an act. Hence, he has performed the act and has fulfilled that legal requirement. This person must theoretically recognize that Allah has witnessed his act. However, that knowledge may not have much or any real affect on his act of worship. The highest level is where one is at a position where he practically sees Allah in front of him. This was the state of the Messenger of Allah (peace be upon him). The middle level is the one who has not reached the level of feeling that he sees Allah

---

[1] Ibn Uthaimin, *Majmu*, vol. 3, p. 218.

[2] Ahmad ibn Muhammad al-Qaastilaani, ***Irshaad al-Saari li-Sharh Sahih al-Bukhari*** (Beirut: Dar al-Fikr, n.d.), vol. 1, p. 140; al-Ubayy, vol. 1, p. 68; Muhammad al-Khidr al-Shanqeeti, ***Kauthar al-Maani al-Daraari fi Kashf Khabaaya Sahih al-Bukhari*** (Beirut: Muassasat al-Risaalah, 1995), vol. 2, p. 349.

[3] Every Muslim should have some level of ***ihsaan***, in the same way that he must have some level of ***imaan***. However, those deserving of the title of ***mu`min*** (believer) should have a higher level of ***ihsaan*** than those who are simply ***muslim***. Next comes those who outdo other believers in ***ihsaan***. Those are the people who are deserving of the title of ***muhsin***, and for them shall be a special reward in the Hereafter.

but he has reached the level that he very much feels that Allah is observing and watching every act he performs. Hence, he also excels in his acts beyond those of the first level mentioned above, but not to the level of the loftiest position. Al-Ubayy then states, "All three of these positions are *ihsaan*. However, the *ihsaan* that is a condition for the soundness of an act of worship is the first level. The *ihsaan* of the last two levels are characteristic of the more devout, special people. Many are not capable of reaching those levels."[1]

The View that Only One Concept is Being Conveyed

An alternative view of this hadith is given by al-Nawawi, al-Sindi and Uthmani.[2] According to this view, the two sentences are just conveying one concept. In other words, it was as if the Prophet (peace be upon him) had said, "Although you do not actually see Allah, you should still excel in your worship because He is seeing you." Ibn Rajab points out that it is as if the second statement is a causal statement for the first.

Uthmani has presented the logic behind the reasoning of this view,

> The first sentence [that you worship Allah as if you see Him] deals with the real objective, but there was a possibility of a doubt arising, which he [the Prophet (peace be upon him)] has answered in the second sentence [that Allah sees you although you cannot see him]. This can be understood by an analogy. Suppose, there are some people present before a king in his palace. Now, how far these will observe the requisite respect and dignity of the

---

[1] Al-Ubayy, vol. 1, p. 68.

[2] See Shabbir Ahmad Uthmani, *Fadl al-Bari Commentary on the Sahih al-Bukhari* (Karachi, Pakistan: Idarah Ulum-I-Shariyyah, n.d.), vol. 1, p. 537.

> court is known to everyone. There are two things here. The one is that the king is looking at them and also that they see the king. What is the reason behind this perfect observance of respect and obedience? Which reason has motivated their attitude of subservience? Is it the seeing of the king or their seeing the king? By a little deliberation, it will be clear that it is the king's seeing them (which really matters). For instance, if there is a blind man amongst them who cannot see the king, would his observance of respect and subservience for the king be in any case less than that of the others?[1]

This argument has some merit to it. However, it seems that the interpretation given by ibn Hajr and others is to be preferred. The analogy or question that Uthmani presented may not be quite complete. In the first case of *al-mushahadah*, the person both feels that Allah is watching him and that he can also see Allah in front of him. Hence, there is a stronger and clearer motivating factor. When a person is being watched but does not feel the presence of the one watching him, he may become forgetful or neglectful of the fact that he is being watched. Allah knows best.

This is Not in Reference to Rites of Worship Only

Nomani has made a very important point with respect to this portion of this hadith. He wrote,

> Often it is maintained about this part of the above Tradition that it applies exclusively to *Namaz* (the Prayer).[2] It is said that only *Namaz* is required to be offered with full humility and devotion. But the

---

[1] Uthmani, vol. 1, p. 537.

[2] *Namaz* is the Urdu word for prayer or *salat*. Nomani's book was originally written in Urdu and then translated into English.

words of the Tradition do not justify it. It speaks of *T'abud* which denotes absolute worship and obeisance. Thus, there is no justification for limiting the Prophet's observation to *Namaz*. Moreover, in another version of this Tradition the word *Takhshi* has been used in the place of *T'abud*, which, when translated into English reads: "*Ihsaan* means that you fear God as if you saw Him." Yet another version has it that "*Ihsaan* means that you perform every act for the sake of God and in such a way that you were seeing Him." Both of these accounts make it clear that *Ihsaan* is not related only to *Namaz* but it covers the entire range of living and doing and its pith and substance is that every act of worship and obeisance should be performed and all the Divine commands carried out and the prospect of Final Reckoning dreaded as if the Lord was present before us and watching every act and movement of ours.[1]

The Reward for *al-Ihsaan* and Its Relationship to This Hadith

The hadith makes it clear that the one who has *ihsaan* either worships Allah as if he is seeing Him or, at the very least, he is fully conscious of the fact that Allah is seeing him. The *muhsin* will receive a special reward for this attitude of worship. Allah has stated in the Quran,

﴿لِّلَّذِينَ أَحْسَنُواْ ٱلْحُسْنَىٰ وَزِيَادَةٌ﴾

"For those who have done good is the best and even more" (*Yunus* 26). In *Sahih Muslim*, it is stated that the Prophet (peace be upon him) explained the meaning of "even more"

---

[1] Nomani, vol. 1, pp. 61-62. In the original work, *Ihsaan* was spelled *Ehsan*. It was changed here for the sake of consistency.

as the bounty of seeing Allah in the Hereafter. Hence, the one who worships Allah as if he is seeing Him or who knows that Allah is seeing him[1] while he is worshipping will be rewarded by the great reward of seeing Allah in the Hereafter.

This is the opposite of the recompense of the disbelievers in the Hereafter:

كَلَّآ إِنَّهُمْ عَن رَّبِّهِمْ يَوْمَئِذٍ لَّمَحْجُوبُونَ

"Nay, surely, they (evil-doers) will be veiled from seeing their Lord that Day" (*al-Mutaffifeen* 15). These people refused to submit to Allah. Instead of worshipping Allah as if they see Him, they behaved as if Allah had no idea of what they were doing. Hence, their recompense is that they will be veiled from seeing Allah in the Hereafter in the same way that they have kept themselves from worshipping Him in this life.

The Hadith Does not Imply Seeing Allah in this World

Both ibn Rajab and ibn Hajr are adamant that this hadith does not imply the possibility of seeing Allah while one is alive in this world. They say that this is how some unfortunate Sufis have incorrectly interpreted this hadith. Ibn Hajr demonstrates that these people are both ignorant of the Arabic language as well as the other narrations of this hadith.[2]

Ibn Rajab also discusses the "seeing" of Allah with one's heart while one is alive in this world. He stated,

---

[1] Every Muslim must believe that Allah is aware of and sees his every action. However, the intensity of this feeling varies from believer. Hence, the corresponding reward in the Hereafter may also vary according to this varying intensity. Allah knows best.

[2] Ibn Hajr, *Fath*, vol. 1, pp. 164-165.

> As for whoever claims that the hearts can reach a level in this life where they can physically see Allah in the same way they will see them by their sights in the Hereafter— as some of the Sufis claim— [it should be known] that this is a false claim. That special level is a level that some of the Companions, such as Abu Dharr, ibn Abbas and others, including one narration from Aisha, stated occurred for the Prophet (peace be upon him) [only] twice...

He states that such was something special for the Prophet (peace be upon him) that distinguished him from others. However, the Sufis claim that some of them reach that level often or are always in such a state. Hence, they consider their "saints" to be superior to the prophets. Ibn Rajab then stated, "Branching off from this belief are many of their aspects of misguidance and ignorance. And Allah guides whomsoever He wills to the Straight Path."[1]

---

[1] Ibn Rajab, *Fath*, vol. 1, pp. 214-215.

Signs of the Day of Judgment

He said, "Tell me about [the time of] the Hour." He answered, "The one being asked does not know more than the one asking."

"Tell me about [the time of] the Hour."

In the narration from Ammara ibn al-Qa'qa'a, the question is explicitly, "When is the Hour?"[1] It is to that question that the Messenger of Allah's (peace be upon him) response is directed. Furthermore, in the narration of Abu Farwa, it is also mentioned that the Messenger of Allah (peace be upon him) lowered his head and did not respond. The Angel repeated the question three times and the Messenger of Allah (peace be upon him) then raised his head and responded.[2]

---

[1] Ibn Hajr, *Fath*, vol. 1, p. 165.
[2] Ibn Hajr, *Fath*, vol. 1, p. 165.

"The one being asked does not know more than the one asking."

This response is not meant to imply that the two of them were equal in some knowledge concerning the occurrence of that Day. Instead, it was meant to say that this knowledge is something that Allah has kept to Himself and has not conveyed to anyone. In fact, in the narration in *Sahih al-Bukhari*, the Prophet (peace be upon him) mentioned that there were five aspects that are known only to Allah. And then the Prophet (peace be upon him) recited the verse,

إِنَّ ٱللَّهَ عِندَهُۥ عِلْمُ ٱلسَّاعَةِ وَيُنَزِّلُ ٱلْغَيْثَ وَيَعْلَمُ مَا فِى ٱلْأَرْحَامِ ۖ وَمَا تَدْرِى نَفْسٌ مَّاذَا تَكْسِبُ غَدًا ۖ وَمَا تَدْرِى نَفْسٌۢ بِأَىِّ أَرْضٍ تَمُوتُ ۚ إِنَّ ٱللَّهَ عَلِيمٌ خَبِيرٌۢ

"Verily, Allah, with Him (alone), is the knowledge of the Hour. He [alone] sends down the rain, and knows that which is in the wombs. No person knows what he will earn tomorrow, and no person knows in what land he will die. Verily, Allah is All-Knower, All-Aware" (*Luqmaan* 34).[1]

One should note how the Messenger of Allah (peace be upon him) responded to the question. At that time, as shall be discussed below, the Messenger of Allah (peace be upon him) was not aware that the questioner was the Angel Gabriel. However, his response was in a general form and its meaning is: "No one being questioned about this matter will have any more knowledge concerning it than any one

[1] According to al-Qurtubi (quoted in ibn Rajab, *Fath*, vol. 1, p. 216), the meaning of the verse is that none of mankind shall ever have definite knowledge of those things before they occur. However, one could have conjecture concerning them based on some signs that are apparent to him (such as concerning rainfall). This conjecture is sometimes wrong and sometimes right. Such conjectures are not what is prohibited or denied in this verse. Allah knows best.

who may ask such a question." That is, no one of mankind will ever have knowledge of when the Day of Resurrection will occur. Hence, anyone who claims to have such exact knowledge is either a blatant liar or a deluded fool.

According to al-Qurtubi, the purpose of this question was to put an end to any further asking of when the Day will occur. Many people— as can be seen by reference to it in the Quran and hadith, such as *surah al-Naaziaat* 42-44 and *al-Araaf* 187— would ask the Messenger of Allah (peace be upon him) about when the Day would occur. Due to the nature of the Prophet's response in this question and the later statement that the questioner was the Angel Gabriel, it became understood that such knowledge would never become available to mankind. The noblest of the human beings and the noblest of the angels have no knowledge whatsoever of when that Day shall occur. Hence, there is no need to ever ask this question again. Therefore, one can also see that the purpose of this question was different from the purpose of the previous questions. The previous questions were posed in order to extract beneficial knowledge while this question was posed to bring an end to the asking of this particular question.[1]

Why is it that the knowledge of the Hour has not been given to mankind? Allah knows best, but there may be two important aspects related to this fact. First, for the individual, the more important matter is not the occurrence of the Hour but the occurrence of his own individual Hour. That is, the more important issue is for the person to realize that he is going to face death. When his death occurs, this is his "Hour," as his deeds will have come to an end and after that there will be only reckoning. This important aspect was alluded to by the Prophet (peace be upon him) when he once asked by a bedouin about the time of the Hour and he pointed to the youngest boy among them and said,

---

[1] Al-Qurtubi was quoted in ibn Hajr, *Fath*, vol. 1, pp. 165-166.

إِنْ يَعِشْ هَذَا لا يُدْرِكْهُ الْهَرَمُ حَتَّى تَقُومَ عَلَيْكُمْ سَاعَتُكُم

"If this [boy] should live, he will not become old and decrepit until your Hour has already been established for you." (Recorded by al-Bukhari and Muslim.)[١]

Again, the time of the Hour is not what is important. The second important aspect is how one spends one's life in preparation for the final Hour. On another occasion, a bedouin asked the Prophet (peace be upon him) when the Hour would come and his response was,

وَيْلَكَ وَمَا أَعْدَدْتَ لَهَا

"Woe to you! What have you prepared for it?" (Recorded by al-Bukhari and Muslim.) Hence, the individual is required to prepare for the Hour by faith and good deeds. He has no obligation with respect to when and how it will occur.

He said, "Tell me about its signs[1]." He answered...

The Importance of the Signs of the Hour

No one can know when the Day of Judgment will occur. However, Allah has mercifully taught His messengers some of the signs that alert one to the fact that the Hour is approaching. These signs play a very important role, especially for those who live at a time distant from the Prophet (peace be upon him) and who did not experience first hand his teaching and example. These signs reinforce one's belief in the Prophet (peace be upon him). More importantly, these signs, if one takes the time to reflect upon them, are a reminder of the Day of Judgment. They should revive the heart of the person and make him recall what he is doing on this earth and to where all this is heading.

There is a very direct and clear relationship between the signs of the Hour and *ihsaan*. When one witnesses these signs around him, they should be clear reminders of Allah and one's future meeting with Allah. They should be a reminder that Allah has foreknowledge of everything that is occurring in this world— this is how He could convey those signs to His messenger. Therefore, Allah also has knowledge of everything the person is doing. Allah is watching and aware of every act of His creatures. At the

---

[1] The question was about "signs," in the plural. In the response, the Prophet (peace be upon him) mentioned only two signs. This is problematic because, in Arabic, the minimum of a plural is generally considered to be three rather than two, which is a dual form only. A response to this is that two can be considered a plural. Another response is that in other narrations of the hadith, three signs are mentioned. (Cf., ibn Hajr, *Fath*, vol. 1, p. 166.) The third sign that is mentioned in the other hadith is that the barefoot, scantily clothed, ignorant people will become the leaders of the people.

very least, this consciousness, which comes about through witnessing the Signs of the Hour, should make the person worship and fear Allah knowing full well that He is seeing him. This is that level of *ihsaan* known as *al-muraqabah*, which was explained earlier.

The signs of the Hour can be divided into two types. First are those that occur as part of the changes in everyday life. The second are the extraordinary or supernatural events that will occur just before the actual Hour. In his reply, the Messenger of Allah (peace be upon him) only mentioned some signs of the former category. Perhaps, Allah knows best, this is because these are the signs that have much more of an effect on one's *ihsaan* in everyday worship, although the recognition of these signs are sometimes more difficult or subtle.

Why it is Called "the Hour"

The "Hour"[1] refers to the Last Day or the Day of Judgment. There are a number of explanations for why it is called the Hour. Some say it is called the "Hour" because, although it will last for a very long time, it will be established suddenly, to the point that a person who is holding some food in his hand will not be able to taste it. For example, Allah says in the Quran,

فَهَلْ يَنظُرُونَ إِلَّا ٱلسَّاعَةَ أَن تَأْتِيَهُم بَغْتَةً فَقَدْ جَآءَ أَشْرَاطُهَا

"Do they then await [anything] other than the Hour— that it should come upon them suddenly? But some of its portents have already come" (*Muhammad* 18). Hence, it is referring to the first event or beginning of the Hour that will come all of a sudden.

---

[1] During the time of the Prophet (peace be upon him), the word *saah* ("hour") did not mean "hour" in the sense of sixty minutes. However, it did mean a portion of time that was neither extremely long or extremely short.

It could also be referred to as the "Hour" because that is with respect to the "timing" of Allah. Allah says,

تَعْرُجُ ٱلْمَلَـٰٓئِكَةُ وَٱلرُّوحُ إِلَيْهِ فِى يَوْمٍ كَانَ مِقْدَارُهُۥ خَمْسِينَ أَلْفَ سَنَةٍ

"The angels and the *Ruh* (Gabriel) ascend to Him in a Day the measure whereof is fifty thousand years" (*al-Maarij* 4). Hence, it is a very long event but as part of that day, it is like but one hour.[1]

Finally, some say it is called an "Hour" in the way of a good omen— hoping that it will pass easily and quickly— in the same way that, in Arabic, an important matter is referred to as the successful matter.

"The slave-girl shall give birth to her master."

The scholars have differed concerning the interpretation of this sign of the Hour. Indeed, it is difficult to explain many of the signs of the Hour that the Messenger of Allah (peace be upon him) stated. In some cases, perhaps only those who actually live through the events being described will have a complete and correct understanding of what the Messenger of Allah (peace be upon him) was actually alluding to. For example, it may be only in modern times that one truly witnesses and understands what the Prophet (peace be upon him) meant by women who are dressed but naked. Before modern times, the scholars could only hypothesize as to exactly what that was referring to.

Ibn al-Tin says that there are seven explanations for this sign mentioned by the Prophet (peace be upon him).

---

[1] There is a hadith in *Musnad Ahmad* that states, "By the One in whose hand is my soul, it [the Hour] will be made so easy upon the believer that it will be easier upon him than an obligatory prayer that he used to pray in this world." However, according to al-Albani, the chain of this hadith is weak. See al-Albani's footnotes to Muhammad al-Tabrizi, *Mishkat al-Masabih* (Beirut: al-Maktab al-Islami, 1985), vol. 3, p. 1544.

Ibn Hajr says that in reality these seven opinions boil down to four separate and distinct opinions. These four are:[1]

(1) Al-Khattabi mentions that its meaning is that Islam will spread, dominate the lands of the disbelievers and take their inhabitants as slaves. Then a man will have a child through his slave-girl and that child shall be like her master because she is the daughter of her master. Al-Nawawi states that this is the opinion of the majority of the scholars. However, this interpretation is somewhat problematic. Ibn Hajr points out that such a thing existed during the time of the Prophet (peace be upon him) and the early years of Islam. The implication of the speech is that such an event will occur close to the Day of Judgment and will be a sign of its coming. Others give a slightly different interpretation by saying that a woman will give birth to a child and then that child will end up being the king of the land. Hence, the woman will fall under his general citizenry and he will be her master. Some even say that the king will later buy his own mother who was a slave, either out of ignorance or knowingly, and then use her as a servant. Hence, the mother has given birth to her own master.

(2) A second interpretation is that the slave-girls who have given birth to the owner's children will be sold by the owners. There will be so much selling of such women that the woman's own son will later buy her and not realize that it is his mother. Hence, the one she gave birth to will become her master. According to some scholars, if a slave-girl gives birth to a child, she cannot then be sold and she becomes free on her master's death. Hence, this sign of the Hour reflects either ignorance of the laws of Islam or disdain for the laws of Islam in the later years. However, some scholars say that such sales are permissible so that is neither a sign of ignorance or disdain. Finally, to reconcile the two views, some say that the woman are sold while they

---

[1] Cf., ibn Hajr, *Fath*, vol. 1, p. 167.

are still pregnant and this is absolutely forbidden according to the consensus of the scholars.

(3) A third interpretation is that a woman gives birth to a child. However, that child was not the result of a completely legal act of intercourse, such as the child being the result of fornication or an improper marriage. Then the mother is sold in a proper and correct manner and she continues to be sold until, finally, her own child buys her.

(4) The fourth interpretation is that the children will disobey their mothers. The child will end up treating his own mother like a slave owner treats a slave girl, showing disdain, perhaps beating her and, in general, treating her simply like a servant. In this case, "her master" is either figurative or in the sense of the one who brings up the other. This is the view that ibn Hajr prefers. He states that it is the most general. Furthermore, it is parallel to the next sign that the Prophet (peace be upon him) stated. That is, it is further evidence that the society has changed so much that things are, in essence, upside down. This is a sign of the coming of the Hour as things are no longer in the way that they should be.

"And you will see the barefooted, scantily-clothed, destitute shepherds competing in constructing lofty buildings."

The point of this sign is, as al-Qurtubi mentioned, that, once again, the affairs will be turned upside down. The bedouins will be in charge, taking over by force and having the wealth in their hands. Their only concern after that will be competition and boasting in constructing tall buildings. Al-Qurtubi, who died in 671 A.H., said, "We have witnessed that during this time."[1]

---

[1] Al-Qurtubi was quoted in al-Shanqiti, vol. 2, p. 362. Al-Qurtubi's statement, "by force," is based on other narrations of this hadith.

In general, it means that those not qualified to be in charge and to have the wealth in their hands will be running the affairs and will be in control of the wealth. They will not know the proper way to deal with their wealth or how to run the affairs. Hence, they will waste their money in extravagance and frivolous pursuits. Other hadith of the Prophet (peace be upon him) give the same impression of what will occur before the Hour. The Prophet (peace be upon him) said,

لا تَقُومُ السَّاعَةُ حَتَّى يَكُونَ أَسْعَدَ النَّاسِ بِالدُّنْيَا لُكَعُ ابْنُ لُكَعٍ

"The Hour will not be established until the happiest of all people with this world is Luka' ibn Luka'."[1] The name Luka' ibn Luka' means "the most ignorant, stupid fool, the son of the most ignorant stupid fool." Another hadith states,

فَإِذَا ضُيِّعَتِ الأَمَانَةُ فَانْتَظِرِ السَّاعَةَ قَالَ كَيْفَ إِضَاعَتُهَا قَالَ إِذَا وُسِّدَ الأَمْرُ إِلَى غَيْرِ أَهْلِهِ فَانْتَظِرِ السَّاعَةَ

"If the 'trust' is lost, then expect the Hour." He was asked, "How will it be lost?" He answered, "When the affairs are in the hands of those who are not qualified for it, then expect the Hour." (Recorded by al-Bukhari.)

Note that the word العراة is usually translated as "naked". However, al-Qaari points out that it also applies to the person who has left a part of his body that should be covered uncovered.[2] This is the most likely meaning here and, hence, the translation "scantily-clothed" has been used. Allah knows best.

---

[1] Ibn Hajr states that this hadith is in ***Sahih al-Bukhari*** but this does not seem to be correct. It was recorded by Ahmad and al-Tirmidhi. According to al-Albani, it is *sahih*. See al-Albani, *Sahih al-Jami*, vol. 2, p. 1238.

[2] Al-Qaari, vol. 1, p. 63.

Summary of the Two Signs Mentioned in the Hadith

Both of the signs indicate that the state of affairs will not be proper. In the first sign, those that are deserving of authority, respect and good treatment— mothers— will be treated with disdain and without their due respect. In the second sign, those that are not deserving of wealth and authority or who do not know how to handle it will receive wealth and authority. One can only imagine what society as a whole must be like when such occurs. Ibn Rajab wrote,

> The points that are mentioned in these signs of the Hour in this hadith go back to the fact that matters are not in the hands of qualified people, as the Prophet (peace be upon him) mentioned in [another hadith quoted above]... If the barefoot, scantily-clothed shepherds— and they are the people of ignorance and crudeness— are the leaders of the people and the owners of the resources and wealth, to the point that they compete in constructing buildings, then the entire structure of the religion and worldly affairs will be ruined and in disarray. If the leader of the people is someone who used to be poor and destitute, and he is the ruler over the people, regardless if that is a general rule or a specific rule only in some matters, then it is hardly conceivable that such a person will give the people their rights. Indeed, instead, he will hide from them what wealth he possesses. One of the early scholars stated, "For you to stretch your hand to the mouth of a sea monster and he bites on to it is better than for you to stretch your hand to the hand of a rich person who used to be poor."[1] If in addition to being ignorant, he is also coarse and harsh, then religion will also be ruined. This is because it is of no importance to him to rectify the religion of the

---

[1] The one who made that statement was Sufyan al-Thauri.

> people nor to teach them their religion. His only concern is to gather and store wealth. He will not be concerned with how the people's religion has become ruined or what poor soul has lost his life out of need....
>
> If the kings and rulers of the people are of that nature, then all of the other affairs will also be turned upside down. The liar will be believed in and the truthful one will not. The deceitful one will be trusted and the trustworthy one will be deceived. The ignorant one will speak while the scholar will remain silent. Alternatively, there will not be any scholars at all. It is authentically reported that the Prophet (peace be upon him) said, "One of the signs of the Hour is that knowledge will be removed and ignorance will be dominant." [Recorded by al-Bukhari.] He also stated, "Knowledge shall be taken away by the taking away of the scholars, until no scholar is left. The people will take ignorant persons as their leaders. They shall ask them and they will reply without knowledge. They are misguided and they misguide others." [Recorded by al-Bukhari and Muslim.] Al-Sha'bi said, "The Hour will not be established until knowledge becomes ignorance and ignorance becomes knowledge." This is all part of the turning upside down of the realities at the end of Time and the affairs being the opposite of what they should be.[1]

Perhaps American society is very much approaching the first sign. Nowadays, children seem to have more rights than their parents. If a parent even somewhat mildly disciplines his or her child, he or she may be arrested and the children taken away. On the other hand, young teens may even beat up their parents, and hardly get more than a slap on the wrist from the authorities.

---

[1] Ibn Rajab, *Jami*, vol. 1, pp. 140-141.

Perhaps one of the greatest signs of this turning upside down of the ways things should be is the place of the Muslims vis-a-vis the disbelievers today. Although Muslims should be witnesses against mankind, leading mankind and demonstrating the truth of Islam, today that is definitely not the case. Indeed, the case is almost completely the opposite. Muslims are under the control and influence of the disbelievers. This is definitely a case of the affairs being in the wrong hands and may be considered a sign that the Hour is approaching.

Al-Qaari also points out that the first sign, concerning the slave girl giving birth to her master, implies the presence of a great deal of injustice, evil and ignorance. These aspects even reach the higher classes of society, as they are the ones most likely to have slaves and so forth. The second sign implies extreme love for this world and a neglect of what this world leads to in the Hereafter. The desire for this world is also exhibited among the lowest classes who can barely clothe themselves.[1]

---

[1] Cf., al-Qaari, vol. 1, p. 63.

The Angel Teaches the Religion

Then he [the Prophet (peace be upon him)] said, "O Umar, do you know who the questioner was..."

Then he went away. I stayed for a long time.

The narrations of this hadith from Umar and Abu Huraira greatly differ as to when the Prophet (peace be upon him) identified the questioner as being the angel Gabriel. Many scholars pointed out that Umar left in search of the person and, upon not finding him, returned to his home which was some distance from the Prophet's mosque. Al-Qadha further speculates that on the following day it was Umar's neighbors turn to be with the Prophet (peace be upon him), as they used to alternate being with the Prophet (peace be upon him) and then they would tell each other what happened on that day. Hence, it was not until the third day, as is explicitly stated in some narrations, that Umar was told by the Messenger of Allah (peace be upon him) who the questioner was. However, the others who stayed around the Prophet (peace be upon him), such as Abu

Huraira, were told shortly afterwards that it was the Angel Gabriel who had asked those questions.[1]

Then he [the Prophet (peace be upon him)] said, "O Umar, do you know who the questioner was?"

In many different narrations of the hadith, it is clear that the Prophet (peace be upon him) himself was not aware of the true identity of the questioner until after the angel had departed. In the narration of Abu Furwah, the Prophet (peace be upon him) said, "By the One who sent Muhammad with the truth, I was not more aware of who he was than any man among you. [I didn't know] that he was Gabriel." In the hadith of Abu Amr it states that the Prophet (peace be upon him) said, "Glory be to Allah, that was Gabriel who came to teach the people their religion. By the One in Whose Hand is the soul of Muhammad, he never came to me before except that I recognized him, except for this time." The narration from al-Taimi is similar and states that the Prophet (peace be upon him) did not know who he was until he departed.[2]

"It was [the Angel] Gabriel who came to teach you your religion (*Deen*)."

Commenting on these words, Ibn Uthaimin stated,

> [He came to teach the religion] although it was the Prophet (peace be upon him), in reality, who was teaching the religion. However, the Prophet (peace be upon him) called Gabriel the teacher. This is

---

[1] Sharf al-Qadha, *Asbab al-Taaddud al-Rawaayaat fi al-Hadith al-Nabawi al-Shareef* (Amman, Jordan: Dar al-Furqan, 1985), pp. 20-21.
[2] For these different narrations, see ibn Hajr, *Fath*, vol. 1, p. 170.

because he was the one who asked and the teaching was due to him. One can conclude from this that the one who is the cause of something is similar to the one who does the direct act. When it comes to capital offenses, the jurists have derived the legal principle: The cause of the act is similar to the one who directly performs the act. For that reason, the Prophet (peace be upon him) called Gabriel a teacher because he was the cause of the teaching of the religion by the Prophet (peace be upon him), through the responses to his questions. Second, if a person asks a question to which he knows the answer and he only asks so that the people would know the answer to that question, he has become a teacher.[1]

The Religion (*Deen*)

The Prophet (peace be upon him) described what the Angel taught as being the *Deen* or religion. The religion comprises the states of Islam, *Imaan* and *Ihsaan*. For a person to try to complete his religion, he must try to complete all three aspects. Nomani summarizes this point,

> In fact, three things make the sum-total of Faith. Firstly [*sic*], the bondsman surrenders himself wholly to God and casts his life into the mold of submission to Him. This is what Islam actually is and its tenets and practices are the signs and symbols of this fundamental reality. Secondly, the major transcendental truths the Apostles of God have revealed[2] and called on mankind to believe in are accepted as true. This is *Imaan*. Thirdly, should God, in His Infinite Mercy, make it possible for one to complete the stages of Islam and *Imaan*, the third

[1] Ibn Uthaimin, *Majmu*, vol. 3, p. 222.

[2] This must be some sort of typographical error in the English text. Most likely, it should read, "received".

and ultimate stage is that the consciousness of God... became so strong that allegiance was rendered to Him and His commands were carried out as if He was present before our own eyes in all His Glory and Splendour, and watching all our deeds and actions closely. This state of feeling is called *Ihsaan*.[1]

[1] Nomani, vol. 1, p. 64.

Summary of the Hadith

- The pillars or foundation upon which Islam, the submission to Allah, rests are five: the declaration of the testimony of faith, the establishment of the prayers, the paying of Zakat, the fasting of Ramadhan and the pilgrimage.
- The articles of faith in which all Muslims must believe are six: belief in Allah, the angels, the messengers, the books, the Day of Resurrection and Divine Decree.
- As for *ihsaan*, Al-Nawawi's following statement provides an excellent summary of the Messenger of Allah's (peace be upon him) answer to the meaning of *ihsaan*: "This is one of the comprehensive expressions that the Messenger of Allah (peace be upon him) was given. This is because if anyone of us could stand in worship while he is seeing Allah, then he would not leave anything that would be in his ability of submission, humility, fear, beautiful features, and combine them all both outwardly and inwardly. One would take care to complete the act in the best possible way.... Hence, the purpose of these words is to encourage purity in worship and recognition by the person that his Lord is watching him, so that he will be as complete as possible when it comes to submission, humility and fear."[1]

---

[1] Al-Nawawi, *Sharh Sahih*, vol. 1, p. 158. Al-Syuti has almost exactly the same words but he does not ascribe them to al-Nawawi. See Jallal al-Din al-Syuti, *al-Deebaaj ala Sahih Muslim ibn al-Hajjaaj* (Al-Khobar, Saudi Arabia: Dar ibn Affan, 1996), vol. 1, p. 6.

- The religion or *deen* is comprised of the three different levels of *islaam*, *imaan* and *ihsaan*. The one who continues only at the level of Islam until he dies will be saved from being forever in the Hell-fire, although he may enter it due to his sins. On the other end, the one who continues in *ihsaan* until he dies will go directly to Paradise and will have the pleasure of seeing Allah in the Hereafter.[1]
- The knowledge of when the Hour will be established is known only to Allah. The noblest of mankind and the noblest of the angels demonstrated that they have no knowledge of when it will occur. Some Shiites and Sufis make outlandish claims that their Imams and saints have knowledge of the Unseen— some even say that the saints look at the Preserved Tablet. In fact, at times they even claim that they have all the knowledge, just like Allah.[2] These beliefs go against the Quran and sunnah and if a person insists on them even after being shown their falsehood, the insistence on this belief takes him out of the fold of Islam.
- Allah has blessed mankind with the knowledge of some of the signs of the Hour. These signs that occur around the person should act as reminders of the coming Hour and Judgment. This should also remind him that Allah sees and knows all things, including what the person himself is doing at any moment.

---

[1] Ibn Rajab, *Fath*, vol. 1, p. 215.

[2] For quotes from Shiite sources, see Sultan, p. 51; for quotes of a Sufi nature, see al-Qaari, vol. 1, p. 62.

References

References in English

Abdul-Khaliq, Abdur-Rahmaan. *The General Prescripts of Belief in the Quran and Sunnah.* The Majliss of al-Haqq Publication Society. 1986.

Ansari, Muhammad Abdul Haq. *Sharh al-Aqeedah al-Tahawiyah.* Fairfax, VA: Institute of Islamic and Arabic Sciences in America. Forthcoming.

al-Ashqar, Umar. "The Wisdom behind the Creation of Satan." *al-Basheer.* Vol. 2, No. 3. Sept.-Oct. 1988.

al-Barbahaaree, Abu Muhammad al-Hasan. *Explanation of the Creed.* Birmingham, UK: Al-Haneef Publications. 1995.

Hasan, Ahmad, trans., *Sunan Abu Dawud.* Lahore: Sh. Muhammad Ashraf. 1984.

Idris, Jaafar Sheikh. *The Pillars of Faith.* Riyadh: Presidency of Islamic Research, Ifta and Propagation. 1984.

Khan, Muhammad Muhsin, trans. *Sahih al-Bukhari.* Beirut: Dar al-Arabia. 1985.

Lane, E. W. *Arabic-English Lexicon.* Cambridge, England: The Islamic Texts Society. 1984.

Nadwi, Abul Hasan Ali. *The Four Pillars of Islam.* Lucknow, India: Academy of Islamic Research and Publications. 1976.

Nomani, Mohammad Manzoor. *Meaning and Message of the Traditions.* Lucknow, India: Academy of Islamic Research and Publications. 1975.

Philips, Bilal. *The Fundamentals of Tawheed.* Riyadh: Tawheed Publications. 1990.

Sabiq, as-Sayyid. *Fiqh us-Sunnah.* Indianapolis: American Trust Publications. 1985.

Siddiqi, Abdul Hameed. trans. *Sahih Muslim.* Beirut: Dar al-Arabia. n.d.

Uthmani, Shabbir Ahmad. *Fadl al-Bari Commentary on the Sahih al-Bukhari.* Karachi, Pakistan: Idarah Ulum-I-Shariyyah. n.d.

Zarabozo, Jamaal al-Din. *The Friday Prayer: Part II: Khutbahs (I).* Aurora, CO: IANA. 1994.

-----*The Friday Prayer: Part III: Khutbahs (II).* Ann Arbor, MI: IANA. 1995.

----- "Questions and Answers," *Al-Basheer.* Vol. 2, No. 1. May-June 1988.

References in Arabic

al-Abdul Lateef, Abdul Aziz. *Nawaaqidh al-Imaan al-Qauliyyah wa al-Amaliyyah.* Riyadh: Dar al-Watn. 1414 A.H.

Ahmad, Salaah. *Dawah Shaikh al-Islaam ibn Taimiya wa Atharuhaa ala al-Harakaat al-Islaamiyah al-Muasirah.* Kuwait: Dar ibn al-Atheer. 1996.

al-Aini, Mahmood. *Umdah al-Qaari Sharh Sahih al-Bukhari.* Beirut: Dar al-Turath al-Arabi. n.d.

al-Albani, Muhammad Nasir al-Din. Footnotes to Ali ibn Abu al-Izz, *Sharh al-Aqeedah al-Tahaawiya.* Beirut: al-Maktab al-Islami. 1984.

----- Footnotes to Muhammad al-Tabrizi. *Mishkat al-Masabih.* Beirut: al-Maktab al-Islami. 1985.

----- *Hukum Taarik al-Salaat.* Riyadh: Dar al-Jalalain. 1992.

----- *Irwa al-Ghaleel fi Takhreej Ahadith Manar al-Sabeel.* Beirut: al-Maktab al-Islami. 1979.

----- *Sahih al-Jami al-Sagheer.* Beirut: al-Maktab al-Islami. 1986.

----- *Sahih Sunan Abi Dawud.* Riyadh: Maktab al-Tarbiyah al-Arabiya li-Duwal al-Khaleej. 1991.

----- *Sahih al-Targheeb wa al-Tarheeb.* Beirut: al-Maktab al-Islami. 1982.

----- *Silsilat al-Ahadith al-Dhaeefah.* Beirut: al-Maktab al-Islami. 1398 A. H. Vol. 1.

----- *Silsilaat al-Ahadeeth al-Saheeha.* Beirut: al-Maktab al-Islami. 1979. Vol. 1.

al-Arnaut, Shuaib. Introduction to Zain al-Din al-Maqdisi. *Aqaweel al-Thiqaat fi Taweel al-Asma wa al-Sifaat wa al-Ayaat al-Muhkamaat wa al-Mushtabihaat.* Beirut: Muassassat al-Risalah. 1985.

al-Ashqar, Umar. *Al-Yaum al-Akhir: al-Qiyaamah al-Sughra.* Kuwait: Maktab al-Falaah. 1986.

al-Ateeq, Yusuf. *al-Tareef bima Ufrid min al-Ahadeeth bi-l-Tasneef.* Riyadh: Dar al-Sameei. 1997.

Baadi, Jamaal. *Al-Athaar al-Waarada an Aimmat al-Sunnah fi Abwaab al-Itiqaad min Kitaab Siyar Alaam al-Nubalaa.* Riyadh: Dar al-Watn. 1416 A.H.

al-Baghawi, al-Husain. *Sharh al-Sunnah.* Beirut: Muassasat al-Risaalah. 1983.

al-Baihaqi, Abu Bakr. *Al-Itiqaad ala Madhhab al-Salaf Ahl al-Sunnah wa al-Jamaah.* Beirut: Dar al-Kutub al-Arabi. 1984.

al-Dausiri, Abdul Rahman. *Safwat al-Athaar wa al-Mafaheem min Tafseer al-Quran al-Adheem.* Kuwait: Dar al-Arqam. 1981.

Haakimi, Haafidh ibn Ahmad. *Maarij al-Qubool bi-Sharh Sullim al-Wusool ila Ilm al-Usool fi al-Tauheed.* Beirut: Dar al-Kutub al-Ilmiyah. 1983.

al-Haitami, Ahmad. *Fath al-Mubeen li-Sharh al-Arbaeen.* Beirut: Dar al-Kutub al-Ilmiyah. 1978.

----- *al-Zawaajir an Iqtiraaf al-Kaba`ir.* Beirut: Dar al-Marifah. 1987.

al-Hammad, Muhammad. A*l-Imaan bi-l-Qadha wa al-Qadar.* Riyadh: Dar al-Watn. 1416 A.H.

----- *Tauheed al-Uloohiyah.* Dar ibn Khuzaima. 1414 A.H.

al-Hamood, Muhammad. *Al-Nahaj al-Asma fi Sharh Asma Allah al-Husna.* Kuwait: Maktaba al-Imam al-Dhahabi. 1992.

al-Hawaali, Safr. *Dhaahirah al-Irjaa fi al-Fikr al-Islaami.* Cairo: Maktab al-Tayyib. 1417 A.H.

ibn Abdul Wahab, Muhammad. *Mualafaat al-Shaikh al-Imam Muhammad ibn Abdul Wahaab.* Maktaba ibn Taimiya. n.d.

ibn Abu al-Izz, Ali. *Sharh al-Aqeedah al-Tahaawiyah.* Beirut: Muassasah al-Risaalah. 1988.

ibn Abu Shaiba, Abdullah. *al-Musannaf.* Beirut: Dar al-Fikr. 1989.

Ibn Battah, Ubaidullah. *Al-Ibaanah an Shareeah al-Firq al-Naajiyah wa Mujaanibah al-Firq al-Madhmoomah.* Riyadh: Dar al-Raayah. 1988.

ibn Hajr, Ahmad. *Fath al-Baari bi-Sharh Sahih al-Bukhari.* Makkah: al-Maktabah al-Tijaariyah. 1993.

ibn Hubaira, al-Wazeer. *Al-Ifsaah an Maani al-Sihaah.* Riyadh: Dar al-Watn. 1996.

Ibn al-Jauzi, Abdul Rahman. *Zaad al-Masair fi Ilm al-Tafseer.* Beirut: Dar al-Fikr. 1987.

ibn Jibreen, Abdullah. *al-Shahadataan.* No city or publisher given. 1990.

ibn Katheer, Ismail. *Tafseer al-Quran al-Adheem.* Kuwait: Dar al-Arqam. 1985.

ibn Muhammad, Fauzi. *al-Adhwaa al-Samaawiyah fi Takhreej Ahadeeth al-Arbaeen al-Nawaiyah.* Amman, Jordan: al-Maktabah al-Islamiyah. 1413 A.H.

ibn Rajab, Abdul Rahman. *Fath al-Bari Sharh Sahih al-Bukhari.* Madina: Maktaba al-Ghuraba al-Athariya. 1996.

----- *Jaami al-Uloom wa al-Hikm.* Beirut: Muassasat al-Risaalah. 1991.

ibn al-Qayyim, Muhammad. *Madaarij al-Salikeen.* Beirut: Dar al-Kitaab al-Arabi. 1972.

----- *Shifa al-Aleel fi Masa`il al-Qadha wa al-Qadar wa al-Hikma wa al-Taleel.* Beirut: Dar al-Marifah. n.d.

ibn Taimiya, Ahmad. *Kitaab al-Imaan.* Beirut: al-Maktab al-Islami. 1988.

----- *Majmoo Fatawaa Shaikh al-Islaam ibn Taimiya.* Collected by Abdul Rahmaan Qaasim and his son Muhammad. No publication information given.

ibn Uthaimin, Muhammad. *Hukum Taarik al-Salaat.* Fairfax, VA: IIASA. n.d

----- *Majmuat Fatawa wa Rasail Fadheelat al-Shaikh Muhammad ibn Salih al-Uthaimin.* Riyadh: Dar al-Watn. 1413 A.H.

----- *Sharh al-Aqeedah al-Waasitiyah.* al-Damaam, Saudi Arabia: Dar ibn al-Jauzi. 1415 A.H.

----- *Sharh Hadith Jibreel Alaihi al-Salaam.* Dar al-Thuraya. 1415 A.H.

----- *Al-Sharh al-Mumti ala Zaad al-Mustaqni*. Riyadh: Muassassat Asaam. 1996.

----- *Sharh Usool al-Imaan.* Fairfax, VA: Institute of Islamic and Arabic Sciences in America. 1410 A.H.

al-Isfahaani, al-Raaghib. *Mu'jam Mufradaat Alfaadh al-Quran.* Beirut: Dar al-Fikr. n.d.

al-Jalood, Mahmaas. *al-Muwaalat wa al-Muaadaat fi al-Shariah al-Islamiya.* Al-Mansurah: al-Yaqeen li-l-Nashr wa al-Tauzee'. 1987.

al-Jarullah, Abdullah. *Bahjah al-Naadhireen fima Yuslih al-Dunya wa al-Deen.* No publication information given. 1984.

Kaamil, Abdul Aziz. *al-Hukum wa al-Tahaakum fi Khitaab al-Wahi.* Riyadh: Dar Taiba. 1995.

al-Khalidi, Salaah. *Fi Dhilaal al-Imaan.* al-Zurqa, Jordan: Maktabah al-Manaar. 1987.

al-Laalakai, Hibatullah. *Sharh Usool Itiqaad Ahl al-Sunnah wa al-Jamaah min al-Kitaab wa al-Sunnah wa Ijmaa al-Sahaabah wa al-Tabieen min Badihim.* Riyadh: Dar Taiba. n.d.

Maash, Abdul Razaaq. *Al-Jahl bi-Masail al-Itiqaad wa Hukmuhu.* Riyadh: Dar al-Watn. 1996.

al-Magharaawi, Muhammad. *Fath al-Barr fi al-Tarteeb al-Fiqhi li-Tamheed ibn Abdul Barr.* Riyadh: Majmuat al-Tahaf al-Nafais al-Dauliya. 1996.

al-Mahmood, Abdul Rahman. *al-Qadha wa al-Qadar fi Dhau al-Kitaab wa al-Sunnah wa Madhaahib al-Naas feeh.* Riyadh: Dar al-Nashr al-Dauli. 1994.

al-Misri, Muhammad Abdul Hadi. *Haqiqat al-Imaan ind Ahl al-Sunnah wa al-Jamaah.* Dar al-Furqan. 1991.

al-Mubaarakfoori, Muhammad. *Tuhfah al-Ahwadhi bi-Sharh Jaami al-Tirmidhi.* Beirut: Dar al-Fikr. n.d.

al-Mudaabaghi, Hasan. *Haashiyah.* On the margin of al-Haitami, *Fath.*

al-Muslih, Abdullah and Salaah al-Saawi. *Ma La Yasa'u al-Muslim Jahla.* Islamic Foundation of America. 1995.

Al-Nawawi, Yahya. *Sharh Sahih Muslim.* Beirut: Dar al-Fikr. n.d.

Al-Qaari, Ali. *Mirqat al-Mafateeh Sharh Mishkat al-Masabeeh.* Multan, Pakistan: Maktaba Haqqaaniya. n.d.

al-Qaastilaani, Ahmad ibn Muhammad. *Irshaad al-Saari li-Sharh Sahih al-Bukhari.* Beirut: Dar al-Fikr. n.d.

al-Qadha, Sharf. *Asbab al-Taaddud al-Rawaayaat fi al-Hadith al-Nabawi al-Shareef.* Amman, Jordan: Dar al-Furqan. 1985.

al-Qaisi, Marwaan. *Maalim al-Tauheed.* Beirut: al-Maktab al-Islami. 1990.

al-Qurtubi, Muhammad. *al-Jaami li-Ahkaam al-Quran.* Beirut: Dar Ihya al-Turath al-Arabi. n.d.

al-Raazi, al-Fakhar. *Al-Tafseer al-Kabeer.* Beirut: Dar Ihya al-Turath al-Arabi. n.d.

al-Rasheed, Abdul Aziz. *Al-Tanbeehaat al-Sanniya ala al-Aqeeda al-Waasitiya.* Dar al-Rasheed li-l-Nashr wa al-Tauzee'.

Ridha, Muhammad Rasheed. *Tafseer al-Quran al-Hakeem.* Beirut: Dar al-Fikr. n.d.

al-Saadi, Abdul Rahman. *Al-Fatawa al-Saadiyah.* Riyadh: Manshooraat al-Muassasat al-Saeediyah. n.d

Salaam, Ahmad. *Muqaddimah fi Fiqh Usool al-Dawah.* Beirut: Dar ibn Hazm. 1990.

al-Sanusi, Muhammad. *Sharh al-Sanusi.* on the margin of al-Ubayy.

al-Sa'uwi, Saleh ibn Muhammad. *Majmuat al-Manaahil al-'Idhaab feema ala al-Abd li-Rabb al-Arbaab.* No city or publisher given. 1414 A.H.

al-Shaadhili, Abdul Majeed. *Hadd al-Islaam wa Haqiqat al-Imaan.* Makkah: Umm al-Qura University. 1983.

al-Shaayi, Muhammad. *Al-Furooq al-Laughawiyyah wa Atharahaa fi Tafseer al-Quran al-Kareem.* Riyadh: Maktabah al-Ubaikaan. 1993.

ali-Shaikh, Muhammad ibn Ibrahim. *Tahkeem al-Qawaaneen.* No city or publisher given. 1411 A.H.

al-Shanqeeti, Muhammad al-Khidr. *Kauthar al-Maani al-Daraari fi Kashf Khabaaya Sahih al-Bukhari.* Beirut: Muassasat al-Risaalah. 1995.

al-Shaukaani, Muhammad ibn Ali. *Nail al-Autaar.* Riyadh: Dar Zamam. 1993.

al-Sudais, Abdul Rahman. *al-Haakimiyah fi Tafseer Adhwa al-Bayaan.* Riyadh: Dar Taiba. 1412 A.H.

al-Syooti, Jallal al-Din. *al-Deebaaj ala Sahih Muslim ibn al-Hajjaaj.* Al-Khobar, Saudi Arabia: Dar ibn Affaṇ. 1996.

al-Tabari, Muhammad ibn Jareer. *Jami al-Bayaan an Taweel Ayi al-Quran.* Beirut: Dar al-Fikr. 1988.

al-Ubayy, Abu Abdullah. *Sharh Sahih Muslim.* Riyadh: Maktaba Tabariyyah. n.d.

al-Uroosi, Jailaan. *Al-Duaa wa Manzalatuhu min al-Aqeedah al-Islaamiyah.* Riyadh: Maktabah al-Rushdi. 1996.

Al-Yahsoobi, Al-Qaadhi Iyaadh. *Kitaab al-Imaan min Ikmaal al-Muallim (sic) bi-Fawaaid Saheeh Muslim.* Riyadh: Dar al-Watn, 1417 A.H.

Glossary[1]

Ahl al-ra`i (أهل الرأي)- this is a term used for those scholars who were more apt to make *ijtehad* or personal reasoning.

Ahl al-sunnah wa al-Jamaah (أهل السنة والجماعة) - "The People of the Sunnah and the Congregation," this refers to those people who follow the way of the sunnah of the Prophet (peace be upon him) and the way of his Companions with respect to beliefs and deeds or a general application of the religion of Islam.

Amal (عمل) - deed, act

Ashaairah, al- (الأشاعرة) - These are the supposed followers of Abu-l-Hasan al-Ashari (260-324 A.H.). This group is known for making *taweel* for many of the attributes of Allah. They also believe that *imaan* is solely *tasdeeq*.

Asharites - a common Western term for the *Ashaairah*

Asmaa, al- wa al-sifaat (الأسماء والصفات) - names and attributes; *al-asmaa* are names and *al-sifaat* are attributes

Auliyaa (أولياء) - devoted servants, friends, associates; the Sufis use this term in a way similar to the English word, "saint" but that is not its proper sense.

Deen (دين) - complete way of life, religion

Dua (دعاء) - supplication, informal prayer

Faasiq (فاسق) - evildoer, unrighteous person

Ghaib, al- (الغيب) - the unseen, unwitnessed

Hajj (حج) - the pilgrimage to Makkah that one must perform once in one's life if one has the means to do so.

Hasan (حسن)- this is a verified hadith of the Prophet (peace be upon him) although it is not as strong as *sahih*.

Hijrah (هجرة) - lit., "emigration, migration," when used in the expression, "Year of the *hijrah*," it is a reference to the Prophet's (peace be upon him) migration from Makkah

[1] The "*al*" preceding words is ignored when putting the words in alphabetical order.

to Madinah that marks the beginning of the Islamic calender.

Ibaadah (عبادة) - "worship," in the Islamic sense, it includes more than the ritual acts but all acts done for the sake of Allah can be considered acts of worship.

Ihsaan (إحسان) - as discussed in the text, the general meaning is the doing of goodness; the particular meaning is to worship Allah as if one is seeing Him or, at least, to know that He is watching.

Ijtehad (اجتهاد)- the use of personal reasoning to determine what is correct from the Shariah's point of view.

Ikhlaas, al- (الإخلاص) - pure sincerity in one's intentions and deeds.

Ilaah (إله) - god, worshipped one, adored one

Imaan (إيمان) - this is "faith," which has its own Shariah definition as explained in the text.

Iqaamat al-salaat (إقامة الصلاة)- this is the "establishing of the prayer," implying performing it properly according to all of the commands of the Shariah.

Islaam, Islam (إسلام) - this implies submission, such as submission to Allah; it is also the word for the religion as a whole.

Jahmites - a common Western term for the *Jahmiyyah*

Jahmiyyah, al- (الجهمية) - the followers of Jahm ibn Safwaan, who was killed for his beliefs by the Muslim ruler. He virtually denied all of Allah's attributes. He claimed that *imaan* is simply a matter of having knowledge that Allah exists.

Jibreel (جبريل) - the Angel Gabriel

Jizyah (جزية) - this is the tax that non-Muslim citizens of the Islamic state must pay in lieu of military service.

Kaabah (كعبة) - the House of Allah in Makkah to which the Hajj is made.

Kaafir (كافر) - a disbeliever

Karramites - common Western term for the *Karraamiyyah*

Karramiyyah, al- (الكرامية) - This heretical group, which have very little influence in the history of Islam, claimed that *imaan* is simply a statement of the tongue.

Khaleefah (خليفة) - the leader of the Muslim nation

Kharijites - a common Western term for the *Khawaarij*

Khawaarij, al- (الخوارج) - one of the first heretical groups in the history of Islam. Known for their extremist views, they even declared the caliphs Uthman and Ali disbelievers. They believed that anyone who commits a major sin falls out of the fold of Islam. The Prophet (peace be upon him) prophesied their coming and stated that they should be fought.

Khushu' (خشوع) - lowering, humbling and submitting oneself

Kufr (كفر) - disbelief, the opposite of *imaan*.

La ilaaha illa-llah (لا إله إلا الله) - "There is none worthy of worship except Allah"

Maaturidiyyah, al- (الماتريدية) - The followers of Abu Mansur al-Maturidi (d. 333 A.H.). This group is very close to the Ashaariyyah in their beliefs.

Madhhab (مذهب)- basically this refers to a person's school of thought or opinion.

Mahram (محرم) - herein, it is a reference to a woman's male relative who is in the prohibited degrees for marriage.

Marifah (معرفة) - knowledge of something

Maturidites - a common Western term for the *Maaturidiyyah*

Muhsin (محسن) - a doer of good, a person characterized with *ihsaan*

Mumin (مؤمن) - a believer

Murjiah, al- (المرجئة) - an early sect in the history of Islam and an opponent to the Khawaarij; they went to the opposite extreme concerning *imaan* and claimed that even the biggest sinner is a complete and perfect believer.

Murjiites - A common Western term for the *Murjiah*

Muslim (مسلم) - one who submits

Mushrikeen (مشركين) - those who commit *shirk* (associate partners with Allah)

Mutazilah, al- (المعتزلة) - an early heretical group in the history of Islam. They were greatly responsible for the spread of Greek thinking among the Muslims. Among their beliefs was that the *faasiq* was neither a believer nor a disbeliever but he would be in the Hell-fire forever.

Nifaaq (نفاق) - hypocrisy

Qabool, al- (القبول) - acceptance, as in accepting whatever the *shahaadah* implies.

Qadar, al- (القدر) - Divine decree and preordainment

Qawl or *qaul* (قول) - "statement," the scholars discuss statements of the heart (beliefs) as well as statements of the tongue

Qudsi (قدسي) - herein, it is used to refer to a hadith in which the Prophet (peace be upon him) transmits Allah's own words.

Rabb (رب) - Lord, creator, nourisher, sustainer

Rububiyyah, al- (الربوبية) - Related to the *rabb* (lord and creator)

Sadaqa (صدقة) - charity, usually used for charity other than the obligatory zakah.

Sahih (صحيح)- this is an authentic or verified hadith of the Prophet (peace be upon him).

Salaf, al- (السلف) - the first three generation of Muslims, in particular, the Companions, and those who follow their path

Salafi (سلفي) - one adhering to the way of the *salaf*

Salat (صلاة) - the Islamic ritual prayer

Shahaadah (شهادة) - "testimony," herein it refers to the testimony of faith, "I bear witness that there is none worthy of worship except Allah and that Muhammad is the Messenger of Allah."

Shariah (شريعة)- Islamic law.

Sharr (شر) - evil

Shirk (شرك)- the associating of partners with Allah.

Sidq, al- (الصدق) - sincerity, the opposite of lying, falsehood and hypocrisy.

Siyaam (صيام) - fast

Surah (سورة)- this is a "chapter" from the Quran.

Surah al-Faatiha (سورة الفاتحة) - This is the opening chapter of the Quran.

Taaghoot (طاغوت) - false god or false object of worship

Takbir (تكبير)- this is the saying of "Allahu Akbar," "Allah is greater."

Taqwa (تقوى) - the fear of Allah, being mindful of Allah, God-consciousness

Tasdeeq (تصديق) - affirmation, belief

Tauheed, al- (also, *tawheed, tawhid, tauhid*) (التوحيد) - Islamic monotheism

Taweel (تأويل)- this is the reinterpretation of a text when one claims that its literal meaning is not what is meant.

Uluhiyyah (ألوهية) - related to the *ilaah* (God, worshipped one)

Umm al-Kitaab (أم الكتاب) - literally, "the foundation or mother of the book," it is in reference to *Surah al-Faatiha*

Ummah (أمة) - "nation, people," it refers either to the Muslim nation or the people who have been adressed by the Prophet Muhammad (peace be upon him), which would be all of mankind from his time until the day of Judgment.

Umrah (عمرة) - the "lesser pilgrimage" that contains less rites than Hajj and may be performed throughout the year.

Yaqeen, al- (اليقين) - certainty, free of any doubt

Zandiqah (زندقة) - a hypocrite who is openly showing Islam but is secretly working against Islam.

Zakah (زكاة) - one of the five pillars of Islam; it is the portion of one's wealth that one must give away for the sake of Allah to certain people as specified in the Quran.

Index of Figures

Figure 1a. The Components of *Imaan* as Viewed by Different Sects 75
Figure 1b. The Components of *Imaan* as Viewed by Different Sects 76
Figure 1c. The Components of *Imaan* as Viewed by Different Sects 77
Figure 1d. The Components of *Imaan* as Viewed by Different Sects 78
Figure 2. Graphical Representation of the Division of *Tauheed* into Three Categories 126
Figure 3. Graphical Representation of the Division of *Tauheed* into Two Categories 145

Index of Quranic Verses Cited

al-Faatiha, surah - pp. 1, 124
4 - p. 147
al-Baqara 8-10 - p. 22
21 - p. 137
25 - p. 117
85 - p. 19, 165
130-1 - p. 159
146 - p. 169
165 - pp. 23-24, 132
183 - p. 58
213 - pp. 148-9
253 - p. 188
256 - p. 25
260 - p. 98
ali-Imraan - p. 144
31 - p. 32
64 - p. 144, 156
97 - p. 66
102 - p. 26
167 - pp. 101-102
173 - p. 100
180 - pp. 53, 55
al-Nisaa 64 - p. 171
65 - pp. 20, 171-2
105 - p. 149
125 - p. 20
171 - p. 160
al-Maaidah 48 - p. 165
51 - p. 155
55-57 - pp. 154-5
77 - p. 160
81 - p. 95-96, 154
93 - pp. 197-8
al-Anaam - p. 144
19 - p. 137
33 - p. 88
46 - p. 137
59 - p. 185
93 - pp. 178-9
124 - p. 27
162 - p. 162
al-Araaf 2 - p. 119
8-9 - p. 175
59 - p. 129
65 - p. 129
83 - p. 129
85 - p. 129
157 - p. 169
158 - p. 27
187 - p. 213
al-Anfaal 2 - p. 99
2-3 - p. 114
4 - p. 114
al-Tauba 24 - pp. 24, 31
31 - p. 150, 152

34-35 - p. 55
45 - p. 18
72 - p. 117
124-125 - p. 101
Yunus - p. 144
26 - p. 207
99 - p. 191
Hood 50 - p. 129
61 - p. 129
84 - p. 129
Yusuf 40 - p. 150
al-Hijr 9 - 167
36 - p. 83
39 - p. 83
al-Nahl 36 - p. 148, 167-8
43 - p. 7
61 - p. 137
al-Israa 23 - p. 128
57 - p. 133
102 - p. 82
al-Kahf 16 - p. 155
26 - p. 152
29 - p. 177, 191
110 - p. 135
Maryam 76 - pp. 99-100
Taha - p. 144
5 - p. 50
11 - p. 50
13-14 - p. 40
71 - pp. 50-51
103 - p. 51
al-Anbiyaa 47 - p. 175
61 - p. 137
63 - p. 137
64 - p. 137
90 - p. 133
104 - p. 174
al-Hajj 41 - p. 52
70 - p. 186
al-Muminoon 23 - p. 129
32 - p. 129
70 - p. 88
84-8 - pp. 127-8
al-Noor 47-51 - pp. 149-50
54 - p. 28
62 - p. 119
63 - p. 12
al-Furqaan 1-2 - p. 189
al-Shuaraa 105 - p. 169-70
al-Naml 59-60 - pp. 136-7
al-Qasas 68 - p. 26
al-Ankaboot 45 - p. 42
al-Room 41 - p. 193
Luqmaan 34 - p. 212
al-Sajdah - p. 144
17 - p. 176-7
al-Ahzaab 21 - p. 31
36 - pp. 19-20
40 - p. 30, 168
64-6 - p. 177
Faatir 32 - p. 116
Ya-Seen 51-2 - p. 173-4
al-Saaffaat 96 - p. 189
Saad 5 - p. 137
82 - p. 83
al-Zumar p. 144
2 - p. 22
54 - p. 20
62 - p. 189
68 - p. 173
Ghaafir 56 - p. 132

78 - p. 171
Fussilat 30 - p. 178
37 - p. 147
al-Shoora 11 - p. 141
al-Zukhruf 26-28 - p. 156
86 - pp. 16-17
Muhammad 18 - p. 216
19 - p. 16
al-Fath 4 - p. 100
al-Hujuraat 7 - p. 89
14 - pp. 103-104
15 - pp. 17, 119
Qaaf 17-18 - p. 163
al-Dhaariyaat 56 - p. 128
al-Qamar 49 - p. 189
al-Rahmaan 29 - p. 187
al-Hadeed - p. 144
22 - p. 186, 195
al-Mujaadilah 22 - p. 96
al-Hashr - p. 144
al-Maarij 4 - p. 217
19-23 - p. 42
al-Mudaththir 31 - p. 100
al-Insaan 29-30 - p. 191
al-Naaziaat 42-4 - p. 213
al-Takweer 27-9 - p. 188
al-Mutaffifeen 15 - p. 208
al-Ghaashiyah 25-6 - p. 175
al-Ala 14 - p. 49
al-Bayyinah 5 - pp. 22-23
7-8 - p. 176
al-Ma'oon 4-5 - p. 35
al-Kaafiroon - p. 144
al-Ikhlaas - p. 144

General Index

Abu Hanifa 67, 93
Ahmad ibn Hanbal 6, 56n, 67, 93
Al-Albani, Muhammad Nasir al-Din 29n, 39n, 41n, 43n, 46n, 47n, 51n, 52n, 56n, 58n, 60n, 61, 64n, 67n, 68n, 79n, 80n, 97n, 107n, 135n, 178n, 202n, 217n, 220n
angels, belief in 161-163

books (revealed), belief in, 163-167
Al-Bukhari, Muhammad 6n, 86n, 117n

Divine decree, belief in, 182-196

Fast (*siyaam*)
- importance of 57-60
- meaning of 57
- ruling concerning one who does not fast 61-62

Hajj - see pilgrimage

ibn Abu al-Izz al-Hanafi 79, 82, 83, 84, 96, 100, 118, 123, 124, 136, 143, 158, 160
Ibn Hajr, Ahmad 1, 6n, 11, 200, 206, 208, 215n, 218, 219, 220n, 226n
Ibn Rajab, Abdul-Rahman 197n, 200, 205, 208, 209, 212n, 221
Ibn al-Qayyim, Muhammad 85, 141n, 143n, 159n, 185, 186, 187, 192
Ibn Taimiya, Ahmad 72, 73n, 84n, 86n, 87, 88n, 90, 91n, 92n, 93n, 94, 95, 96n, 99n, 102, 103, 106n, 107, 112, 114, 115, 116, 133, 141n, 150, 154, 177, 234
Ibn Uthaimin, Muhammad 85, 127, 161, 162, 164, 165, 174, 179, 181, 188, 189, 193, 194, 203, 204, 226
Ihsaan 197-209
Imaan
- complete and lacking 103-116
- components of 85-92

concept of 71-74
definition of 74-85
increases and decreases 99-103
relation to deed 92-99
vis-a-vis Islam and ihsan 117-120
Islam , meaning of 13-14

Last Day, belief in, 172-181

Malik ibn Anas 67, 93, 138n
messengers, belief in, 167-172
Musnad Ahmad, hadith from 6, 29, 39, 41, 43, 47, 48, 58, 64, 67, 68, 79, 97, 202, 217, 220
Muwatta al-Imam Malik, hadith from, 43, 47

Al-Nawawi, Yahya 2, 6n, 11, 205, 218, 229

pilgrimage (*hajj*)
delaying 67-70
importance of 63-65
meaning of 62-63
obligatory upon 65-66
prayers
Importance of 40-44
meaning of "establishing the prayer" 35-40
meaning of *salat* 33-35
ruling concerning one who does not pray 44-48

Qadar - see Divine decree

Sahih al-Bukhari, hadith from, 6, 21, 24, 27, 32, 38, 44, 53, 54, 59, 63, 64, 79n, 84n, 97n, 98n, 104, 106, 107, 117n, 119n, 174n, 201n, 212, 214, 220, 222
Sahih Muslim, hadith from, 6, 16, 18, 23, 24, 25, 27, 38, 44, 46, 56, 59, 63, 64, 79, 84, 97, 98, 102, 104, 106, 107, 115, 119, 170, 173, 174n, 183-4, 186, 193, 207, 214, 222
salat - see "prayers"
Al-Shafii, Muhammad ibn Idris 92, 93
Shafii school 67
shahaadah, conditions of 14-26
meaning of second part 26-33
siyaam - see "fast"

tauheed 123-125
divided into three categories 125-142
divided into two categories 142-157
tauheed al-asma wa al-Sifaat 137-142
tauheed al-rubuiyah 126-128
tauheed al-uluhiyah 128-137

tauheed in practice 146-157
tauheed in theory 145-146

Zakat
imporance of 49-55
meaning of 48-49
ruling concerning one who not give zakat 55-57